BORN FOR FRIENDSHIP

BORN FOR FRIENDSHIP

The Spirit of Sir Thomas More

by

BERNARD BASSET, S.J.

"He seems born and made for friendship"
—Erasmus, 1517

SHEED AND WARD: NEW YORK

DE LICENTIA SUPERIORUM ORDINIS

———

NIHIL OBSTAT: JOANNES M. T. BARTON, S.T.D., L.S.S.
CENSOR DEPUTATUS
IMPRIMATUR: PATRITIUS CASEY
VICARIUS GENERALIS
WESTMONASTERII: DIE 5a SEPTEMBRIS 1964

Library of Congress Catalog Card Number 65-20862

Manufactured in the United States of America

TO

BROTHER ANDREW ATKINSON, S. J.

IN GRATITUDE

ACKNOWLEDGEMENTS

Fordham University Press for Stanley Morison's *The Likeness of Thomas More*, New York, 1964; P. J. Kenedy & Sons for E. E. Reynolds' *Margaret Roper*, New York, 1960, *Sir Thomas More*, New York, 1954, and *The Trial of St. Thomas More*, New York, 1964; Alfred A. Knopf, Inc. for Garret Mattingly's *Catherine of Aragon*, New York, 1960; The Macmillan Company for H. F. M. Prescott's *Mary Tudor*, New York, 1953.

Contents

Foreword

Is THERE any need for another book about Sir Thomas More? Surely, the facts of his life are so well established that no new disclosures now seem possible. In his case, history has retained few secrets and research is restricted to small, unessential points. A new biography, it may be urged, will add nothing to the story so well told by Roper, Stapleton and Harpsfield and can only repeat the salient facts of an uncomplicated life. For More's story is straightforward, as befits one of the most candid characters in modern history. Though he held high office in the State, he never occupied the centre of the stage. At best, for a few minutes, he was in the centre of the scaffold, at nine o'clock in the morning of Tuesday, 6th July, 1535.

The excuse for this book must rest less on new information, more on the painful alterations which we see happening to ourselves. Our world has experienced shattering upheavals in the past five decades and these help us to see More from a more lowly but better point of view. Just as the grandeur of a great building is revealed with the demolition of the slums around it, so Sir Thomas grows in stature as the partisan causes against which he struggled play themselves out and fade away. This was the justification for G. K. Chesterton's impressive prophecy made at Chelsea in 1929. "Sir Thomas More is more important at this moment than at any moment since his death, even perhaps the great moment of his dying; but he is not quite so important as he will be in a hundred years time. He may come to be counted the greatest Englishman, or, at least, the greatest historical character in English history."[1]

This powerful assertion made by a shrewd, informed man may

[1] *The Fame of Blessed Thomas More*, Sheed and Ward, 1929, p. 63.

well be verified. Indeed, after thirty years, one may trace its likely fulfilment in five different ways:

1. The present earnest search for peace, the groping towards World Government and peaceful co-existence, must make us regard *Utopia* with far greater honour and respect. This little book, so long regarded as a delightful extravaganza, now appears as one of the wisest contributions to sane living devised by man. More almost has the answer to the bomb. So many of his imaginative schemes have, over the centuries, been adopted without recognition; today, *Utopia*, in the hands and heads of statesmen, would give us peace.

2. With the increase of leisure, thanks to automation, the need for true education must become increasingly felt. Life will prove unbearable for those who have been educated for one purpose only, to get and to hold a job. The right use of leisure, the value of crafts, the danger of idleness, in a word, the full implications of education, were elaborated in theory and in practice at Chelsea four hundred years ago. Is it fanciful to dream of a Thomas More University in some English-speaking country or to suggest that students who followed its curriculum would be happier, better adjusted, more integrated citizens than their less fortunate contemporaries?

3. Sir Thomas has increased in stature now that so many men have lived under dictatorship and tyranny and know far better the importance of human liberty. It has taken four hundred years for us to grasp the wisdom and courage of his attitude to kings. The situation has been well expressed in the verdict passed on Cranmer by Jaspar Ridley, the latest biographer of a man who thought it right to trim his sails. "We are often told that it is unfair to judge him [Cranmer] by present standards and that we must take into account the century in which he lived; but though some future historian may seek to excuse the acts of Hitler's followers by pointing out that they lived in the twentieth century and must be judged by the standard of their age, this argument does not dispose of the problem." What is true of Cranmer is true of More who faced the same issue which

was also placed before so many in Hitler's day. More chose
to die.

4. As the Reformation blows itself out and Christians of every
kind seek for unity and reconciliation, the eyes of all may turn to
the last great Christian figure, universally respected, before
Christendom split into many warring camps. More knew neither
Protestants nor Roman Catholics, as we use these labels; he heard
the word "Papist" with sorrow not long before his death. He was
not martyred by Protestants but by his friend, a Catholic king.
Within a decade of his death, Europe was divided and, post-
humously, he became the champion of the Roman Catholic cause.
One cannot blame the Catholics for claiming so great a saint or
the Protestants for rejecting the rival protagonist, but these
partisan disputes had nothing to do with Thomas More. He whose
strange destiny in life had been to grasp and to face the true issues
may well show to both sides the tragedy of division and the way
in which Christian unity might be restored. A genuine reformer,
the enemy of all forms of superstition, he foresaw the tragedy,
struggled to prevent it and may now help to heal the wounds of
centuries. Those on either side who are great enough to admit
their errors must be willing to retrace their steps. This would
mean going back to look once more at the issues, the errors and
abuses which More faced before he died.

5. One further, modest excuse may be urged in defence of this
book. Sir Thomas More died on Tower Hill and our very preoccupation with the Reformation issues may have obscured our
vision and distracted our attention from his primary role. He was a
saint before he was a martyr; his life came before his death. His
was an astonishing approach to life; had he not been a martyr, his
unique position in Christian history would still have been recognized. It would be difficult to name any other layman in
Christian history whose approach to holiness was as impressive
as his. Now, in an age when the position of the laity in the
Church is attracting attention, we may turn to the Lord Chancellor with awe. For Thomas More was a mystic long before he
was a martyr, in wisdom he comes near to being a Doctor; he is,

surely, one of the most profound of spiritual writers that the
English Church has ever known.

Here is the purpose of this book. It would be vain to set out all
the dates afresh, to enter into the politics of the time, to discuss
the social and religious trials of Tudor England, but it may not
be wholly a waste of effort to return to Chelsea, to meet one of
the greatest saints of modern times.

Many more people love Thomas More than love English history
and this offbeat biography is intended for them. It selects facts
and presents them in an irregular order to bring out less the
historical details, more the humanity and sanctity of the man.

It is not strictly necessary to know much history but, for the
sake of clarity, it may help us at the beginning to take a quick
view of the whole of More's life.

Ours is the story of a man who was born in the reign of King
Edward IV, spent most of his life in London and was executed for
treason by King Henry VIII. A lawyer by profession, he became
a Member of Parliament, Speaker of the House of Commons and
finally Lord Chancellor. He married twice, had four children,
eleven grandchildren in his day. He lived for many years near
the Mansion House in London and then moved to Chelsea; his
epitaph may still be read in old Chelsea Church. His most famous
book is *Utopia*, now an English classic; he is perhaps better
known today as the subject of Holbein's famous paintings and
the hero of Bolt's *Man for All Seasons*, one of the most successful
of modern plays.

Though the facts of More's life are all known, it is less easy
to assign any accurate dates. Experts differ but the following
dates may be taken as certain and will serve as a rough outline
of his life.

He was born in 1478, studied at Lincoln's Inn in 1496, became
a Member of Parliament in 1504. Henry VIII came to the throne
in 1509. More was married in 1505. He moved to Chelsea in
1524 and became Lord Chancellor in 1529. He was a courtier
for fifteen years, resigned the Chancellorship in 1532, was arrested

in 1534 and, after fifteen months in the Tower of London, was executed on 6th July, 1535. He was fifty-seven when he died.

Our offbeat biography opens normally with his description of London as he knew it and the details of his early years. When he was twenty-two, he underwent a spiritual crisis and this we pause to consider in detail in Chapter Two. After establishing the main principles and motives of his life, we go forward with him, watching as he applies his decisions to his marriage, his home, his professional duties, the education of his children and, finally, to his career at Court. Less attention is paid to the legal details of his trial and execution, more to his psychology. He may well prove to be the greatest man in English history and for this reason, if for no other, it should be rewarding to study his advance in holiness.

BOURNEMOUTH
    21st February, 1964.

CHAPTER ONE

Young More

I. SMALL BOY IN A BIG CITY

PART OF THE charm of the historical novel lies in the reconstruction of past scenes. The novelist goes to great pains, poring over maps and plans, studying diaries, letters, broadsheets, drama, woodcuts, that every detail of his description may be exact. He may even read the novels of those who have attempted the same before him, to see if these can add to his fund of facts. Last of all, he summons his imagination for the final touches, to provide that precision which the documents too often lack.

As this is not an historical novel, all such titivations would be out of place. The author has made no effort to reconstruct a Tudor setting in which the story of Thomas More may be neatly placed. Indeed, no imaginative effort is required, for More himself tells us so much of the London in which he dwelt. So observant was More, so shrewd in judgement, so deeply committed to the folk about him, that he gives us far more facts about London than details about himself. His was the type of mind that nourishes itself on the living world of people; his living world was London and in his merry comments on this city he provides, unconsciously, a comment also on himself.

To omit particular scenes which may occur later, More, in his general impressions of the city, describes a more simple, homespun world than we have ever seen. London looked great to him with its "broad high street" and high roofs which shut the sun out, but he also knew the squalor of its slums. With no trace of squeamishness and in considerable detail, he speaks of the joys and sorrows of its people and gives us a glimpse of many types of

home. From him, if we trouble to learn, we may read of court-
ships, wedding rings and weddings, fires, sickness, doctors, can-
cers, deathbeds and funerals.

More is especially vivid about funerals. In the streets he points
out "the rabble of ragged beggars" bawling abuse, the groups of
worshipful folk about their business, the gangs of children locked
in mock battle from which, in the past, not a few "have taken
great hurt". Less dangerous for the children and more amusing
are the antics of the performing bear. The men play dice at night,
deciding in advance the value of the counters which will represent
their stakes. They probably drink too much beer or wine and
More mentions one pub, "The King's Head". In the London that
he knew, the favourite jokes, then as now, were about nagging
women; one of whom was so determined to get her husband to
the gallows that she provoked him until he "upped with his chip-
axe and, at a chop, chopped her head off indeed". He was re-
prieved, the lucky fellow, because neighbours came forward to
reveal his late wife's wicked plan.

London to More was an exciting city with merchantmen from
many distant countries lying along the City reaches of the river
to discharge their wares. Greatly intrigued, More proved a ready
purchaser for rare and unusual objects brought from foreign
lands. He loved the Thames and watched its tides with awe. From
him we hear of the silversmiths, fashioning their delicate thread,
of the glass blowers, of the new craft of printers, moulding the
red hot metal to prepare their type. He looks down a little on
"the butchers, confectioners, fishmongers, carriers, cooks and
poultrymen, all occupied in serving sensuality". He chatted to
men on their way to execution, tells of a man in the stocks for
faking a miracle, describes strange goings-on in the City jails.
There were pageants galore with Cheapside gay with bunting,
some of which his brother-in-law designed. He also saw London
torn with scandal, shaken with riots and the cannon from the
Tower of London turned on to its citizens.

When More was a young man, he saw private gardens in the
centre of the City, raspberries could be gathered by Holborn,

Chelsea and Stepney were in the country and Lambeth was best reached by boat.

The City, in his day, was still feudal, almost patriarchal in its government, with its apprentices, journeymen, masters, aldermen and guilds. He himself was a freeman of the Mercers' Guild. He watched with sorrow the slow decay of the old system, for the trek of the aristocracy from London had begun. The rich were building their mansions round the court at Westminster and along the river strand. What must have been the first printing press to come to Fleet Street was opened in his day.

The King came less frequently to London, preferring his palaces at Greenwich and Richmond round which were gathering a new type of courtier and a new and more frivolous type of Court life. Cardinal Wolsey was to give the lead even to his royal master with his monster palaces in Whitehall and at Hampton Court. More deplored these new developments, especially the unwieldy bands of idle serving-men. These ignorant servitors caused trouble in the City, brawling, drinking, dicing and unsettling the apprentices. Londoners were turning into the common people and the Mores had been for generations City men.

London still had its royal occasions and More describes them, studying the behaviour of the country bumpkins who came to London especially to see the King. In verse he told the tale of one poor fellow who stood gaping in the crowd as the procession passed. He heard the cheering, saw the glittering dress, then gave vent to his disappointment thus:

> "The King, The King, O where is he?"
> The clown began to cry,
> Quoth one—with finger pointed out,
> "Lo, there he sits on high!"
> "Tush, that is not the King," quoth he,
> "Thou art deceived at best,
> That seemeth just a man to me,
> In painted vesture dressed."

As an introduction to our story, can we better More's casual comments on the City in which he lived for fifty-seven years? Of

all his vivid pictures, none are more colourful than those which
sketch the religious life of London, its faith, its superstitions,
shrines, relics, festivals set to the music of innumerable bells. Often
smiling, always kindly, More rivals Chaucer in his wit. We see the
devout praying at shrines, praying for Kitty's lost keys, thinking
that the statue of Our Lady by the Tower is looking at them, back-
ing Our Lady of Ipswich against Our Lady of Walsingham. "A
few doting dames make not the people," he comments slyly and
then remarks that some think that their prayers are better answered
in St Paul's Cathedral by the north rather than the south door.

Not all his dames are devout. While the holy ones are praying
and putting up candles, the less pious are off on pilgrimage,
more for company than for devotion, "dancing a reel" on the
way home when they are a little drunk. So bad was the reputation
of the Willesden pilgrims that Friar Donald, a sturdy Scot, from
the pulpit of St Paul's, warned the men of London: "Ye men of
London, gang on your self with your wives to Willesden in the
devil's name, or else, keep them with you at home." While the
adults thus mixed pleasure and devotion, the children played at
funerals, chanting a dirge in mumbo-jumbo as they carted an
imaginary coffin through the streets.

When the Scottish friar warned the men of London of the
goings-on at Willesden, he was standing in the outside pulpit
at Paul's Cross, to the north-east of the cathedral and not so very
far from Thomas More's first home. And if buildings affect our
lives and characters—few who have lived in famous cities would
want to deny this—then More's life was dominated by old St
Paul's. He lived almost in the shade of this astonishing building,
one of the largest cathedrals in medieval Europe; its spire, according to Dugdale, fifty feet higher than that at Salisbury, its length
a hundred feet longer than the great cathedral of Milan.

St Paul's was the spiritual and civic centre of old London and
More's life moved in circles round it for fifty-seven years.
With its shrines, its votive candles, forty daily Masses, high cere-
monial, celebrated preachers, bulging alms-chests, it represented
all that was good and bad in those good or bad old days.

More loved St Paul's. He often went to the sermons, criticized the more pompous preachers, visited Dean Colet, was intimate with William Lillie, first High Master of St Paul's school. The pavement round St Paul's was the social centre of the City, the resort of beggars, wandering minstrels, servants seeking work. Here started all the rumours—More gives one, by a man who claimed to have seen a huge bird hovering over the cathedral, spanning its width with its wings. By the next morning, another, not to be outdone, admitted that he had not seen the bird but had found in the churchyard an egg so large that it could barely be shifted by ten men. Rumours went round, trade was done, stocks were sold, business discussed in the cloisters, which also housed the gruesome "Dance of Death". Young More was fascinated by these pictures, each with a verse by Skelton and an appropriate text. We meet the "Dance of Death" again on a later page.

More's life centred round St Paul's. On his way to and from Milk Street, to and from Lincoln's Inn and Bucklersbury, its spire can rarely have been out of sight. The spire of Old St Paul's could be seen as far as Richmond, almost certainly, then, at Chelsea; More saw it for the last time when he mounted the scaffold on Tower Hill.[1]

Thomas More was born between two and three in the morning on Friday, 6th February, 1478. This was the Friday after the feast of the Purification of the Blessed Virgin Mary, as his pious father duly recorded in his notes. Thomas was the second child— his sister Joan was three years older—while Agatha, John, Edward and Elizabeth were one, two, three and four years younger than himself. His parents, both of respected City families, lived in a large house in a residential district in the parish of St Giles, outside Cripplegate.[2]

Our only glimpse of More as a baby is delightful, for his nurse,

[1] More's description of London is drawn from many sources too numerous to quote. Cf. *Dialogue of Comfort*, pp. 255, 309, 313, 339; Letter to Colet; Stapleton, pp. 11–13; *Utopia*, p. 23; *English Works*, 1, pp. 468 seq; 2, pp. 40–62.

[2] The exact date of More's birth is still disputed, not, I think, the year. Cf. Chambers, pp. 44–46; Reynolds, p. 24.

when her horse stumbled at a river-crossing, for safety threw the baby Thomas over a nearby hedge. Afterwards, when she ran to look for him, she found him "safe and sound, quite unhurt and smiling at her"—a fact which shows his merry nature, if not her further conclusion that he would live to be a great man.[3]

When he is a little older, we catch sight of him again, this time in one of his own stories which makes us wonder whether children, sitting by the fire of an evening, wore dressing-gowns in Tudor days. "My mother had, when I was a little boy, a good old woman that take heed to her children; they called her Mother Maud. She was wont when she sat by the fire with us to tell us, that were children, many childish tales. . . . I remember me that among other of her fond tales, she told us once that the ass and the wolf came upon a time to confession to the fox." It was a complicated story but More could recall all the details after fifty years. He retained through life a weakness for *Aesop's Fables* and tales of animals that talked.[4]

Of the brothers and sisters who listened with him to Mother Maud's fond stories, two seem to have died when they were small. Infant mortality ran high in the fifteenth century; an extreme example, that of Dean Colet who alone reached manhood of a family that may once have numbered twenty-two. More may never have known his sister Agatha but he should have remembered Edward, born when he himself was three years old. As the stark reality of death was to fascinate More in adolescence, these unrecorded deaths of a small brother and sister may have played a part in moulding his character. We may link them with the "Dance of Death" in St Paul's cloister and with children singing their mumbo-jumbo in the streets.

Later in life, More was to fill his books with merry stories, many of which may refer to himself. He rarely gives a clue. The quaint little boy listening to old Mother Maud by the fire grew into a very reticent young man. More loved to create a fictitious setting and to write in the form of a dialogue. His

[3] Stapleton, p. 2.   [4] *Dialogue of Comfort*, p. 245.

very jokes were often a disguise. He knew himself well and once allows one of his imaginary characters to say to him, "You so often look sad when you are joking that men are not sure whether or not you are joking, when you speak so earnestly."[5]

There was much of Hamlet in More, much of Touchstone and, hence, much of Shakespeare; both had the skill of conveying through others the joys and panics which they had experienced themselves. After a time one knows with More when he is speaking of himself. How much of himself he reveals in the sentence which describes a soul coming back from the dead to gaze at its former riches "as an old man that has found a bag of cherry stones which he laid up when he was a boy".

The following reminiscence of his is often quoted to describe him in his schoolboy days. He tells the yarn to criticize the behaviour of those spiritual directors who, to avoid any unpleasantness in the present, fail to warn sinners of their state.

> In such wise deal they with him as the mother doth sometime with her child; which when the little boy will not rise in time for her, but lie still abed and slug, and when he is up, weepeth because he has lien so long, fearing to be beaten at school for his late coming thither, she telleth then that it is but early days and he shall have time enough, and biddeth him "Go, good son, I warrant thee, I have sent to thy master myself, take thy bread and butter with thee, thou shalt not be beaten at all." And thus, so she may send him merry forth at the door that he weep not in her sight at home, she studieth not much upon the matter, though he be taken tardy and beaten when he cometh to school.[6]

Young More had a happy life in a loving but severe home. If he was beaten at school—a practice much in fashion—he does not write bitterly about it as Erasmus was to do. Once, in an aside, he mentions evil masters "which be readier to beat than to teach their scholars" but he remained on most friendly terms with his headmaster, John Holt. More's mother is not mentioned again

---

[5] *English Works*, 2, p. 37.   [6] *Dialogue of Comfort*, p. 182.

and it would seem that she, like so many mothers of the period, died relatively young.

2. FATHER AND SON

The deep affection between father and son cannot be doubted, and young More took after his father in a great many ways. They shared a pride in their profession, a love of London, loyalty to the Crown with a special attachment to the memory of King Edward IV. Old More, in his will, left money for Masses for a king who had been dead for fifty years. Young Thomas, copying his father, abstained from drink. He quoted his father often; such phrases as "I have heard my father say", "once when talking to my father", "my father declares", occur frequently in his books. Old More had a salty wit which showed itself in his remarks about women, their nagging, their fashions, their interference, their chatter, their vanity. His humour was the humour of the music hall, bantering but kindly, and young More imitated this. Old More was unsubtle and an extrovert; if we look at his portrait in the famous Holbein picture, we see at a glance the type of man he was.

To supplement the Holbein portrait, painted in the last years of his father's life, More himself wrote about his father after the latter's death. Indeed, he carved it in stone when he composed his own epitaph, still standing in Chelsea parish church. More wrote this epitaph with care at a critical moment in his career. One is surprised, perhaps, to note how much space he devoted to his father when setting out the facts of his own life.

At last John More his father, Knight and chosen by the prince to be one of the justices of the King's bench, a civil man, pleasant, harmless, gentle, pitiful, just and uncorrupted, in years old but in body more than for his years lusty, after he had perceived his life so long lengthened that he saw his son lord chancellor of England, thinking himself now to have lived long enough, gladly departed to God. His son then, his father being dead, to whom as long as he lived, being compared, was wont both to be called young and himself so thought too, missing his father departed and seeing four children of his own and of their offspring eleven, began in his own conceit to wax old.[7]

After reading this moving tribute there is no need to elaborate further or to try to describe in detail the mutual respect which united father and son. As lawyers they worked together, shared, in a sense, the same practice, attended the same legal and civic functions, enjoyed the family pride in Lincoln's Inn. Roper recalls how More as Chancellor, on his passage through Westminster Hall, would kneel for his old father's blessing when he came to the Court of the King's Bench. Sir John died with his son's arm around him, comforting him. One would expect that young More who was to write so feelingly of the duty of love and respect towards one's parents would maintain and protect his old father to the end. Old Sir John was about seventy-six when he died and Holbein has captured and preserved the moment of his greatest glory, seated by his son, soon to be Lord Chancellor. He died just in time and was spared the last chapter of his son's story in which he may claim a share.[8]

Old Sir John affected his son's career in many ways. He lived so long—and lived so long as senior partner—that Thomas was known as young More for over fifty years. The fact is significant and he recorded it in stone. Old John More was no passenger; he married for the fourth time when he was in his middle-sixties and on his death his possessions passed, not to Thomas, but to his third stepmother. A situation such as this may easily alter a son's or daughter's character. Young More loved his stepmothers and they loved him. His father's extraordinary stamina had the very effect which he recorded, it kept him young. Further, love for his father gave him a touch of that ambition which he otherwise completely lacked. Each time one reads the epitaph and looks at the Holbein portrait, the thought recurs that John More's pride in his son and Thomas's desire to please his father played a part in the first steps towards the Lord Chancellorship. It was his father who used

[7] Rastell's translation. Cf. Bridgett, pp. 250–251.
[8] For More's devotion to his father, Stapleton, p. 3; Roper, p. 22; Harpsfield, p. 84.

his professional influence to have his eldest son placed at Lambeth as page in Archbishop Morton's court. Thomas was only twelve when he first left home.

One point is certain, that, but for his father, Thomas would not have chosen to study law. He was barely fourteen when the Archbishop sent him to Oxford, a brief interlude in his carefully planned career. For the first and only time in many years, he lived outside London and away from his father's watchful eye. The poor little boy was kept very short of money and could not afford to have his shoes repaired without his father's leave. He was later to admit that his Oxford fare was the worst that he had known.

It never crossed More's mind to disobey his father and, later, he was to assert that his father was right. "Thus it came to pass," he would say, "that I indulged in no vice or vain pleasure, that I did not even know the meaning of extravagance and luxury, that I did not learn to put money to evil uses and, in fine, I had no love or even thought of anything beyond my studies."[9]

Though it cannot be held that Thomas disagreed with his father in the choice of his profession, it is abundantly clear that in leaving Oxford and the world of learning, he had to do violence to himself. Whether or not he learned Greek as Erasmus says, whether or not he met the great contemporary scholars as Seebohm doubtfully conjectured, he certainly showed signs of considerable promise in many fields. Harpsfield, both scholar and lawyer, expressed the situation in this way:

> where, for the short time of his abode there (not being fully two years) and for his age, he wonderfully profitted in the knowledge of the Latin and Greek tongues; where, if he had settled and fixed himself and run his full race in the study of the liberal sciences and divinity, I trow he would have been the singular and only spectacle of this our time for learning, but his father minded that he should tread after his steps and settle his whole mind and study upon the laws of the realm. And so being plucked from the Universities of study and learning, he was set to the studies of the laws only of this realm.[10]

[9] Stapleton, p. 3.   [10] Harpsfield, p. 59; Seebohm, pp. 24–26.

Young More had not yet met Erasmus when he went to Oxford and the great Dutch scholar had his information on this particular at secondhand. Nevertheless his remarks on the point deserve special attention, not only because Erasmus had exceptional powers of observation, but also out of respect for his intimate friendship with Thomas More at a later date. Five years later, they were to walk together from Greenwich to Eltham, and on this or some similar occasion, More may have unburdened himself. Erasmus wrote:

He had drunk deep of good letters from his earliest years; and when a young man, he applied himself to the study of Greek and of philosophy; but his father was so far from encouraging him in this pursuit that he withdrew his allowance and almost disowned him, because he thought he was deserting his hereditary study, himself being an expert professor of English law. For, remote as that profession is from true learning, those who become masters of it have the highest rank and reputation among their countrymen; and it is difficult to find any readier way to acquire fortune and honour. Indeed a considerable part of the nobility of that island has had its origin in this profession, in which it is said that no one can be perfect until he has toiled at it for many years. It was natural that, in his younger days, our friend's genius, born for better things, should shrink from this study; nevertheless, after he had had a taste of the learning of the schools, he became so conversant with it that there is no one more eagerly consulted by suitors; and the income that he made by it was not surpassed by any of those who did nothing else; such was the power and quickness of his intellect.[11]

With a character as subtle as Thomas More's, so sensitive, so ready to make a joke to divert attention, we may hardly glimpse the years of frustration which were to stem from his father's four-square attachment to English law. Young More left Oxford at sixteen to return to London, probably lived with his father in Milk Street, studied law at Lincoln's Inn. He began to earn his living without any outward sign of discontent. He was

[11] Erasmus to Hutten, Nichols, 3, p. 393.

successful with his studies from the first. It would be wrong to suggest that he did not enjoy his professional work or his legal studies but, despite many similarities, his character differed profoundly from his father's and he could find in the law none of the satisfaction which he sought. Young More lacked any ambition—surely a prerequisite for a full professional life? He was entirely disinterested in money-making, played no games and was unattracted to society life. While he was always competent in practical affairs and often brilliant, his heart was never committed to them. Even today, one may sense his enthusiasm mounting when he is writing or conversing on intellectual pursuits.

John More may have wanted his son to "settle his whole mind" to his legal studies and Thomas would have intended to obey his father, but with only partial success. He was a scholar born. Grace of expression both in Latin and in English gave him exquisite pleasure, though it must always be remembered that, at this time and for years later, he never had the publication of his writings in mind. He studied law by day but continued to practise his style, to read the classics, to exercise his talent for translation late into the night. Stapleton reports: "More's natural bent was entirely to a literary life and often did he bewail the multitude of business he had to attend to and the constant interruptions to which he was subject". In one of the very earliest of his letters he wrote to Colet: "Meantime I pass my time with Grocyn, Linacre and our dear friend Lillie," not one of whom was a lawyer, all three of whom were enthusiasts for the new learning, scholars who, like Colet himself, had made the long trek to Italy.[12]

The point may seem unimportant but the fashioning of More's character was much affected by this struggle within himself. His greatness is whittled away by those biographers who see him as always witty, calm, earnest, at peace with others and with himself. The sense of frustration survived long after adolescence and was still with him when he had climbed to the highest offices of State. Twenty-two years after he had left the University More was to write to Erasmus:

[12] Stapleton, pp. 11, 30.

You bid me, dear Erasmus, to write fully to you about everything, which I am all the more disposed to do as I understand that you were pleased with my former letter as a proof of my love. But when you say that you were also pleased with it because it showed my proficiency in power of expression, you invite me at once to be silent. For how can I be disposed to write to you if my letters are to be curiously weighed and examined? And when you compliment me on my scholarship, I blush to think how much I am losing every day of the less than little that I ever had; which cannot but be the case with one constantly engaged in legal disputations, so remote from every kind of learning. If therefore you weigh my words, that is to say, if you count my errors and barbarisms, you bid me hold my tongue; but if you are content to hear about your business and mine in whatever speech comes to my pen, I will tell you about your money, as of most importance.[13]

Young More remained always a scholar at heart and when, as we shall see, he turned to the education of his children, he drew up for them a very different syllabus to the one which he had been forced to follow in his youth. Almost at the end of his life, he wrote to Erasmus with the same note of sorrow after he had resigned the Lord Chancellorship: "From the time I was a boy I have longed, dear Desiderius, that, what I rejoice in you having always enjoyed, I myself might someday enjoy also namely, that being free of public business, I might have some time to devote to God and myself." The poignancy of this heartfelt relief comes home to us vividly when we remember that More never had this respite, was never free of public office; he changed from Lord Chancellor to traitor and martyr inside three years.[14]

Weighing both sides, the years of frustration and the loss to scholarship against his legal achievements, it seems clear in retrospect that old Sir John was right. Thus, it may be questioned whether More as a wholetime scholar would have written better than he did. By instinct and prejudice, Sir John reached the possibly wise conclusion that much of what passed for the new

---

[13] Nichols, 2, p. 293.   [14] Cf. Bridgett, p. 245.

learning would eventually prove to be ephemeral. In the end More outstripped all his friends. Two, at least, of his books, *Utopia* and *A Dialogue of Comfort against Tribulation* have surpassed in wisdom any other book written in his day. The *Dialogue of Comfort*, for so many centuries ignored, may, one day, in a new translation, be seen to rival St Augustine himself. The genius of More, his thought, his wit, his spiritual approach to life was fashioned by the active, selfless round of engagements which he was forced to fulfil. What would he have been like had he remained at Oxford and, like Erasmus, given his life to books? As it turned out, More never became a great scholar, nor was he in the fullest sense one of England's greatest lawyers, but he certainly became one of Europe's greatest and most noble characters. Sir John did not foresee it but, only as a statesman and a lawyer, could his son have made his last, heroic stand.

3. THE YOUNG CITY MAN

In outline the life of Thomas More is simple with but a few ambiguities as to facts or dates. The date of his birth is now almost certainly settled and, as his life was spent in public service, we may follow his career through his promotions recorded in the public registers. One period alone presents any problems, those ten years between his leaving Oxford and his marriage in the spring of 1505. Facts are not lacking; only the sequence is obscure. During this decade, young More was unimportant and very few of his letters have been preserved. Yet, in anyone's life, the spell between sixteen and twenty-six holds the secret of future failure or success. An analysis of these ten years of More's story is fascinating for we find there the adolescent problems and struggles of so very human and imitable a saint.

Most saints are martyred by their own biographers, who already know what they want to find before they begin their research. Few saints are lucky enough to have as biographers their exact contemporaries who knew them in their formative and less perfect years. Most biographers are younger than their heroes and, if they knew them at all, saw them through young, ardent and innocent eyes. Thomas More is not exceptional in this. Though he had three of the best biographers that any great man could hope for, all three were younger and two of the three, Stapleton and Harpsfield, drew their material from More's friends and children, all of whom knew him as a martyr and a saint. They were not wrong in this and their stories are both factual and honest, but, in the fervour of their devotion to his memory, they make him seem almost impossibly good. Not a single fault is recorded of him unless we count as a fault the story of his daughter that she could remember her father losing his temper twice. Nor is much told about his struggles, those inner conflicts, doubts, misgivings which would have shown in detail the kind of man he was. Poor Professor Chambers yearns "for some stories which might have dissipated that atmosphere of blamelessness which is the greatest difficulty with which More's biographer has to cope."[15]

Thomas More was, in fact, blameless but, unlike so many other saints, he has been spared an air of priggishness. Erasmus was his contemporary. This extraordinary man, illegitimate by birth, scholar, cynic, a semi-dispensed religious, knew young More intimately. Erasmus was not particularly pious, rarely missed the chance of a bitter comment and certainly would not have liked More if More had been a prig. The gist of Erasmus's tribute to More, written long before More was either a statesman or a martyr, is a defence against the very suggestion of priggishness. Erasmus seems to say in all that he wrote that this friend of his who was in all things blameless was also so witty, so amusing, such very good company.

If Erasmus saves More from seeming unendurably good, he also does him considerable service in emphasizing some of the problems which More had to face. One has been mentioned, the threat of his father to disown him unless he studied law. No later biographer dared to state the situation so bluntly and few of us who gaze at father and son in the Holbein portrait could have imagined such a crisis in the martyr's early life. No one will

[15] Chambers, p. 98.

accuse Erasmus of trying to create a saint and his evidence is the more telling when we remember the egocentricity of his own character and the mordant nature of his wit.

Add to Erasmus's evidence all that we learn of More through his own writings, some published, some never intended for publication, and we see more clearly the imposing array of fears, hesitancies, misgivings against which he struggled throughout his life. His jokes put many off the scent. He was certainly scrupulous and often unsure of himself. Had it not been for Erasmus, I doubt if he would ever have published a book. His confidence increased throughout the years but, in his final meditations in the Tower of London, we grasp with amazement the kind of battle which he had had to fight. One sees very clearly why he always liked to hide his identity, to argue both sides to every question and to fall back on dialogue.

Oddly enough, the only adverse criticism which I can find of More, though from a suspect source and not well authenticated, may, in fact, come near to the truth. Archbishop Cranmer of all people is quoted to have held that he found More "somewhat too conceited and too fond of laying himself out to gain approval and admiration of those around him; never willing to vary anything which he had once expressed, whether right or wrong, lest he should damage his reputation thereby". The charge is not proved —one would naturally expect such a remark from Cranmer— but it helps us to see More in a less celestial light.[16]

Another contemporary, Richard Pace, throws a further light on young More's problems when he describes an argument between More and two professional theologians on a very silly point proposed by them. Pace remarks: "I regret to say that More has frequently the ill-luck that, whenever he says something very learned or acute among such dignified fathers in reference to their science, which is also quite as much his own, they always oppose him and call his words puerile. It is not that they really think him wrong or that he says anything puerile but that they are jealous of his marvellous talent, of his knowledge of so many

[16] *Philomorus*, p. 5.

other things of which they are ignorant." On this particular occasion, Pace, in a final sentence, hits off More perfectly: "When he saw that they did not understand his meaning, he laughed to himself and went on his way."[17]

In considering young More in these first ten years of his life in professional London, we might well follow the example of Erasmus in his famous letter to Ulrich von Hutten in 1517. Erasmus began with a description of More's appearance and though he was writing of More some twenty years later, he adds a very significant detail, "What charm there was in his looks when young may even now be inferred from what remains."[18]

Young More was unusually attractive—one might almost say beautiful—after studying the one certain likeness of him, the sketch painted by Holbein when More was in his fiftieth year. The verdict of Erasmus may be tested even in our day, "What charm there was in his looks when young may be inferred from what remains." This strange attraction was admitted implicitly by a long line of distinguished men. Cardinal Morton fell for the charm of the small boy of thirteen. Colet, Grocyn, Linacre, Lillie and Erasmus felt a similar attraction and, many years later, Henry VIII was to walk in the garden for an hour with his arm around More's neck. Erasmus neatly expresses all this in a question for which he had the answer, "What has nature ever created more gentle, more sweet, more happy than the genius of Thomas More?" Professor Reed adds a significant detail: "In his younger days, More took pleasure in the company of older men whilst later in life young people became his devotees."

He was of average height, boyish, delicate, well proportioned, with brown hair, a blond rather than a pale complexion and an occasional flush which suffused his whole face. This flush reveals his gay, ardent disposition, quick in sympathy, sharp in retort, fascinated by everything going on around him, matched by a gift of spontaneous expression which makes all that he says vivid and personal. We see him as a small boy darting on to the stage at

[17] Richard Pace, *De Fructu*, Bridgett's translation, p. 13.
[18] Nichols, 3, p. 389.

Lambeth during a Christmas pageant and, unrehearsed, delighting the adult audience with an extempore part. Latimer brings out the same ardour in a later letter to Erasmus: "I first read your letter on the very day I fell in with More and he took the opportunity of discussing both matters carefully with me. You know yourself how quick More is, how eager his intellect and with what energy he pursues any work that he has begun." Perhaps the best example of all is the letter he wrote to John Holt, his former schoolmaster, describing the wedding of Princess Catherine of Aragon to Prince Arthur at St Paul's. "You would have burst with laughing if you had seen them (the Spanish escort); they looked like devils out of hell. . . . As to the Princess everyone is singing her praises. There is nothing wanting in her that the most beautiful girl should have."[19]

Young More, laughing, flushed, intense is also often anxious, a trait observed by many and later captured by Holbein in the famous portrait, an anxiety conveyed in the earnest gaze of his bluish grey eyes. He unconsciously reveals himself in a letter to Erasmus when Peter Giles his friend was ill: "So anxious a thing is love that I am driven to fear things which, perhaps, may be worse than reality."[20] There is much of the true More of the *Dialogue of Comfort* in this remark.

If we follow Erasmus, More was indifferent about his dress—his clothes were often crooked, crumbled, even dirty; he was always anxious not to appear effeminate. Not physically robust, not attracted to sport, all his life abstemious, he was happiest with a group of scholars and clerics, all many years older than himself. At this period of his life, he rarely mentions his brothers and sisters or their friends. There is occasional mention of one Staverton who later married Joan, his eldest sister, and once, on a visit to Erasmus, lodging at Greenwich, More took with him another young lawyer, Edward Arnold, and the three went to

---

[19] Latimer to Erasmus, Nichols, 3, p. 236. More's letter to John Holt is found in Rogers, p. 3. More wrote: "*At Hispanorum comitatus, proh deorum atque hominum fidem, qualis erat! Vereor ne si aspexisses, ruptus ridendo fuisses ita ridiculi erant,* etc., etc." The above translation is from Chambers, p. 4.

[20] Nichols, 2, p. 585.

Eltham to see the royal children in their nursery. This incident occurred during the first visit that Erasmus paid to England during which started a friendship which was to last throughout More's life.

In the main young More was much more at home with older men and scholars with whom he could polish up his Latin, learn Greek and sharpen his precocious wit. Another explanation of this exclusiveness must be considered later, for More was restless and unsettled throughout these years. Though he was ten years younger than these distinguished European scholars, intellectually they saw him as an equal while his youthful enthusiasm gladdened them. Throughout his life, few could resist More's extraordinary appeal. Writes Erasmus to Hutten: "In company, his extraordinary kindness and sweetness of temper are such as to cheer the dullest spirit and alleviate the annoyance of the most trying circumstance. There is nothing that occurs in human life from which he does not seek to extract some pleasure, although the matter may be serious in itself. He is not offended even by professional clowns as he adapts himself with marvellous dexterity to the tastes of all." Anyone who knows the querulous, self-pitying Erasmus of his other letters, will grasp from such tributes just how attractive and winning Thomas More must have been.

There can be no doubt at all that during these early years young More gave his mind to his legal studies; his subsequent honours and promotions suggest that he was one of the outstanding students of his year. His heart may have been elsewhere but his nose was in his books. No more is heard of his father who, having won his point, had little about which to complain. Young More spent two years at New Inn and entered Lincoln's Inn in 1496 when he was just eighteen. During these years he seems to have taken some part in the social life of the City and Erasmus, ever watchful, records the fact. While with the ladies, in general More's talk was a mixture of playfulness and teasing; there can be little doubt that he was invariably courteous, shy, uncertain and that on one occasion at least he fell in love. Erasmus writes: "When of a sentimental age, he was not a stranger to the emotions of love but without loss of character, having no inclination to press his advantage and being more attracted by a mutual liking than by any licentious object." It is surprising that Professor Chambers should deduce from this that "More's youth had not been altogether blameless", for no blame need be attached to an adolescent love affair. One thing is certain, that so reticent and sensitive a man would keep all such affections entirely to himself. Young More could joke about women in public, in the music-hall fashion of his father, but his heart lay very much deeper than his sleeve.[21]

We may never now know exactly who Eliza was or whether or not she ever existed, but the poem about her gives us another glimpse of the inner More. He merely tells us that he had loved her in his youth.

> Thou liv'st Eliza, to these eyes restored,
> O more than life, in life's gay bloom, adored.
> Many a long year, since first we met, has rolled,
> I, then, was boyish and I now am old.
> Scarce had I bid my sixteenth summer hail,
> And two in thine were wanting to the tale,
> When thy soft mien—ah, mien for ever fled;
> On my tranced heart, its guiltless influence shed. . . .
>
> Now on my memory breaks that happy day,
> When I first saw thee with thy mates at play.
> On thy white neck the flaxen ringlet lies,
> With snow thy cheek, thy lip with roses vies.
> Thine eyes, twin stars with arrowy radiance shine,
> And pierce and sink into my heart through mine.
> Struck as with heaven's own bolt, I stand, I gaze,
> I hang upon thy look in fixed amaze.
> And as I writhe beneath the new-felt spear,
> My artless pangs our young companions jeer.
>
> So charmed me thy fair form; at least to me
> Fairest of all the forms it seemed to be.
> Whether the glow that fills our early frame,

[21] Nichols, 3, p. 392; cf. Chambers, pp. 80, 83.

Lit in my breast the undecaying flame,
Or some kind planet at our natal hour
Deigned on our hearts its common beam to pour;
For one who knew with what chaste warmth you burned,
Had blabbed the secret of my love returned.
Then, the duenna and the guarded door
Baffled the stars and bade us meet no more.

Severed, our different fates we then pursued,
Till this late day my raptures are renewed.
This day whose rare felicity I prize
Has given thee safe to my delighted eyes.
Crimeless, my heart you stole in life's soft prime,
And still possess that heart without a crime.
Pure was the love which in my youth prevailed,
And age would keep it pure if honour failed.
O may the Gods who, five long lustres past,
Have brought us to each other well at last,
Grant that when number'd five long lustres more,
Healthful, I still may hail thee healthful as before.[22]

[22] Archdeacon Wrangham's translation; cf. *Philomorus*, p. 53. The Latin verse
is entitled: "*Gratulatur quod eam repererit incolumen quam olim ferme puer amaverat.*"

CHAPTER TWO

The Realist

I. YOUNG MORE GOES TO THE CHARTERHOUSE

How MUCH WE would like to have known more about Eliza, to have questioned Colet, Grocyn, old John More and, most of all, Erasmus about young More's early love affairs. Apart from Colet, his confessor, they probably could have told us little, for this young man, so attractive, so full of the joy of life, who "seems to have been born and made for friendship", was remarkably reticent about himself. In all matters of deep, emotional commitment, young More said little to anyone. An extraordinary silence runs through his life, so much at variance with his social urbanity, that his baffled biographers have been forced to concentrate mainly on his political achievements and to fill up the gaps with reminiscences pieced together after his untimely death. Had More died a natural death, his secrets might well have ended in that tomb at Chelsea which he had so thoughtfully provided for himself. There they would have rested under an epitaph deliberately written to tell only half the tale.

No one knew Thomas More very well. Even those who lived in his house and loved him dearly were often baffled and surprised. His children for many years failed to grasp all that went on at Chelsea in a place which they called "the new building", erected by More at some distance from the house. They only knew that he retired there on Fridays to read and to say his prayers.

One hot summer evening when More sat at supper "singly in his doublet and hose, wearing thereupon a plain shirt without ruff or collar" his daughter-in-law spotted the edge of his hairshirt and laughed at it. Meg, his daughter, warned him secretly and he, embarrassed, hastily covered it.[1] Anne Cresacre was not the only one puzzled by his hairshirt. Years earlier Dame Alice, his wife, had found out about it; she consulted his confessor, begged this good man to dissuade her husband, was puzzled how her husband had his laundry washed. Now Meg, his eldest daughter, knew all about his penances and washed his hairshirt for him but even she did not know so much about her father's spiritual life. In the Tower, he opened her eyes about a point or two. William Roper, after sixteen years in the More household, was deeply surprised on one critical occasion when his father-in-law was so preoccupied with his spiritual struggle with the devil that he forgot to ask the commissioners at Lambeth for the concession he had come for, to have his name removed from a treason Bill. These scenes may be considered later but the mystery of More's life is sensed even in his teens.

Even as a boy, young More kept his own counsel where, normally, one so friendly and enthusiastic would have been quick to seek advice. What did his father think? What was the reaction of Grocyn who was teaching him Greek, when young More decided to go and live in the Charterhouse? All his friends knew a little, but Erasmus, the only contemporary to touch the subject, did not know much. Erasmus writes: "Meantime he applied his whole mind to religion, having some thought of taking orders for which he prepared himself by watchings and fastings and prayers and such like exercises; wherein he showed much more wisdom than the generality of people who rashly engage in so arduous a profession without testing themselves beforehand. And indeed there was no obstacle to his adopting this kind of life, except the fact that he could not shake off his wish to marry. Accordingly he resolved to be a chaste husband rather than a licentious priest."[2]

This famous but misinformed statement from Erasmus shows us how little More told his friends about himself. Only after his death did the full truth come to be known. Erasmus says nothing about the Carthusians or the London Charterhouse. Nor does Stapleton, who informs us that More once thought of being a

---

[1] Roper, p. 25.   [2] Nichols, 3, pp. 393-394.

Franciscan and that he and his great friend Lillie talked much of becoming priests. It is Harpsfield who gives us the whole story; Harpsfield who had his information, in the main, from William Roper and, hence, from More's beloved daughter Meg.

Possibly Meg alone knew during his lifetime that her father had thought of becoming a Carthusian, that his strong inclination was towards a solitary life. Meg, and her husband William Roper, had had a hint from More at the time of Meg's serious illness but even they grasped the full truth only when More was in the Tower of London waiting for death. Then, on three occasions, More revealed some of his inner thoughts. Harpsfield alone of the biographers seems to have grasped the crisis through which More passed so early in his life. He alone points out that young More, in his early reading, cut time from his legal studies to give his mind to St Augustine's *City of God*. Harpsfield sets out the crisis well.

And all the while was he unmarried and seemed to be in some doubt and deliberation with himself what kind of trade of life he should enter, to follow and pursue all his long life after. Surely it seemeth by some apparent conjectures that he was sometime somewhat propense and inclined either to be a priest or to take some monastical and solitary life; for he continued after his aforesaid reading four years and more full virtuously and religiously in great devotion and prayer with the monks of the Charterhouse of London without any manner of profession or vow, either to see or to prove whether he could frame himself to that kind of life or, at least, for a time to sequester himself from all temporal and worldly exercises.[3]

Four years is a large slice from a young man's career. The Carthusian rule was and is one of the strictest, not to be undertaken without much self-denial even by one who does not bind himself by vows. The decision to live in the Charterhouse, made by a young and attractive man in the early twenties, argues a determination which, previously, few who knew him would

[3] Stapleton, pp. 9-10; Roper, p. 4; Harpsfield, p. 62.

have guessed. These four years proved to be the turning-point in Thomas More's attitude to life.

First, certain small points must be considered and despatched. In Tudor times it was by no means uncommon for monasteries to welcome long-term guests. Ammonio and Erasmus both lodged with the Augustinians, while Colet in old age retired to the Charterhouse at Sheen. We will now never know whether or not More lodged in the guest house, lived with the brothers or occupied his own cell. His own remarks suggest that his room was cramped. It seems likely that he continued with his studies and that he went into London from time to time. Yet Harpsfield is emphatic that More was not just a boarder; he followed the monastic schedule and cut himself off, as far as he could, from the world outside the Charterhouse. Lillie may have joined him for a time.[4]

More must have known the London Charterhouse well. Dedicated to the Annunciation of Our Lady and popularly known as the Salutation, it stood just outside the walls of the City, not five minutes' walk from his father's house. As a small boy, More must often have passed the Charterhouse, seen the high walls and heard the bells. To judge from old prints, the ancient monastery boasted an imposing group of buildings, some of which still remain. For four years More must have passed it every day.

Of the two most honoured of contemplative orders bound to prayer and silence, the Cistercians live their lives in common, sleep in dormitories together and spend their days toiling in

---

[4] Many problems arise over More's stay at the Charterhouse. The fact can hardly be disputed but it is difficult to assign the years. More could have lodged with the monks soon after he returned from Oxford, in which case he would have done his legal studies there. Or he went to the Charterhouse after his studies, say from 1500 to 1503. It is certain that he took no vows, was not even a novice, and it seems likely that for part of his stay he continued his secular career. Contemplative orders, even in our day, meet men in just such an undecided state. We have no record of More's life inside the Charterhouse. The study of his subsequent career, of his method of prayer, of his writings, reveals his secret and explains his attitude. Had Roper and Harpsfield told us nothing about the years in the Charterhouse, we might still have come near to guessing More's contemplative yearnings from what he shows us of himself. Exactly as with Picus, we would have wondered why More had not tried his vocation as a contemplative.

the fields. The Carthusians, on the other hand, follow a solitary vocation, each monk inhabiting a four-room "cell". The Carthusians come together in church for the solemn celebration of the Divine Office, after which each monk retires to his cell. More was later to refer to this. The Divine Office is never interrupted, its exact performance being the central duty of each succeeding day. The community rises for Matins soon after midnight and observes the sequence of hours throughout the day. In their cells, the monks divide the time between prayer, study and the care of their small enclosed gardens; those who wish may practise some solitary craft. No meat is eaten and the fare, distributed daily by the brothers, is frugal, each monk eating in his cell. The Carthusian vocation is suited only to those who are drawn to be hermits and who wish to live their days alone with God.

We may never hope to understand Thomas More unless we are ready to recognize in him this deep and genuine desire for such an austere and solitary life. His jokes, his charm, his love of friends, his scholarly pursuits must all be judged against the background of the Charterhouse. Not only did he love the life, not only was he, in so many ways, ideally suited for it but he missed it when, after four years, he returned to the world which he had hoped to quit. If we are astonished that so merry and gentle a man should have considered for a moment so austere and chilly a vocation, it is because More has foxed us along with most of his contemporaries. He was the complete realist.

This realism of More's deserves our careful attention if we are to know him better and to copy his sanity. His martyrdom was, in a sense, accidental whereas his wisdom has carried down the ages and is available for the men and women of our age.

Richard Pace, King Henry VIII's very able secretary, describing the fruits which may be derived from learning, makes an apt comment on the genius of Thomas More. Pace was not concerned with spiritual things. In fact, he was dealing with More's skill as a translator, yet he throws considerable light on the Charterhouse episode. Treating of translators, Pace writes:

"Here I will remark that no one ever lived who did not first ascertain the meaning of the words and from them gather the meaning of the sentences which they compose—no one, I say, with one single exception and that is our own Thomas More. For he is wont to gather the force of the words from the sentences in which they occur, especially in his study and translation of Greek. This is not contrary to grammar but above it and an instinct of genius."[5]

Whether or not More had this skill—Richard Pace, his colleague and friend, was well placed to know it—he certainly enjoyed a similar width of vision in the spiritual life. Pace's example is a good one, for who does not know the tedium of translation when words taken out of context are turned up one by one in the dictionary? Those who can see at a glance the meaning of a full sentence may be sure that their whole translation will spring to life. In much the same way, the religious man who comprehends at a glance the whole vision of spiritual reality avoids the friction between the law and the spirit and enjoys the freedom of the contemplative.

The ways of God are certainly unusual; we will never know why More was granted this exceptional grace. Somehow we have come to think of sanctity as either running in families or, as in the case of Augustine or Ignatius of Loyola, resulting from a sudden shock. Not so with More whose home was ordinary and who received no shock. His parents were, undoubtedly, virtuous and devout but showed none of those spiritual yearnings traditionally to be expected from the parents of a saint. His mother was said to have had a dream foretelling her son's greatness but as More himself was the one who told the story, we need not take it too seriously. More, unlike Augustine, had no Monica to egg him on. Nor was he marked off by any special signs in childhood; God is not mentioned by his biographers until after his stay in the Charterhouse. We cannot be sure of his age at the time of his experiment; it seems most likely that he resided with the Carthusians from the age of twenty-one to twenty-four. Until

[5] Cf. Bridgett, p. 12.

that event was over, he appears no more than an attractive, witty and good-living boy.

Cardinal Morton and others foretold for him a great career in this world but few of his friends were much concerned with the next. Linacre, though a priest, was not very pious, Grocyn was devout but far more concerned with learning, Erasmus, an ex-claustrated monk, sounds genuinely relieved when More decides for the married life. Colet alone was of a calibre sufficient to carry More upwards but Colet himself had certain curious limitations of which More was well aware. The younger man consulted Colet on many occasions but there is no evidence that the future dean of St Paul's could offer him more than straightforward, commonsense advice. Now and throughout his life, More needed encouragement and reassurance and Colet gave him that.[6]

No biographer claims for Thomas More any of those heavenly visitations so frequently reported in the lives of other saints. He seems to have heard no voices, seen no visions, endured no spiritual shocks. Reginald Pole, a personal friend of the More family, is reputed to have said that More endured great doubts at one stage, later in his story, which were suddenly dispersed "by a light supernatural and a supernatural love given him by the mercy of God". Though not in the least unlikely, such a statement lacks further proof. The sum total of our knowledge of More's spiritual life from outside sources is neatly expressed in Harpsfield's apt expression, "that always he had a special and singular regard and respect to Godward," and the seed of his spirituality may be found in that. Godward is for More the *mot juste*.

Young More's vision to Godward was comprehensive, penetrating every corner of his being and every phase of his later life. His style of prayer did not follow the method which proved so successful in the next four centuries; it stood closer to that of St Bernard or St Augustine than to St Teresa of Avila or St Francis de Sales. The spirituality of the Church changed at the Reforma-

---

[6] More to Erasmus, Nichols, 2, p. 393. More writes: "He [Colet] is apt, as you know, to resist persuasion for the sake of a dispute, even if one wants to persuade him to do the very thing to which he is himself most inclined."

tion; More belonged in prayer to the medieval world. He knew none of those subtle rules and regulations, preludes, points and colloquies which were used with effect by later saints. Nor did he share their fears of Jansenism or Quietism, worries which began to feature in the manuals eighty years after his death.

To us looking back, he may be classed as medieval, though the great medieval contemplatives might also have found his methods a little strange. St Bernard or St Anselm could hardly have visualized a layman and successful lawyer praying like a hermit and knowing far more about theology than most priests. They might have been surprised to meet a saint who delighted in the pagan classics and found these an aid on his way to God. Perhaps, of all the saints, Augustine would have understood More most fully just as More knew Augustine best.

More was, in fact, the saint of his own transitional age. It is curious to note that he studied the same books as Fisher, Cranmer, Latimer, Luther and Erasmus and shared with Luther many aspirations and doubts. Indeed, at the very time when young More was leaving the Charterhouse for marriage, Luther, a layman, plagued with worries, was entering the Augustinian novitiate at Erfurt to escape from similar doubts. More had much in common with Luther but he solved his problems differently. He also had very much in common with Ignatius of Loyola, then serving as a knight in the army of Isabella of Castile. More and Ignatius never met but they were in London together for one summer, between 1529 and 1533.

Had they met, they would instantly have discovered much in common, the cure of scruples, the use of the imagination in prayer, the vexed question of obedience, the value of the humanities in education, the reality of the devil and, above all, a vivid, personal loyalty to Christ our Lord. On one point only would there have been considerable disagreement, for Ignatius of Loyola regarded Erasmus, at best, as dangerous.

More was the child of his age, an age of transition and, hence, an age with many problems similar to our own. The realism of his approach to Godward would match many of our moods. In

his outlook on life, More has so much in common with Shakespeare, so much in common with Hamlet, a Hamlet who found
the answer to his problems in the Charterhouse.

More's spiritual realism may best be considered under four
clear headings, for his approach to God follows the classic Christian pattern and may be seen as the blending of four basic ingredi-
ents. All four were present in his youth, matured together, and
gave to his spiritual vision its striking colour and integrity. Other
great Christian writers may have covered a wider canvas, touched
on more subjects, shown themselves more confused. The simplicity of More's approach is scriptural and satisfying, a tonic to
simple people in any age. Further, so many of his writings were
private and never intended for publication; as we read them we
are conscious of their intimacy, of what went on in his mind and
heart during those four years at the Charterhouse.

2. A SENSIBLE APPRECIATION OF DEATH

A vivid appreciation of the reality of death is the first and
cardinal notion to absorb More's recorded thoughts. With the
exception of *Utopia*, it would be hard to find a page in any of
More's writings which does not lead back to this central fact.
This preoccupation with death might, in fact, be termed obsess-
ional if it had been found in a less witty and less balanced man.
How much one would have liked to find the natural cause, if any,
for the sober fascination which death held for him. In his quaint,
delightful English he can express his philosophy so lightly, "from
our beginning to our ending one continual dying, so that wake
we, sleep we, eat we, drink we, mourn we, sing we, in what
wise soever live we, all the same while, die we."[7]

Some general explanation may be found, no doubt, in the
fashion of the age. More was the child of an age which derived a
morbid satisfaction from so grim a topic, witness the stone skele-
tons on graves, the sombre soliloquies of Shakespeare, the enorm-
ous popular appeal of *Everyman*, that stark, early sixteenth-century
morality play. Undoubtedly his century provided More with a

[7] *English Works*, I, p. 475.

black-edged background and with many timely reminders in the outbreaks of the plague. Both plague and sweating sickness were endemic and thousands died in London and in other English towns. Yet More, who found the subject of death so all-absorbing, was also always merry and not physically afraid. Though Erasmus and Henry VIII were both terrified of the sickness and rushed from place to place to avoid contagion, More remained calm. Thus he wrote to Erasmus in 1517:

We are in the greatest sorrow and danger. Multitudes are dying all around us; almost everyone in Oxford, Cambridge and London has been ill lately and we have lost many of our best and most honoured friends; among them—I grieve at the grief I shall cause you in relating it—our dear Andrew Ammonio, in whose death both letters and all good men suffer a great loss. He thought himself well fortified against the contagion by his moderation of diet. He attributed it to this, that, whereas he met hardly anyone whose family had not been attacked, the evil had touched none of his household. He was boasting of this to me and many others not many hours before his death, for in this "Sweating Sickness" no one dies except on the first day of the attack. I myself and my wife and children are as yet untouched and the rest of my household have recovered. I assure you there is less danger on the battlefield than in the city. Now, as I hear, the plague has begun to rage in Calais, just as we are being forced to land there on our embassy, as if it was not enough to have lived in the midst of the contagion but we must follow it also. But what would you have! We must bear our lot. I have prepared myself for any event. Farewell in haste. London. 19th August.[8]

I give this one letter in full to contrast its courage and calmness with the gruesome meditations on death in which More indulged. Young More was not afraid of death. His was a much deeper and philosophical attraction, death at any moment was for him reality. When he tells us that the London urchins liked to play at funerals, we may be sure that he was one of them.

[8] Nichols, 3, p. 2; Bridgett, p. 75.

We are only guessing when we suggest that the early death of his little brother and sister may have coloured his outlook, but we know for certain how deeply he was affected by the "Dance of Death" in the cloister of St Paul's. The memory of this Dance was to draw from him one of his most vivid, almost repulsive, descriptions, written when he was living at the King's Court. One might, by omitting it, preserve the image of More as a merry jester at the cost of the true More, the determined realist, praying in the Charterhouse. I make no excuse for offering a hybrid version of the passage for we are not here studying More's English but the vividness of his attitude towards death. He writes:

For nothing is there that may more effectually withdraw the soul from the wretched affections of the body than may the remembrance of death; that is, if we recall it attentively and not as one who hears a word and lets it pass by his ear without any receiving of the sentence into his heart. But if we not only hear this word death but also let sink into our hearts the very fantasy and deep imagination thereof, we shall perceive that we were never so greatly moved by the Dance of Death pictured at Paul's as we shall be stirred and altered by the feeling of that imagination in our hearts. And no wonder. For those pictures show only the loathsome sight of our dead, bony bodies with the flesh bitten away; which, though it is ugly to behold, yet neither the light thereof nor the sight of all the dead skulls in the charnel house, nor the sight of a very ghost is half so grisly as the deep concept of the nature of death which a lively imagination engraves in thine own heart. For there you see not just one grievous sight of bare bones hanging by the sinews but, if you picture your own death as by this counsel you are advised, you see yourself, if you die no worse death, yet lying on your bed, your head shooting, your back aching, your veins throbbing, your heart panting, your throat rattling, your flesh trembling, your mouth gaping, your nose sharpening, your legs cooling, your fingers fumbling, your breath shortening, all your strength failing, your life vanishing and your death drawing on.[9]

[9] *English Works*, I, p. 468.

The scene given above is not exceptional but one of twenty in which young More paints for himself the reality of death. He is ready even to joke about it, missing no detail of the degradation which must come man's way. Below is another description, given not because the subject is pleasant but because More saw life this way.

> Have you not in the past in a time of grave illness, felt it very grievous to have folk babbling to you and asking you questions when it was a pain to speak? Have you never thought what it will be like when we lie dying, all our body in pain, all our mind in trouble, our soul in sorrow, our heart all in dread while our life walketh awayward, while our death draweth forward, while the devil is busy about us, while we lack stomach and strength to bear any one of these heinous troubles; as I say, have you not thought how it will feel to see before your eyes and to hear in your ears a rabble of fleshly friends, skipping about your bed and your sick body, like ravens about your corpse, now almost carrion, crying to you on every side "What shall I have? What shall I have?" Then your children will come to ask for their share; then your sweet wife will come and, where in your health she probably spoke not one sweet word in six weeks, now she calls you her dear husband and weeps with much work to ask you what she shall have; then your executors ask for your keys and what money is owing and what substance you have and where it is kept. And to you in that state, their words will seem so tedious that you would want to throw them all on the fire so that you could lie just half an hour in peace.[10]

Only once have I come across an outlook on death comparable to More's and this was in Granada where an unknown Carthusian artist had painted a Spanish version of the "Dance of Death" in the cloister of the Charterhouse.

More did not confine himself to this grave-digger approach to death. The two passages quoted above are taken from *The Four Last Things*, a short, unpolished treatise written for his children; it represents his own attitude in boyhood and an outlook on death

[10] *Ibid.*, I, p. 469.

which he wished his children to share. Modern educators may
wince, but modern educators are not all as witty or as spiritual as
Thomas More. In this particular exercise on "The Four Last
Things", Meg was invited to compete with her father but, alas,
her contribution has not survived.

In his own life, More's grasp of the immediate threat and
reality of death showed itself in many other forms. It accounts for
his deep appreciation of Christ's agony in the Garden and bitter
Passion about which he was to write in the Tower of London and
towards which, in his last years, his mind so frequently turned.
Again, his sublimation of the fear of death on which he worked
throughout his lifetime is the heroic theme of his *Dialogue of
Comfort against Tribulation*, written in the Tower to console his
family after his death. Though the ghoulish approach to death
breaks through on occasion, these dialogues are sublime in their
courage and show forth the magnificence of More's victory.
Finally there is his philosophic approach to death, the approach
of Shakespeare by way of Touchstone whom More anticipated by
almost a hundred years.

The mind of young More on this subject is introduced to us
first in a most pleasing manner through some of the first English
verses that he wrote. Their date is uncertain but they were probably written before or during his stay at the Charterhouse.
Whatever their history, they tell us much about More, much
about his father's house, much about life in London and show his
mature grasp in early age of the reality of life.

In Rastell's great collection of his uncle's works, we come early
on the following heading:

"Mayster Thomas More in his youth devysed in hys fathers
house in London, a very good hangyng of fyne paynted clothe,
with nyne pageauntes and verses over every of those pageauntes
represented; and also in those pageauntes were paynted, the
thynges that the verses over them dyd (in effecte) declare, whiche
verses here folowe."

The old-time spelling here adds to the charm and quaintness of
young More's unusual display. We can only guess at the size and

shape of this fine painted cloth, its colour, its design, its purpose, just as we can only guess at the dimensions of old John More's house in Milk Street and his own reactions to this inspiration of his son's. We do not know the name of the artist who painted the nine pageants, but young More it was who wrote both the headings and the verses and who, presumably, decided the illustrations and the sequence of scenes. Maybe the banner was designed for display on some civic occasion and may have hung for many years in his father's hall. The verses are undistinguished but their theme is deeply spiritual and reveals the motive which led young More to the Charterhouse.

More hit on an unusual device. The boy who is whipping his top in the first picture is lying on the ground in the second picture when a fine young man rides in on a horse, with hawk and greyhounds, ready for the chase. In turn, the fine young man is lying on the ground when, in the third picture, Venus and Cupid arrive. Venus and Cupid are prostrate when, in the fourth picture, we see seated, an honourable old man. The old man lies down when the image of death is triumphant just as death cowers before Fame and Fame before Eternity. We have, in fact, More's version of the stages of man, much deeper than Shakespeare's; More, after only four stages in this world, adds Death, Fame, Time, which is killed by Eternity.

The lad in the first scene is amusing but wholly frivolous; his verse may be roughly rendered:

> "I am a child; I give my mind to play,
> I'm good at quoits, cock-shying and at ball,
> I set my top and whip it on its way,
> But, would to God, my wretched school-books all
> Were on the fire; reduced to ashes small,
> Then, I could give my life to endless play,
> Which, Good God, grant me to my dying day."

At the other end, Eternity appears as a lady "sittyng in a chayre under a sumptious clothe of Estate, crowned with an imperial crown". Says Eternity, with Time beneath her feet:

"Why need I boast; I am Eternity,
My very name my Empire doth foretell,
As infinite I will for ever be,
While Time is mortal, but a passing spell;
What are you but a slight mobility,
Marking each change of sun and moon you see,
When these two cease their course, you will be brought
For all your pride and boasting back to nought."

One might well guess that young More would not stop his
pageant here. In the end a poet appears, to pronounce in limpid
Latin a warning of the emptiness of fragile, earthly pleasures and
to direct the hope of men towards God. Eternity herself leads us
to the God who made us.

> *Qui dabit eternam nobis pro munere vitam,*
> *In permansuro ponite vota Deo.*[11]

Young More's views on life and death, outlined in his early
verses, remained remarkably consistent throughout his life. He
expressed them first in his lovely translation of the life of Picus,
Earl of Mirandola, a work which he possibly undertook during
his Charterhouse days. The words of the devout Italian nobleman
exactly describe his own sentiments.

"Now to make an end with this one thing, I warn thee that
thou never forget these two things; that both the son of God died
for thee and that thou shalt also thyself die shortly, live thou never
so long. With these twain as with two spurs, that one of fear, that
other of love, spur forth thine horse throughout the short way of
this momentary life to the reward of eternal felicity since we
neither ought or may prefix ourselves any other end than the endless fruition of the infinite goodness, both the soul and body in
everlasting peace." More was to use these expressions many
times.[12]

Twenty years later, when he was at the start of his highly
successful career at Court, his mind was still centred on the short-

---

[11] *Ibid.*, I, pp. 332 seq. The verses have been slightly altered to bring out the sense.
[12] *Ibid.*, I, p. 368.

ness and uncertainty of life. He propounded to himself one of the best known of his parables, often quoted, and enhanced for us by the knowledge of the fate which lay in wait for him:

> So that we never ought to look towards death as a thing far off, considering that although he made no haste towards us, yet we never cease ourselves to make haste towards him. . . . I will put thee an homely example, not very pleasant but none the less very true and very fit for the matter.
>
> If there were two, both condemned to death, both carried out at once towards execution; of which two, the one was sure that the place of his execution were within one mile, the other twenty miles off, yea, an hundred an ye will, he that were in the cart to be carried an hundred miles would not take much more pleasure than his fellow in the length of his way, notwithstanding that it were a hundred times as long as his fellow and that he had thereby a hundred times as long to live, being sure and out of all question to die in the end.[13]

The same ruthless logic which More had learned from Picus and taught to his children, he, at the moment of his suffering and triumph, applied rigidly to himself. More was a prisoner in the Tower and it is Stapleton who tells the tale:

> Nothing then could move More from his purpose or cause him any fear. His wife, then, was sent into prison to tempt her husband, to weaken his resolution with soft words and womanly wiles or to move him to pity for his family. She came, and after greeting him, entreated him with all earnestness not to sacrifice his children, his country and his life which he might yet enjoy for many years. As she kept on pleading and harping upon a long life, he interrupted her. "And how long, my Alice, shall I be able to enjoy this life?" "A full twenty years," she replied, "if God so wills." "Do you wish me, then," said More, "to exchange eternity for twenty years? Nay, good wife, you do not bargain very skilfully. If you had said some thousands of years, you would have said something but yet what would that be in comparison with eternity?"[14]

[13] *Ibid.*, I, p. 475.   [14] Stapleton, p. 176.

More's was an astonishing consistency. From boyhood to the last painful moments in the Tower, this vivid realization of death was his predominant attitude. His answer to Dame Alice, at the end of his life, varies little from the poems which he wrote and the banners which he designed for his father's house when he was a child.

3. THE FOLLY OF THE WORLD

Thomas More's sense of humour should never be regarded as accidental; it is the first fruits of his attitude towards death. Convinced as he was that this life is but a passing phase to be ended at any moment, he was unable to take it seriously. Here is the second ingredient of his spiritual wisdom, a feature so unusual that many of his biographers are unable to deal with it. They forget not only that More was always in deadly earnest but that wise men are at their funniest in a crisis, a truth well illustrated in the London blitz.

Those who have not read Thomas More's writings must take it on faith that he was a very witty man. His jests, his puns, his merry stories and quaint verses, the skill with which he engineered amusing situations have been praised and imitated both by his enemies and friends. Indeed, a wide variety of apocryphal yarns have been told about him, few of them typical, many in doubtful taste. Professor Chambers does well to warn us of them; they are a form of flattery with which a humorist as great as More may well dispense.[15]

All his contemporaries recognize in him this humorous vein. If men like Hall found his joking excessive, others, Henry VIII, Morton and Erasmus, loved it and Erasmus pays an unusual tribute as one whose own mordant humour was notorious. Erasmus writes:

> From boyhood he was always so pleased with a joke that it might seem that jesting was the main object of his life; but with all that, he did not go as far as buffoonery nor had ever any inclination to bitterness. When quite young he wrote

[15] Chambers, p. 37.

farces and acted them. If a thing was facetiously said, even though it was aimed at himself, he was charmed at it, so much did he enjoy any witticism that had a flavour of subtlety or genius. This led to his amusing himself as a young man with epigrams and taking great delight in Lucian. Indeed, it was he that suggested my writing the *Moria* or *Praise of Folly* which was much the same as setting a camel to dance.[16]

More was, then, a very witty man. His humour presents us with a twofold problem, for humour is not normally associated with holy people, nor do we expect to find it in one who is toying with life in the Charterhouse. Certain saints have had a delightful sense of humour, Teresa of Avila high on the list. Yet it would not be unfair to assert that most saints seem to be serious, even grim. We may blame this partly on their biographers, partly to the fact that sanctity involved so many of them in leaving father, mother and home for Christ's sake. They placed themselves in a situation which did not lend itself to merriment. Had More remained in the Charterhouse, we would have known next to nothing of his wit. Teresa of Avila is at her best in her *Foundations*, when she is dealing with the world outside her convent walls. Augustine, too, is highly amusing but only when he comments on worldly shams. More is unique because he found his holiness as a layman and his vision to Godward did not rob him of the contrasting situations of his day-to-day professional life.

The majority of saints left the world, renounced its pleasures, guarded themselves from its allurements and, from a safe distance, condemned its folly and trivialities. More, also, thought of leaving it but eventually was persuaded to remain. He never despised the world or condemned it but it offered him few allurements and, such were his views on the threat of death, he could not stop laughing at all forms of human pomposity. I emphasize this point because it is a trait in More which is so unusual that few expect or allow for it. The world which was so sore a temptation to many holy people was, to More, ridiculous.

One might align More with those—there are many of them—

16 Nichols, 3, p. 391.

who can derive small pleasure from watching a conjuring show. As they know that they are being fooled, that the performance is a trick, that the man on the stage is not chewing razor blades or swallowing fire, they find themselves too adult to be much impressed. A similar cynicism is felt by those who work in a TV studio and are now no longer able to share our excitement as we watch a thriller on the screen. They know too much, see all the gimmicks, have themselves played a part in the great illusion and are no longer naïve enough to sit before a set. Mind you, they are still able to appreciate an amusing act and the skill of the great performer and one may often see the technicians watching, fascinated, as some great singer or dancer rehearses a future act. The same men who can appreciate true talent more fully than we can derive small pleasure from the make-believe.

Now More saw through life in this very fashion without any conscious effort on his part. So clear was his intuitive vision of the Eternal that he could only see life in this world from God's point of view. So much of what he saw looked so very much like play-acting that he could not take it seriously. Indeed he expresses this attitude in a vivid passage which might be rendered loosely in modern English thus: "If you noticed that some silly actor was inordinately proud of wearing a gold coronet while taking the part of an Earl in a stage play, would you not laugh at his foolishness, knowing full well that when the play is finished, he must put on his own shabby clothes and walk home in them? But don't you yourself also feel very smart and proud to wear an actor's outfit, forgetting that when your own part is completed, you, too, will walk off the stage as poor as he? Nor do you care to note that your play may end just as soon as his."[17]

In this passage two of More's deep, spontaneous reactions to life are intertwined. The reality of death and its immediacy make those look ridiculous who take themselves too seriously. As a consequence of this attitude, all More's humour springs from an appreciation of sham. It would be difficult to find one humorous passage in his writings which does not poke fun directly or in-

[17] *English Works*, I, p. 479. Text altered slightly.

directly at vainglory and hypocrisy. As this is so, one will find that almost all More's jokes are directed against the worldly and the wealthy and that he rarely mocks the poor, the sick, the sinner or the unfortunate. Occasionally, in his Latin verse, he laughs at the physical defects of fictitious characters of his own creation, the man with a nose so long that it was out of reach for blowing and out of earshot for sneezing; the little fellow, too, who was to end so sadly:

> Weary of life, the tiny elf
> A cobweb took—and hung himself.

In the main, More's verse is a bitter exposure of sham in all its forms. He makes fun of the woman who thinks that she is lovely, of the ignorant doctor who kills all his patients, of the courtier who looks so brave but runs away in battle; More suggests that, as his feet have served him proudly, he should wear his rings not on his fingers but his toes. He mocks his friend Lalus who is ashamed of everything English but dresses, struts and swears in French like a parrot who knows a little Latin by rote. His most severe criticisms fall on kings and bishops, roguish friars, pompous theologians and one extraordinary character whom he calls Candidus, a parish priest who is a perfect model to hold up to his parishioners:

> As a faithful mirror view it,
> Showing what to do—what shun;
> All he shuns, take care to do it,
> All he does, take care to shun.[18]

To grasp More's humour, with the contempt of hypocrisy and love of sincerity which lies behind it, we can hardly find a more perfect lesson than his most moving account of Jane Shore. The situation itself is extraordinary, for here we have a saint commenting on an adulterous woman, King Edward IV's mistress, when she was compelled to do public penance at the command of the usurper Richard III. More did not see the scene himself—he

[18] *Philomorus*, pp. 126, 238.

would have been a baby—but he had many sources of information, his father and Cardinal Morton to mention but two. Whether or not More's history of Richard III is partisan, there can be no doubt at all that his dislike for the usurper is based on the latter's duplicity and that his sympathy for Jane Shore reveals his deep sincerity.

More tells us that Richard III tried in many other ways to disgrace the mistress of the dead King but, all these failing,

he laid heinously to her charge the thing that she could not deny, that all the world knew to be true and that, nevertheless, every man laughed to hear would be taken so seriously, namely that she had been too easy with her virtue. And for this cause, playing the goodly, continent prince, clean and faultless in himself and sent from heaven into a vicious world to amend men's morals, he ordered the bishop of London to make her do public penance, walking before the cross in procession on a Sunday with a candle in her hand. So she walked with a countenance and carriage so demure and so womanly, even though out of all array save her kirtle only, and she looked so beautiful and comely, with a slight and unusual blush as the crowds were staring at her, that her humiliation won her much praise among those who were more attracted by her body than curious about the state of her soul. And many good folk that had disliked her in her living and were now glad to see her punished, were yet more sorry for her in her shame when they grasped that the Lord Protector had arranged it more from a corrupt intention than from any virtuous affection on his part. . . .

She was once beautiful and fair with nothing in her appearance that one would have wanted to change, except that some would have liked to see her rather more tall. So say those who knew her in her prime, while others, who have only seen her today, for she is still living, maintain that she can never have been beautiful. Such a verdict is like one passed by those who might judge the beauty of one long dead from looking at the skull, salvaged from the mortuary. Today she is old, lean, withered and dried up with little left but parched skin over her bones. Even so, those who study her face can see from its structure, how fair it would be, if some parts were filled out.

Yet men delighted not so much in her beauty as in her kindly behaviour. She used to have a ready wit, could read and write, was jolly in company, quick in repartee, never surly, not full of babble, sometimes teasing but never bitterly and always with much fun. . . .

I doubt not that some will think this woman too insignificant a thing to be written about in the history of more important matters, especially those who judge her as they see her today. But it seems to me that this fact, of itself, is worthy of remembrance that she should now be in so beggarly a state without friend or acquaintance, seeing that once she was so popular, so favoured by the prince, so useful to those who wanted preferential treatment, as important in her time as many men who, through infamy, are famous today. She was important then but now she is not remembered because her wickedness was not so very great. For if someone does us a bad turn, we seem to record his fame in marble where good turns are only written in the dust. The moral of this is proved in her story who now goes begging from those who would, at this day, themselves have been begging had it not been for her.[19]

Standing out sharply in this lovely passage is More's tender appreciation of Jane Shore's genuine virtue and his contempt for the hypocrites who had abandoned her. Through all his humour runs his revolt against pretence. His is, in a sense, the superb example of a man whose sense of humour stemmed from his prayer and mirrored his love of God. Seeing this life as a stage and all the men and women merely players, he could only see the funny side of human conceit. His most amusing passages, the description of Wolsey's speech with the frantic rivalry of the flatterers, the pretensions of the friar at Coventry, the merry tales about Dame Alice, draw their laughter from his sly exposure of make-believe. He poked gentle fun at the pomp of Wolsey, the conceit of preachers, the talkativeness of nuns, the ludicrous snobbery of courtiers, all the vain conceits of worldly men. He even jokes at the elaborate liturgy of death. He sees the devil distracting the sick man from more salutary exercises by persuading

[19] *English Works*, I, pp. 431–432. Text altered slightly.

him on his bed of suffering to plan his funeral. "And instead of sorrow for our sins and care of heaven, he putteth us in mind of provision for our honourable burying—so many torches, so many tapers, so many black gowns, so many merry mourners laughing under black hoods and a gay hearse with the delight of goodly and honourable funerals; in which the foolish, sick man is sometimes occupied as though he thought that he should be in a window and see how worshipfully he shall be brought to Church."[20]

One could fill a whole book with the examples of More's ruthless rejection of humbug and of his devastating attacks on the Establishment. In a sense he may be said to have written just such a book himself, for *Utopia*, when you study it quietly, proves to be exactly this. Its sarcasm, cunningly disguised, seems the more biting when we remember that the Utopians, who are but pagans, offer to Christians a lesson in sincerity:

> For they marvel that any man be so foolish as to have delight and pleasure in the doubtful glistering of a little trifling stone when he may behold the stars or else the sun itself. Or that any man is so mad as to count himself the nobler for the smaller and finer thread of wool, which self-same wool (be it now so finely spun) a sheep did once wear and yet she, all the time, was no other than a sheep. They marvel also that gold, which of its own nature is a thing so unprofitable, is now among all people in so high estimation, that man himself, by whom, yes, and for the use of whom, it is so much set by, is in much less estimation than the gold itself. Insomuch that a lumpish blockheaded churl with no more wit than an ass, and just as full of naughtiness and folly, shall have, nevertheless, many wise and good men in subjection to him only for this, because he has a great heap of gold.[21]

4. WONDER AND WORSHIP

The quotation from *Utopia* given above is of double importance, for the Utopians cannot take gold and jewels too seriously, for they are silly trifles to those who may enjoy the sun and stars. Here More is unconsciously bringing us to the third of his basic

[20] *Ibid.*, I, p. 470.   [21] *Utopia*, p. 81.

spiritual principles, an awareness of God's presence in the small but wonderful happenings of everyday life. More was filled with wonder at the ingenuity of nature which spoke to him forcefully of God.

Though never a poet himself—he wrote occasional verses in a sophisticated manner—More had a poet's vision and was overwhelmed by the signs of God's love and protection which he could see on every side. In his translation of Picus of Mirandola, he uses a fine expression which exactly reveals his own attitude. "Occupy thy mind with these meditations and such other that may waken thee when thou sleepest, kindle thee when thou waxeth cold, confirm thee when thou waverest and exhibit the wings of the love of God while thou labourest to heavenwards." In the manner of St Francis of Assisi, More saw the wings of God everywhere.

Yet he was a City man and as such no lover of nature in the full-blooded, Wordsworthian sense. In a society which was entirely agricultural, the craving to escape back to nature was not so intensely felt. More puts such an urge into words on one occasion only, in a letter to Colet which is not typical:

I really cannot blame you if you are not yet tired of the country where you live among simple people, unversed in the deceits of the towns. Wherever you cast your eyes, the smiling face of the earth greets you, the sweet fresh air invigorates you, the sight of the heavens charms you. You see nothing but the generous gifts of nature and the traces of our primeval innocence. But yet I do not wish you to be so enamoured of these delights as to be unwilling to return to us as soon as possible. But if you are repelled by the unpleasantness of town life, then let me suggest that you come to your country parish of Stepney.

Though More here says all the conventional phrases in praise of living in the country, his letter was written at a time of crisis and does not represent his true mind. No doubt he liked the country but he thrived in towns.[22]

---

[22] Rogers, p. 6; Stapleton, p. 11.

Far from yearning for the country, More disliked travel and in
his letters rarely mentions the countryside. Indeed we know that
his real desire was to be a hermit and to enclose himself for good
in a Carthusian cell. Each Carthusian had a small private garden,
enclosed by a high wall. When More was in the Tower of
London, his cramped quarters were no trial to him. In explaining
this, he remarked: "The holy monks of the Charterhouse order
never leave their cells but only to go to the Church which is set
near their cells and thence to their cells again. It is much the same
with St Bridget's order and St Clare's and in all enclosed religious
houses; and with anchorites and anchoresses it is especially so,
for their whole room is less than a fairly large chamber and yet
are they there as well content many long years together and more
content than other men that walk about the world."[23]

More's love of nature was both Carthusian and cockney and,
as always, he left it to the Utopians to show us what he thought.
"They set great store by their gardens. In them they have vine-
yards, all manner of fruit, herbs, and flowers, so pleasant, so well
furnished and so finely kept, that I never saw anything more
fruitful or better trimmed in any place. Their study and diligence
in this comes not only from pleasure but also of a certain strife
and contention that is between street and street concerning the
trimming, husbanding and furnishing of their gardens, every man
for his own part." More himself did no more and no less. In both
his houses he was much concerned with the garden and with its
cultivation; family, staff and servants all had to help to tend it; it
was for him not mere pleasure but a necessity for a reasonable
life.[24]

To a love of gardens he added a great interest in animals.
These he often mentioned in his writings and he delighted in
Aesop's Fables and in any stories in which a lesson is taught
through animals. A few of these tales are deeply moving as when,
at the end of his life, he was to explain the political situation under
cover of two harts chased by "an urchin bitch". The story was
Aesop's, the poignancy came from More. So, too, he compared

[23] *Dialogue of Comfort*, p. 385.   [24] *Utopia*, p. 61.

the heretics to sparrows twittering on the hedgerows and likened the worldly Christian to a snail burdened by his house. More disliked the fashionable sports, he was bitterly opposed to hunting, but he saw the love of God in the antics of animals.[25]

Erasmus could not miss so characteristic a trait in his friend's approach to life:

> One of his amusements is in observing the forms, characters and instincts of different animals. Accordingly there is scarcely any kind of bird that he does not keep about his residence and the same of other animals not quite so common, as monkeys, foxes, ferrets, weasels and the like. Besides these, if he meets with any strange object, imported from abroad or otherwise remarkable, he is most eager to buy it and has his house so well supplied with these objects that there is something in every room which catches your eye as you enter it; and his own pleasure is renewed every time that he sees others interested.

Much is revealed in this description, especially in the final lines. More was a born collector but he valued his exhibits not on their market price or on current fashion but entirely on their intrinsic merit and interest. His greatest pleasure in this hobby was to amuse and interest his friends. He was also anxious, especially with his children, that they should come to a right understanding of God's love. His menagerie was, in concept, spiritual. One puzzle only remains, how he managed in a house in the very centre of the city to cope with such a zoo.[26]

More's monkey was later to become very famous for it sat beside Dame Alice when Holbein came to Chelsea to paint the family group. Another animal was also painted by Holbein for, between the sketch and the final portrait, Holbein or More, or both of them together, decided to balance the monkey by introducing a little dog. In the sketch the monkey sits alone. In the portrait a little dog, as cheeky as one could wish, stares at the general public from within the folds of the future Lord Chancellor's gown.

More's appreciation of life and his lasting sense of God's love

[25] *Dialogue of Comfort*, pp. 393, 401.   [26] Nichols, 3, p. 392.

and protection is best seen in his attitude to miracles. And first we must note that More was one of the least gullible of Christians, condemning in religious practice all superstition or hypocrisy. Richard Pace informs us that More "has declared open war against such as give utterance to things that are neither true nor probable and beyond the capacity and knowledge of the speaker". The point is worth stressing for a twofold reason, showing, as it does, why More attacked or seemed to attack religion and, further, the strength of his own belief in God's paternal intervention in everyday affairs. His delightful passage of arms with the furious old friar at Coventry turned on exaggerated claims for the rosary which More knew to be unwarranted. He never sought the quarrel but he was prepared, as a layman, to defend the exact truth even in opposition to a priest.

More himself stated his position clearly in a letter to the bishop of Durham, not long after he had left the Charterhouse. He had been translating Lucian's Dialogues in which he delighted because the pagan writer exposed the "common appetite for lying". He then gives his exact view on credulity in religious matters, even rebuking his hero, St Augustine, for showing himself too gullible on one small point. More writes:

> We shall lead a happier life when we are less terrified by those dismal and superstitious lies which are so often repeated with so much confidence and authority that even St Augustine himself, a man of the highest intelligence and with the deepest hatred of a lie, was induced by some imposter, to narrate, as a true event which had happened in his own life, that story about the two Spurini, one dying, the other returning to life, which, with only a change of name, had been ridiculed by Lucian in this very Dialogue so many years before. No wonder, then, if ruder minds are affected by these fictions of those who think that they have done a lasting service to Christ when they have invented a fable about some saint or a tragic description of hell which either melts an old woman to tears or makes her blood run cold. There is scarcely any life of a martyr or virgin in which some falsehood of this kind has not been inserted; an act of piety, no doubt, considering the risk that Truth

would be insufficient unless propped up by lies. Thus they have not scrupled to stain with fiction that religion which was founded by Truth itself and ought to consist of naked Truth.

They have failed to see that such fables are so far from aiding religion that nothing can be more injurious. It is obvious, as Augustine himself has observed, that where there is any scent of a lie, the authority of the Truth is immediately weakened and destroyed. Hence a suspicion has more than once occurred to me that such stories have been largely invented by crafty knaves and heretics, partly for the purpose of amusing themselves with the credulity of persons more simple than wise and, partly, to diminish the authority of the true Christian histories by associating them with fictitious fables, the feigned incidents being so often so near to those contained in Holy Scripture that the allusion cannot be mistaken. Therefore, while the histories commended to us by divinely inspired scripture ought to be accepted with undoubting faith, the others, tested by the doctrine of Christ as by the rule of Critolaus, should either be received with caution or rejected if we would avoid both empty confidence and superstitious fear.[27]

Here we have More setting out boldly his own strict rules for testing Truth. He was to involve himself in a great many small skirmishes with credulous theologians, friars and priests. He would tell many pointed stories to expose all forms of religious deceit. Indeed, when he came to write his celebrated *Dialogue Concerning Tyndale* he would himself, in arguing both sides of the controversy, express the heretical case against pilgrimages, relics and miracles with astonishing force. He has much in common with Chaucer and, though he is vigorous against all forms of superstition, he never drops his sense of humour or condemns those legendary stories which were part of London life. He has the sense to distinguish between amusing legends and downright lies.

His own profound piety stands out more strikingly in contrast to his strictures of all forms of ecclesiastical lies. Throughout his life he never lost his sense of wonder but would maintain, against those who denied miracles, that God's power and genius was

[27] More to Dr Thomas Ruthall, Nichols, 1, pp. 403 seq.

manifest in the ordinary happenings of an ordinary day. While he was prepared to examine the evidence for any particular miracle by strict, judicial standards, he could see no reason at all why God should not lengthen a short beam in the roof of Barking Abbey to please his friend St Erkenwald.

Reading his *Dialogue Concerning Tyndale*, I myself came to think for a time that More was too gullible, that, in fact, he was dodging his own strict principles and falling into his own trap. He seemed to accept divine intervention too easily. Too late it came home to me that, while I shared More's own suspicion of man's veracity, I lacked his sense of wonder and his calm confidence in God's love. Such confidence one might expect in children but it appears more moving when found in so shrewd a man.

Perhaps the most beautiful of his passages in defence of wonder occurs in the Dialogue when the Messenger, who follows the views of Tyndale, has argued strongly against miracles. More, with consummate skill and delicacy, tells the story of a young couple, perhaps of his own family, certainly well known to himself.

"Forsooth," said I, "because we speak of a man raised from the dead to life; there was in the parish of St Stephen's in Walbrook in London, where I dwelt before I came to Chelsea, a man and woman who are both still living, and at that time they were both young. The elder of them was not past twenty-four. It happened to them as it does among young people, that they fell in love. And after many delays, for the maiden's mother was much against it, at last they came together and were married in St Stephen's Church which is not greatly famous for any miracles though, yearly, on St Stephen's day, it is somewhat sought unto and visited with folks' devotion.

But now, to keep the story short, as the custom is with brides—as you know well—this young woman was brought to bed by honest women. And then, after that, went the bridegroom to bed and everyone went their ways and left them twain there alone. And that same night—yet wait a minute, let me not lie, for in truth I am not sure of the time, but certainly, as it appeared afterwards, it was probably that same night or

some other time soon afterwards, or perhaps a little before. ..."
"The time does not matter," said he.

"Exactly," said I, "and as for the matter, all the parish would
testify that the girl was known to be very honest. But for the
conclusion, the seed of these two turned in the woman's body
first into blood and after that into the shape of a man child.
And then it came alive and she grew great with it. And within
a year she was delivered of a fair boy, and, forsooth it was
not then—for I saw it myself—more than a foot in length.
And yet I am sure that he has now grown an inch taller than
I. . . . In good faith, I have yet to meet a man who could claim
for himself any other kind of beginning and this seems to me as
great a miracle as raising a man from the dead."

The Messenger having conveniently asked the right question,
More with great simplicity gives us his vision of life.

Acquaintance and familiarity take away our wondering so
that we wonder no more at the ebbing and rising of the sea, or
of the Thames for that matter, because we see it every day.
But he that had never seen it or heard of it, would, at first
sight, wonder sore thereat, to see that great water come wallow-
ing up against the wind, keeping a common course, to and fro,
with no cause perceived that driveth him. If a man born blind
had suddenly his sight, what wonder would he make to see the
sun, the moon, and the stars; whereas one that hath seen them
sixteen years together, marvelleth not so much at them as he
would wonder at the first sight of a peacock's tail. For this
reason, I cannot understand why we should hold it more wonderful to revive a dead man than to witness the breeding, birth
and growth of a child into a man. No more marvellous is a
cuckoo than a cock, though the one be seen only in the summer
and the other the whole year round. And I am sure that if you
saw dead men as commonly recalled to life by miracle as you
see men brought forth by nature, you would reckon it less
wonderful to bring the soul back into the body which still
has its shape and is not much perished, than from a little seed
to make all the gear anew and make a new soul thereto.[28]

[28] *English Works*, 2, pp. 46–47.

This abiding sense of wonder lies at the centre of More's spiritual life. I am unable to find in any of his works a passage which reveals him more completely and which may possibly suggest the reason why he left the Charterhouse. His children, God excepted, were his life. One can find no saint more wholly fascinated by God's providence over babies and more aware of the dignity and responsibility of parenthood. More made his children into his living prayerbook; they, it was, who stopped him from becoming a solitary. Had he not married, he might have become a contemplative saint through the magnitude of his sacrifice. But without his children he would never have been the Thomas More whom the world has so admired and loved. His children, their birth, their home, their education, their growth in holiness, was for him the only sure path that would lead him to God. His relationship with them may be considered later but his sense of God's presence in the tides on the Thames, in the peacock's tail, in the sacrament of marriage, gave to every moment of his life a value which he could not find in the self-centred affairs of worldly men.

5. WHAT PICUS, EARL OF MIRANDOLA, TAUGHT HIM

The fourth and final principle in More's spiritual life, the one without doubt which led him to the Carthusians, was his vivid awareness of the love of God. This was to deepen throughout his life and, in the end, as his death drew closer, to absorb all his other affections and, alone, to satisfy him. Yet it was present early in his life with such unusual power that it drove him to become a solitary.

C. S. Lewis, taking the four relationships supplied by Scripture, has more clearly than any other English writer described the four ties which join God to the human soul. First, there is the relationship of a potter to the pot which he has fashioned, in which the pot has no more than an independent but inanimate existence, owing shape, size, colour and material to the artisan who fashioned it. For the potter there is the pleasure of achievement and of seeing his mental image expressed in clay before his eyes.

Next, comes the bond expressed both by Christ and by King David when they speak of the shepherd and his sheep. Here the sheep are animate and enjoy the power of movement, the shepherd tends, protects, leads and nourishes his sheep. This relationship is not personal but there is in it a semblance of exchange. One stage higher up and we come to the common New Testament image of a father and his son. Now the bond is personal. Though the father gave to his son a body, fosters, educates and loves him, yet the son is a human person with personal rights. He owes all to his father and yet the father cannot force him without surrender of his love. The relationship between God and the soul is filial and paternal and the bond, when grasped, provides the motive for a Christian view of life.

There is a further stage, outlined in the Canticle of Canticles, hinted at by Christ, mysteriously associated with the mission of the Holy Spirit, and directly experienced only by a few. Such a relationship may only be described by use of lovers' language, by speaking of the love between a boy and a girl. Language fails and may even produce wrong images for an intimacy which is sensed rather than spoken, which proves itself far too subtle for words.[29]

There had been a strong mystical tradition in English spirituality throughout the Middle Ages for which Walter Hilton, Richard Rolle, Juliana of Norwich and the unknown author of *The Cloud of Unknowing* may be cited as witnesses. Should Thomas More also be assigned to this company? One becomes increasingly aware, when studying his life or examining his writings, that an unexplained and probably unfathomable secret lies behind so much of what he said and did. We are faced at the very start of his life with extraordinary decisions, not the least of them the four-year stay at the Charterhouse. It is surely unusual for a young man, so affectionate, friendly and amusing, to be seriously attracted to a solitary life; still more that he should for four years take up residence in so austere a monastery, not five minutes' walk from his father's house. His departure from the Charterhouse is equally mysterious, for the attraction to solitude

[29] C. S. Lewis, *Problem of Pain*, Geoffrey Bles, 1940, pp. 30-35.

remained firmly in him and, both as a father and as a successful
lawyer, he was to find satisfaction in following a mitigated form
of the Carthusian rule. Twice he was to reveal the strong temptation in him to abandon his career for the sake of solitude. Mystery
also surrounds the private oratory which he, later, was to build at
Chelsea, in which he spent so many hours at his prayers. Long after
his death, the world was to discover in his private papers some
clue to his private aspirations, secret undertakings, hidden prayers.
In a practical, middle-class English way, this London lawyer
seems to have been involved in a spiritual love affair. His awareness of God's love proved no less acute than the similar attraction
to which a saint like St Augustine confessed. One is led to suspect
that young More was rather more than a martyr, that his death on
the scaffold may have confused the issue, that the conflicts of the
Reformation may have distracted our attention and prevented us
from viewing his holiness, free of the shadow of the Tower axe.

It may be that Picus, Earl of Mirandola[30] still guards the missing
clues. In some ways, Picus is a bore. This rich Italian nobleman, sincerely drawn to the new learning, swayed by the austere eloquence
of Savonarola, died suddenly in Florence on 17th November, 1494.
In the same year, More, sixteen years old, was moved by his
father from Oxford to London, experienced adolescent friendships, possibly met Eliza "whom he had loved in his youth".

The biography of Picus, written by his nephew, was published
in 1496. We do not know how or when More obtained a copy but
he was immediately and powerfully attracted to the man. We
are still able to study this attraction, for More translated a selection of Picus's writings and a shortened form of his biography.
We know from Stapleton that More undertook this, his first
literary exercise, less to make the life of Picus known to others
than to impress the example of the Italian on his own mind.

There was much in Picus to attract More, for the Italian had
enjoyed a brief, brilliant and turbulent career. Steeped in the spirit
of the new learning, Picus had clashed with traditional theology

---

[30] Usually referred to as Pico della Mirandola, but as Thomas More himself
calls him Picus, Earl of Mirandola, this title has been used throughout.

and had been censured by the Roman authorities. He had studied the classics, as More was then doing, and had mastered several Eastern languages. Of a sudden, Picus had thrown up his secular career, disposed of his riches and retired to give himself to prayer. He had informed his nephew that when certain books were finished he proposed "fencing myself with a crucifix, to journey about the world barefoot, preaching Christ in every castle and every town." Picus died suddenly. Young More did not know that his hero was probably poisoned by his servants and blames a sudden fever for his untimely death. He dutifully translated an extraordinary passage in which Savonarola, preaching the funeral oration in a church in Florence, claimed to have seen Picus suffering in purgatory for rejecting a religious vocation, "not being generous enough for so great a blessing from God or held back by the tenderness of his flesh; as he was a man of delicate complexion, he shrank from the labour and thought perhaps that the Church had no need for him". More records that, later, Picus changed his mind and decided to enter the Dominican order but he died before he could carry out his purpose and, according to the theatrical Savonarola, went to purgatory for his hesitancy.

Books still play an influential part in the lives of thoughtful people; their power was, perhaps, greater in the early sixteenth century when they were rare. This Latin Life of Picus produced an extraordinary effect in Thomas More. We cannot be sure how he obtained his copy; Colet, his spiritual director, may well have lent it to him, for Colet was back from Italy soon after Picus died. William Lillie, with whom More discussed the subject of a vocation, had also studied in Italy. Skelton, the poet, had corresponded with Picus and another source might well have been Antonio Bonvisi, the Italian banker, More's lifelong friend. As far as we know, More made his own decision in attempting a translation, but whoever lent him the book had a share in the staggering results.

How much it would help us to know the date on which More read the Life of Picus, for this might even explain his motive for retiring to the Charterhouse. His translation appeared in print in

1510 and was probably written in 1504. More may have read the biography at an earlier date—one would like to think so—he almost certainly translated it during his stay at the Charterhouse. Only one near-contemporary refers to More's attraction for Picus and he, though often quoted, may perhaps be wrong. Stapleton tells us that when More had decided not to be a monk, he looked around to find an example of a model layman on whom to base his life. He could find no better a type than Picus, Earl of Mirandola, and made his translation "thoroughly to familiarize himself".

That More admired and imitated Picus cannot be disputed; to read the Life of Picus is almost to read in advance the life of More himself. So we have Picus disposing of his silverware, eating plain fare, scourging himself on days connected with Christ's Passion, shunning the Court, attaining to that stage of indifference in which "he little cared whether his written works went under his own name or not". More followed him in this. Or, take this explanation given by Picus and applicable to More:

> The great fortunes lift a man high to show him off but often, like a fierce or skittish horse, they later throw their master off. Certainly they always grieve and vex him and rather tear him than bear him. The golden mediocrity, the mean estate is to be desired that shall bear us like a draught-horse more easily, that shall obey us and not master us. I, therefore, firmly abide by this opinion, setting more by my little house, my study, the pleasure of my books, the rest and peace of my mind than by all your glory, all the advantages that you hawk after and all the favour of the court.

More certainly took Picus as his model in all but one respect. Stapleton must surely be mistaken when he sees More imitating Picus after he has decided not to continue in the religious life. Picus was no model in this. More knew very well that Picus had delayed such a vocation and that Savonarola claimed to have seen him in purgatory, suffering for this. One need not accept Savonarola's strange pronouncement but one should consider its effect on More. Throughout his life he was a scrupulous man. Though he finally decided to remain a layman, he had no doubt about the perfection of the religious state. His vivid appreciation of death made this life seem hollow and empty and Picus, who shared this outlook, would have stood as a warning to him. If, as is certainly possible, More first read the Life of Picus when Colet or some other friend acquired a copy, in 1498 or later, then the example of the Italian would have drawn More to the Charterhouse. Picus was not so much an example of a model layman as of a layman who was told that he should be a priest. When More and Lillie were debating their vocations, the Life of Picus could have been a turning point. After all, the Life of Picus as we read it today teaches one clear lesson, that a wise man will shun wealth and human learning to find happiness with God. Picus may well have been responsible for More going to the Charterhouse.

Whether or not More read the biography before he entered, he translated it during his years with the monks. His introduction to this book is worth consideration for he presented his translation to Joyce Leigh, a family friend, then a nun in the convent at Aldgate. His preface is typical.

For a long time, my well beloved sister, it has been a custom for friends to exchange gifts and presents as a sign of love and friendship at the start of the New Year. Such gifts express the hope to one another that the year that has started well should continue prosperously. Commonly all these presents given to friends pertain only to the body in the form of food, clothing and other delights. By this it would seem that such friendships are only fleshly and extend only to the body and nothing beyond. But as the love and friendship between Christians should be spiritual rather than carnal, I, therefore, mine heartily beloved sister, in good luck for this New Year, have sent you such a present as may bear witness to my tender love and zeal for a continual and gracious increase of virtue in your soul; and where the gifts of other folk show that they wish their friends worldly prosperity, mine shows that I desire for you Godly success. These works, more profitable than extensive, were made in Latin by one John Picus, Earl of Mirandola, a lordship in Italy, of whose cunning and virtue we need not here speak . . . which works I would ask you gladly to receive if only because they contain such excellent material (however translated) that they will delight and please anyone who has even a moderate desire and love of God. You are such a one and because of your virtue and fervent zeal towards God, you cannot but rejoice to receive anything which reproves vice, commends virtue and sings the praise and honour of God— may he look after you.

More tells Joyce Leigh and, through her, tells us also, that Picus will please those who have "even a moderate desire and love of God". Here, undoubtedly, lay the Italian's power over More. Other influences are discernible in More's methods of prayer but Picus may claim to be the first. Picus set out his method of prayer in a letter to his nephew which More selected for his book.

When I stir thee to prayer, I stir thee not to the prayer that standeth in many words but to that prayer which in the secret chamber of the mind, in the privy closet of the soul with very affection speaketh to God and in the most lightsome darkness of contemplation not only presenteth the mind to the Father but also uniteth it with Him by unspeakable ways which only they know that have essayed. Nor care I how long or how short your prayer be but how effectual, how ardent and rather interrupted and broken in between with sighs than drawn on long with continual row and number of words. If you love your own health, if you desire to be safe from the snares of the devil, from the storms of this world, from the await of thy enemies; if you long to be acceptable to God; if you covet to be happy at the last—let no day pass you but you once at leastwise present yourself to God in prayer and falling down before Him flat to the ground with an humble affection of devout mind, not from the extremity of your lips but out of the inwardness of your heart, cry these words of the prophet: "The offences of my youth and my ignorance remember not, good Lord; but after thy mercy, Lord, for Thy goodness remember me."[31]

[31] "Life of Picus," *English Works*, Introduction, 1, pp. 347–348.

Thirty years later, More, lying a prisoner in the Tower of London, was suddenly to break his accustomed silence about his own spiritual methods and to set out for the comfort of his children his methods and views on prayer. He seems almost to use the words of Picus in describing his own prayer in his private oratory. He writes: "Let him also choose himself some secret, solitary place in his own house, as far from noise and company as he conveniently can and thither let him sometimes secretly resort alone, imagining himself as one going out of the world even straight unto the giving up of his reckoning unto God of his sinful living. Then let him before an altar or some pitiful image of Christ's bitter passion, kneel down or fall prostrate as at the feet of Almighty God, verily believing Him to be there invisibly present as without doubt He is."[32]

So Picus prayed and More prayed, flat on their faces before God. More was so attracted by this gesture of adoration that he even introduced it in his description of Utopia. The Utopians at the start of their pagan services "fall down everyone reverently to the ground with so still a silence in every part that the very fashion of the thing strikes into them a certain fear of God as though He were there personally present".[33]

Both men had this acute awareness of God's presence, both adored God prostrate and in silence, both made much of the affection of the inward senses in place of many words. The sentiments expressed thus "in the privy closet of the soul" were for both men the aspirations of King David in the psalms. More's own knowledge of the psalms is quite extraordinary and, in his selection from the two-volume life of Picus, he chose to translate the whole of the Italian's commentary on the fifteenth psalm. "*Deus Meus es Tu;* My God art Thou" is the theme repeated and, in the thoughts of Picus, we come very near to understanding why young More went to the Charterhouse. Many years later in the Tower of London, More in his *Dialogue of Comfort* was to reveal unconsciously other details of his prayer. On one occasion when he has been laughing at prayers in which "while our tongue

[32] *Dialogue of Comfort*, p. 287.   [33] *Utopia*, p.129.

pattereth upon our prayers apace, while, Good God, how many mad ways our mind wandereth", he suddenly describes the prayer of men in pain. "God", he writes, "requires no such long prayers of them, but the lifting up of their heart alone without any word at all, is the more acceptable to Him of one in such a state, than long service so said as folk use to say it when in health."[34]

Beyond the method of prayer and the content of prayer lies the motive and affection and, on this most delicate point, More goes forward alone. The love of God was so ardently felt by him in early manhood that he attempted to express himself in verse. Probably at the Charterhouse, when he was translating the life and works of Picus, he came upon that good man's list of the twelve properties of Love. Whether or not Picus fully intended it, More decided to apply these properties to God. He went even further, allotting to each property two stanzas, the first showing the behaviour of human lovers, the second transposing this human affection to the living God. The verses are quaint and sometimes inelegant but the thought behind them is overwhelmingly beautiful. It has been suggested that More wrote these verses in the time of crisis when he was deciding whether or not to marry, whether or not to give his whole life to God. Be this as it may, these verses, written in his early twenties, afford us a glimpse of the inner life of Thomas More. As space does not permit the inclusion of all these verses, let it suffice to give the most famous, the one which assumes so profound a meaning in the light of More's death. So he writes of human love:

> If love be strong, hot, mighty and fervent,
> There may no trouble, grief or sorrow fall,
> But that the lover would be well content,
> All to endure and think it eke too small
> Though it were death, so he might therewithal,
> The joyful presence of that person get,
> On whom he hath his heart and love yset.

[34] *Dialogue of Comfort*, pp. 199–200.

And of God:

> Thus should of God the lover be content,
> Any distress or sorrow to endure,
> Rather than to be from God absent,
> And glad to die, so that he may be sure,
> By his departing hence for to procure
> After this valley dark, the heavenly light,
> And of his love the glorious blessed sight.[35]

This vision did not wane nor did the love of God grow weaker in him as year followed year. At the very end of his life, at the very end of the words that he wrote before going to the scaffold, More was to return to this Charterhouse theme.

Would God we would consider what hot affection many of these fleshly lovers have borne and daily do to those upon whom they dote. How many of them have not hesitated to jeopardise their lives and how many have willingly lost their lives indeed, without great return shown them ... but they were happy and contented in their minds that by their death their lover should clearly see how faithfully they loved. ... Oh, if he that is content to die for his love from whom he looks for no reward and by his death yet goes from her, might by his death be sure to come to her and ever after in delight and pleasure dwell with her, why such a lover would not hesitate to die for her twice. And how cold lovers we be, then, unto God if rather than die for Him once, we will refuse Him and forsake Him for ever that both died for us before and hath also provided that if we die here for Him, we shall in heaven everlastingly both live and also reign with Him.[36]

[35] *English Works*, I, p. 390.   [36] *Dialogue of Comfort*, pp. 416–417.

CHAPTER THREE

Licentious Priest

I. CHASTE HUSBAND OR LICENTIOUS PRIEST

ONLY AN EXTREME lack of sympathy and understanding could have led some writers to a gross misjudgment of the next phase of More's life. The remark made by Erasmus has already been quoted and this, we should remember, remains our one contemporary account. The Dutchman tells us that More gave up all thought of the priesthood "because he could not shake off his wish to marry" and that "accordingly he resolved to be a chaste husband rather than a licentious priest".

To read into this, as some have done, an implied criticism of the Charterhouse community, would be to contradict Thomas More himself. His own praise for these austere and devoted men has many times been mentioned and, in quitting their convent, More certainly thought of himself as choosing the second best. One may, further, question the embroidered gossip of Cresacre More and others who see in More's decision a criticism of the religious life as practised in his day. Erasmus makes it abundantly clear that the motive for More's choice must be found in More himself.[1]

How strange are the ways in which history is written; this casual comment by Erasmus, tucked away in the middle of a lengthy letter, has so tickled the world's fancy, so often been quoted, that it has come to be regarded as gospel truth. Yet, at best, it remains only an impression, possibly based on a facetious excuse made by More himself. He often joked in this way. It is worth remarking that Erasmus was never fully abreast of More's spiritual development. He knows or says nothing about the Carthusians, shows no interest in Picus and passes only a super-

[1] Cf. Seebohm, pp. 149–150; Stapleton, p. 10.

ficial judgment about the method of More's prayer. One need not deny this verdict of Erasmus, an affectionate observer, but it would be foolish not to check his statement or to treat it too authoritatively. It should not be twisted to imply that More disapproved of celibacy, that he was himself passionate or overmuch tempted, that he left the Charterhouse simply because of sex.[2]

First, let us consider More himself. The purity and innocence of his personal life is so overwhelmingly attested that no trace of scandal has ever been adduced. Every scrap of evidence that has survived points to his virtuous living, so much in contrast, as Harpsfield remarks, to the impurity and moral decadence of the society of his day. Even at the time when the Court sought to blacken his reputation, no sexual rumours could ever be whispered about More. He never thought or wrote or acted impurely, showed scant interest in women, gave no sign that he was passionate. Indeed, the opposite criticism has been made against him that he was too perfect, that there was little love even in his married life. More's innocence is the more extraordinary in that he was not ignorant of vice. As a police court magistrate he was fully aware of all the moral squalor in the London of his day. He mentions sexual abuses, witnessed scandals, dealt with all manner of impure people, lived amid the licence of the Royal Court for many years. In the education of his children he was never prudish but rarely spoke of sex. He certainly was aware of the dangers to himself and others, occasionally wrote about them, touched with wisdom on the need for controlling one's thoughts. Any theory, read into Erasmus's words, that More left the Charterhouse panting for marriage would afford a wholly wrong impression of Thomas More.

Though More himself chose deliberately to marry, he never

[2] Erasmus used the Latin word *impurus* and this has been translated in different ways by different authors, licentious, impure, unchaste. Reynolds, whom I consulted on this, first accepted the word *licentious* but now feels that it is rather too strong. He suggests "a faithful husband rather than an indifferent priest". All turns on what Erasmus had in mind when he wrote *impurus*. He cannot have wanted to imply that More was much tempted or too passionate. Such a suggestion would contradict his own verdict of More and the facts of More's life. Further, Erasmus's letter to Hutten was published in More's lifetime, and More would surely have objected if the phrase implied licentiousness in himself or in the monks.

altered his views on the perfection of the celibate state. In *Utopia* he allowed a married clergy as he had to, for Utopia was governed by human reason not by divine or Church law. To suggest from this that More wanted a married clergy is a plain contradiction of the facts. He was many times to maintain that fewer priests should be ordained after better training and with more careful selection, but he was explicit in his defence of celibate life. As to the vow of chastity, freely taken in imitation of Christ's example, he held it to be an act of self-denial more perfect than the chastity of married life. He certainly set a very high standard for priestly behaviour and his own decision may have been affected by this. As a police court magistrate, he was very well aware of the moral decadence of certain priests. He did not hesitate to record such misbehaviours for he was scrupulously honest in arguing against the charges of the heretics. Yet he could write, "For so dare I boldly to say, that the clergy of England, and especially that part in which you find most fault, namely that part which we call commonly the secular clergy, is, in learning and in honest living, well able to match and overmatch, number for number, the clergy of any other Christian nation."

More was to reveal himself in a typical way on one occasion. Pointing out how some pagan religions used to castrate their priests to make sure of exact observance, he judged that the Christian method was far in advance of this. With such physical compulsion "would be lost the merit that good men have in resisting the devil and restraining their fleshly motions".

More was the champion of the clergy though he himself had chosen to marry and though he knew much more than most about clerical defects. His last word on the subject came in an argument with a fictitious heretic which he finishes thus: "Well," said I, "since I am already married twice and, therefore, cannot be a priest and you be so set in mind for marriage that you will never be a priest, we two be not the most suitable people to ponder what might best be said in this matter from the priests' point of view."[3]

[3] *English Works*, 2, pp. 215, 227–229, 25.

2. MORE'S NATURAL DIFFIDENCE

In discussing More's motives for leaving the Charterhouse and in seeking to understand so complex a character, we must look beyond his desire for marriage to a far more fundamental struggle against a natural hesitation and diffidence.

From our position looking back to Tudor England, we see More as a calm, shrewd and confident man. Ours is the advantage and, possibly the disadvantage, of knowing how the story is going to end. Remembering his courage on the scaffold, we may start to see signs of it at an earlier stage. He appears to us so sure of himself in the courts of law, in the company of scholars, in controversy, in all his dealings with Cardinal Wolsey or with the King. Even the Holbein portrait may come to stand both for sanctity and serenity. Yet Professor Brewer, who knew the period so well, could recognize More's anxiety even in the portrait; whether or not the artist intended this impression, it is the one which exactly fits the facts.[4]

Almost all men and women suffer from diffidence in one form or another for, knowing their limitations, they cannot believe that they have it in them to achieve success. A few are brave enough to risk the failures, the majority dodge any major commitment and go through life safely but without fully extending themselves. It is, perhaps, encouraging to see how a man as successful as More, and as holy, was forced to master so many misgivings and a host of fears.

To cover this important subject by easy stages, we should first note the social situation which he faced. Unlike King Henry VIII, Cardinal Wolsey, Colet or Erasmus, More was exceptionally sensitive and diffident. He lacked ambition and, in his youth, never expected to succeed. Partly this may have been due to his upbringing, to being junior partner to his father, but some of it may have sprung from class. The Mores were respectable City

---

[4] Brewer, I, p. 292, note. "The face of More is remarkable for its peering anxious look as of a man endeavouring to penetrate into and yet dreading the future."

people with few pretensions, wholly committed to the law. All high offices of State were held by the nobility or by churchmen and the universities were still a clerical preserve. A layman of More's class hardly expected to achieve much. It can never have crossed his mind that he might one day be Lord Chancellor any more than he would have expected to write a book. During his boyhood, printing was also in its infancy. Books were rare and precious, mostly theological, copied laboriously by hand.

Young More was very conscientious about his studies; he taught himself Greek and, as we learn from Erasmus, took endless care to polish and perfect his Latin style. He ranks among the pioneers of English prose. To boys of his day, studies were not, as now, a means towards money or promotion. More read, wrote, translated, turned out epigrams and verses simply for the satisfaction to himself. He did not translate Picus with a view to publication and *Utopia*, which brought him European fame, was written in a hurry; he did not want it printed and never expected its success. Had More not met Erasmus in 1498 to become fast friends with this natural promoter, he might well have lived and died without publishing a single book. Erasmus not only made More's reputation for him but he gave to his young friend some of his own infectious confidence. Everything that Erasmus wrote he thought worth printing; his influence had a profound effect on More.

We are now able to see that More was lovable and that he owed his promotion to a great number of influential and devoted friends. He "who seemed to be born and made for friendship" had no inkling of his virtues and frequently disparages himself. It is not easy with More to distinguish diffidence and humility. As he grew older, he grew more and more humble but, at the start, there was also a lack of confidence. We catch a glimpse of this in the years of hesitation which marked almost every grave decision in his life. So he took four years to choose between the monastic or married life. Another marked period of hesitation precedes his decision to go to Court. When it came to the King's great question, More spent seven years of worry and, as he told his daughter in the Tower, "many a restless weary night". Before his martyrdom he endured and fought a natural diffidence which amounted to agony. So many signs of this anxiety are shown by More that it would be impossible to quote them all. Nor can we, knowing of his spiritual life, behave in the style of the redoubtable Dame Alice who chided her husband in good round terms.

This wife, when she saw that Sir Thomas More, her husband, had no wish to grow greatly upward in the world, nor neither would labour for office of authority, and over that, forsook a right worshipful room when it was offered to him, she fell in hand with him and all too rated him and asked him:
"What will you do that you desire not to put forth yourself as other folk do? Will you sit by the fire and make goslings in the ashes with a stick as children do?"[5]

It is clear from all that has gone before, and especially from our knowledge of More's love for God and of his contempt for worldly honour, that his desire not to promote himself, "just to draw goslings with a stick in the ashes", sprang in large measure from his spiritual view of life. Not entirely. In a certain sense it was his love of God which gave him the courage and urged him on. We see both his anxiety and his courage in that most revealing scene, given by his son-in-law, who went by barge with him to Lambeth Palace when More was first called before the Commissioners. More was going to Lambeth to clear himself and to have his name removed from the Bill before Parliament in connection with the treason of the Holy Maid of Kent. When More came out of the Council Room in high humour, Roper presumed that his father-in-law had pleaded successfully and had achieved his end. This was not so. The short and famous dialogue, which Roper reports exactly, describes the kind of battle which More continually had to face.

Then took Sir Thomas More his boat towards his house at Chelsea, wherein by the way he was very merry, and for that I was nothing sorry, hoping that he had got himself discharged

[5] Harpsfield, p. 106.

out of the Parliament Bill. When he was landed and come home, then walked we twain in his garden together, where I, desirous to know how he had sped, said, "I trust, Sir, that all is well because you are so merry."

"It is indeed, son Roper, I thank God," quoth he.

"Are you then put out of the Parliament Bill?" I asked.

"By my troth, son Roper," quoth he, "I never remembered it."

"Never remembered it, Sir," said I, "a case that toucheth yourself so near, and all of us for your sake! I am sorry to hear it, for I verily trusted, when I saw you so merry, that all had been well."

Then said he, "Wilt thou know, son Roper, why I was so merry?"

"That I would gladly, Sir," quoth I.

"In good faith, I rejoiced, son," quoth he, "that I had given the devil a foul fall, and that with those lords I had gone so far, as without great shame, I could never go back again."

At which words waxed I very sad, for though himself liked it well, yet liked it me but a little.[6]

This astonishing scene, set on a barge in the Thames, with a great saint laughing with delight and surprise at his own courage, should open our eyes to the full meaning of his spiritual life. After so much thought, so many prayers, scourgings, hairshirts, fasts, psalms and litanies, More was happy so to have committed himself that he could not with honour go back. So overcome was he at his own courage that he had forgotten to attend to his vital business, to see that his name was removed from the Parliament Bill. The scene is typical. It prepares us for all that we will learn about More later and for all that we may expect from ourselves. Given a true crisis—for More this confrontation at Lambeth proved to be mortal—we too would be equally glad to have committed ourselves. This incident on the river is the climax of More's life. Yet it is possible that the earlier decision to leave the solitary life of the Charterhouse was of equal pain and importance in his progress towards God.

⁶ Roper, p. 34.

3. MORE'S SCRUPLES AND FEARS

Spiritually, at least, More lacked all confidence in himself. He lived coldly and entirely by faith. Such fundamental humility, more startling in him than in most other people, was partly hidden for many years by the ceaseless activities of his busy life. Watching him climb from Under-Sheriff to Lord Chancellor of England, seeing him walking with the King at Chelsea or travelling abroad on important State business, we find it hard to believe that he was all the time struggling to be true to himself.

Only when the battle had been both lost and won and he was housed in a cell in the Tower of London can he reveal, for the comfort and guidance of his children, the nature of the battle which he had had to endure. Now he was old and sick and garrulous, less prepared to arrange his thoughts in order or to polish his style. He still uses all his favourite tricks and devices to confuse the issue and not fully to reveal himself. In the hostile surroundings of the Tower, there was an added reason for such subterfuge. More places his two characters, a weary old uncle and a more bumptious but just as frightened nephew, in Budapest. Instead of naming Henry VIII, Cromwell and the other courtiers, he pictures a similar situation in Hungary threatened by the Turks. Uncle and nephew face enemy occupation of their country, persecution for religion, disgrace, dishonour and, perhaps, a martyr's death.

Anyone who reads with care the *Dialogue of Comfort* composed by Thomas More in the Tower of London becomes aware immediately that More's book is unique. As a commentary on life, it has had no rival and we are conscious, as we read it, that its author ranks with Teresa of Avila, Augustine, Francis de Sales or Ignatius of Loyola as a master of the spiritual life. One can think of no other book in Christian history more revealing or more heroic, describing as it does in the simple, uninhibited language of a layman, the fears and misgivings of one who, all his life, has trusted God.

One dare not claim that More experienced in himself all the

trials and perplexities which he here sets out in detail, for in his
life he had met so many people and had many sources from which
to draw. One can, however, assert without fear of contradiction
that no author could probe so deeply or so expose the ramifica-
tions of spiritual anguish who had not endured, in one form or
another, as much and more than he describes.

One might claim that the *Dialogue of Comfort against Tribulation*
is, in the main, a treatise about fear: fear of loneliness, fear of the
devil, fear of the past, fear of pain, fear of death, fear of salvation,
and—for More the situation is peculiar—fear that he will not
match up to martyrdom. All the years at the Charterhouse, all
the prayers and penances of his life, all his hesitations, the reason
why he abandoned a contemplative vocation are here explained.
We may be sinning against chronology in thus taking the end of
the story at the beginning, but you and I, who already know the
last act of More's drama, will be helped in watching the gradual
unfolding and blossoming of his courage during thirty years.

Plainly, it would be ridiculous to attempt a synopsis of such a
treatise or to pretend that a few haphazard quotations give an
adequate impression of More's thought. We may return to the
Dialogue of Comfort on a later page. Here we are concerned only
with More's diffidence and hesitation and with the need to know,
if possible, why he left the Charterhouse. In general, it may be
claimed that More's treatment of fear goes far deeper than that of
most other spiritual writers, for he is prepared to devote many
pages to the agony of the temptation to suicide. Whether or not
he experienced such a trial himself he does not tell us; it would
not surprise me, for St Ignatius of Loyola certainly endured the
same. More shows much insight on the matter but lessens the
tension by introducing one of his merry tales. Or, again, he suddenly introduces into the discussion of a monk's vision the complicated and common psychological experience of not knowing
whether you are asleep or awake. In writing of this, More shows
himself aware of that strange sense of unreality which can make
life itself seem to be a dream. It is impossible to read the *Dialogue
of Comfort* without deriving considerable comfort, mixed with

astonishment. How rare to find a spiritual writer whose experience reaches down to street level and to the lunacies of a humdrum day.

Sufficient here to limit attention to one particular topic which gives us so great a light on More himself. He was a very scrupulous man. Hence his remarks on scruples are not only of considerable assistance but enable us to judge his own worries and perplexities. Could one find anywhere a better description than this?

> Thus fareth the scrupulous person who frames for himself more than double the fear that he needs and many times a greater fear when there is no cause for fear at all. Of that which is no sin at all he makes a venial sin, that which is venial he imagines to be mortal and yet, for all this, continues to fall into them because of their very nature, they are things which no man can live long without. Next, he fears that he is not fully and properly confessed, nor never fully contrite and, then, that his sins will never be forgiven him; so then he confesses and confesses again to the burden both of himself and his confessor. Then, every prayer that he recites, though he said it as well as the frail infirmity of man will ever suffer, yet he is not satisfied unless he says it again and, after that, again. And when he has said one thing thrice, he is as little satisfied with the last as with the first and, then, his heart is forever heavy, restless, and in fear, full of doubt and dullness without comfort or spiritual repose. With this fear of the night, the devil sorely troubles the mind of many a right good man and reduces him to some great inconvenience. For he will drive him, if he can, so much to think of the rigour of God's justice that he will keep him from pondering on the comfortable remembrance of God's great mighty mercy and so make him do all his good works wearily and without consolation or quickness.[7]

Thus far we have from More a straightforward description of a scrupulous person but, later, he enters more fully into the psychology of a scrupulous man.

[7] *Dialogue of Comfort*, pp. 244–245.

Some at the sudden appearance of a horrible thought, experience a violent revulsion from it, which revulsion is virtuous. But the devil, using their melancholy humour and their natural inclination to fear his machinations, causes them to conceive such a deep dread that they begin to feel that such a terrible thought has made them fall into an outrageous sin. He makes them despair of grace, judging that God has abandoned them forever. Whereas in fact, that thought, no matter how horrible or abominable, is for those who never wanted it, still abhor it and for merit strive against it, no possible sin of any sort.

Some people, holding a knife in their hands, have suddenly had the thought of killing themselves and afterwards, in considering what a terrible thing it would be if they should suddenly do it, have fallen into a fear that they might, in fact, do it and have with long thinking thereon, imprinted the fear so firmly in their imagination that some of them cannot cast it off without great difficulty. But just as the devil uses the blood of a man's own body to provoke him towards the sin of impurity, though the man must and does with grace and wisdom resist it, so, too, must the other man act whose melancholy humours have been used by the devil to put such a desperate dread into his heart.[8]

Later, More returns again to the same subject and, this time, he seems to me to go even further in his examination of scruples and of their cure.

He must also consider that a great part of this temptation is, in effect, but the fear of his own imagination, the dread that he has, lest he shall sooner or later be forced to do a thing which all the devils in hell can never impose on him, where, if he is silly enough, his own foolish imagination may. For just as some man, crossing a high bridge, becomes so afraid through his own fantasy that he falls off indeed, though the bridge may be crossed, in fact, without any danger; and just as some man would fall off on such a bridge if people call out to him "look out, you are falling", whereas he would cross over quite merrily if people said "there is no danger", so it is with this temptation.

[8] *Ibid.*, p. 275.

The devil finds a man afraid of his own imagination and cries into the ear of his heart, "you are falling, you are falling," and makes the poor man sick to death that he will fall indeed. And the devil so wears him out with this continual fear, if he gives the ear of his heart to the devil, that finally he takes his mind from the right remembrance of God and so drives him to this deadly mischief indeed. Therefore, as in sins of the flesh, victory is found not always in fight but sometimes in flight . . . in this temptation also, a man must not always resist it with reason but, sometimes, treat it as nothing and despatch it whence it came and not regard it as worth thinking about.[9]

These quotations are long but, I hope, not tedious. They explain many of More's hesitancies, his frequent confessions and the spiritual distress which he suffered there.

At the time when More was deciding to marry, he wrote his well-known letter to Colet, already partly quoted, which he starts thus:

Thomas More to his dear John Colet, greeting. As I was walking in the law-courts the other day, occupied with business of various kinds, I met your servant. I was delighted to see him, both because I have always been fond of him, and especially, because I thought he would not be here without you. But when I heard from him, not only that you had not returned, but that you would not return for a long time yet, my joyful expectation was changed to unutterable grief. No annoyance that I could suffer is to be compared with the loss of your companionship which is so dear to me. It has been my custom to rely on your prudent advice, to find my recreation in your pleasant company, to be stirred by your powerful sermons, to be edified by your life and example, to be guided, in fine, by even the slightest indications of your opinions. When I had the advantage of all these helps, I used to feel strengthened, now that I am deprived of them, I seem to languish and grow feeble. By following your footsteps I had escaped from almost the very gates of hell and now, driven by some secret but irresistible force, I am falling back again into the gruesome darkness.[10]

[9] *Ibid.*, p. 278.   [10] Rogers, pp. 6–9; Stapleton, p. 11.

This letter was written when More was about twenty-four. Thirty years later in the Tower of London, he was to give this advice to his children:

> Let them, therefore, that are in troublous fear of their own scrupulous conscience, submit the rule of their own conscience to the counsel of some other good man, who according to the variety and nature of the scruples, may temper his advice. Yea, although a man be very well learned himself, yet let him in this case learn from the custom used among physicians. For be one of these never so cunning, yet in his own disease and sickness he never likes to trust himself but sends for such of his colleagues as he knows to be competent and puts himself into their hands.[11]

One may feel sure that John Colet knew the reasons why More left the Charterhouse. It is very likely that Colet decided for the younger man. The remark of Erasmus that More chose "to be a chaste husband rather than a licentious priest" may well be part of the explanation for his decision, once allowance has been made for scrupulosity. Many young men today are brought to the same decision for the same reasons, being temperamentally unfit for so great a mental strain. Fear and diffidence in their case, as in More's, is less easily managed in the contemplative life.

More's decision, however, may have gone deeper, for, in the Tower, he seems to reveal a further significant point.

More is describing with great vividness the dangers which a man of the world must face. The uncle says to his nephew:

> For as it is a thing right hard to touch pitch and not defile the fingers, to put flax on the fire and yet keep it from burning, to keep a serpent in thy bosom and yet be safe from stinging, to put young men with young women without danger of foul, fleshly desire, so it is hard for any person, either man or woman, in great worldly wealth and much prosperity, so to withstand the suggestions of the devil and the occasions given by the world that they keep themselves from the deadly desire of ambitious glory. Whereupon there followeth if a man falls in this, a whole

[11] *Dialogue of Comfort*, p. 251.

flood of unhappy mischief, arrogant manner; high, sullen, solemn carriage, despising of the poor in word and countenance, unpleasant and disdainful behaviour, ravin, extortion, oppression, hatred, cruelty.

Now, many a good man, cousin, coming into great authority, turning in his mind the peril of such occasions of pride ... is sore troubled therewith. Some are so afraid that even in the day of prosperity, they fall into the night's fear of pusillanimity and fearing that they might misuse themselves, leave the things undone which they might have done well and so mistrusting the aid and help of God in keeping them straight in their temptations, give way to the devil and fall into the opposite temptation, whereby, through a faint heart, they quit their good works in which they were well occupied. *Under pretext as it seems to them of a humble heart and meakness and of serving God in silence and contemplation, they unconsciously seek their own ease and earthly rest, and with this God is not well content.*[12]

Given a character as sensitive and as scrupulous as More's, it may very well be that the urge to live in the Charterhouse was a form of escape. When he took the plunge and returned to face life's ordinary troubles and temptations, bravely but with grave misgivings, he made the first heroic step towards martyrdom.

We might end this chapter on a different note and with another story, one which Professor Chambers describes as "one of the greatest stories in the world". More's life is over: on the way to execution he is moving towards the scaffold on Tower Hill:

Afterwards as he passed, there came to him a citizen of Winchester who had been once with Sir Thomas More before. ....
This poor man was grievously vexed with very vehement and grievous temptations of desperation and could never be rid of it, either by counsel or prayer of his own or of his friends. At last a good friend of his brought him to Sir Thomas, then chancellor. Who, taking compassion of the poor man's misery, gave him the best counsel and advice he could. But it would not

[12] *Ibid.*, p. 284.

serve. Then fell he to his prayers for him, earnestly beseeching Almighty God to rid the poor man of his trouble of mind. He obtained it; for, after that, the Hampshire man was never troubled with it any more, so long as he would come to Sir Thomas More; but, after he was imprisoned and could have no access to him, his temptation began again more vehement and troublesome than ever before. So he spent his days with a heavy heart and without hope of remedy.

But when he heard that Sir Thomas was condemned, he posted from Winchester, hoping at least to see him as he should go to execution and so determined to speak to him, come what would of it. And for that cause, he placed himself in the way. And at his coming by, he thrust through the throng and with a loud voice said, "Mr. More, do you know me? I pray you, for Our Lord's sake, help me. I am as ill-troubled as I ever was." Sir Thomas answered, "I remember thee full well. Go thy ways in peace and pray for me and I will not fail to pray for thee." And from that time, so long as he lived, he was never troubled with that manner of temptation.[13]

[13] Ro Ba., pp. 263–265; Stapleton, p. 71.

CHAPTER FOUR

At the Barge in Bucklersbury

I. MORE'S PATTERN OF LIFE AFTER LEAVING THE CHARTERHOUSE

WE KNOW LITTLE of More's routine while he was lodging at the Charterhouse; for part of his stay, at least, he seems to have gone about his professional business, returning to the monastery at night. We have already seen from his letter to Colet that he was much occupied in the law courts in Westminster Hall. During the same period he was called to the Bar, appointed lecturer at Furnivall's Inn, elected a Member of Parliament, rather less of an honour and much less exacting an office than it is today. Roper alone records an incident which caused More some worry, when he opposed in the Commons a grant of money to the King. Also, during his Charterhouse days, More gave considerable time to the study of the Fathers, delivering in the church of St Lawrence adjoining Guildhall a series of lectures on St Augustine's *City of God*. Stained-glass windows of More and Grocyn now adorn this church.

The effect of the Charterhouse on More's outward behaviour was not great. Erasmus was later to record his habits thus:

I have never seen any person less fastidious in his choice of food. As a young man he was by preference a water-drinker, a practice he derived from his father. But, not to give annoyance to others, he used at table to conceal this habit from his guests by drinking out of a pewter vessel, either small beer almost as weak as water or plain water. As to wine, it being the custom where he was for the company to invite each other to drink in turn out of the same cup, he used sometimes to sip a little of it, to avoid appearing to shrink from it altogether, and to habituate himself to the common practice. For his eating he has been accustomed to prefer beef and salt meats and household bread thoroughly fermented, to those articles of diet which are commonly regarded as delicacies. But he does not shrink from things which impart an innocent pleasure, even of a bodily kind, and has always a good appetite for milk-puddings and for fruit and eats a dish of eggs with the greatest relish.[1]

Erasmus, though a good man, was not deeply spiritual, while More was painfully reticent about himself. The Carthusian regime affected him very much more than Erasmus or his other friends could guess. It was only after his death that the full story was pieced together from small incidents which one or other of the family recalled. It seems certain that he rose each morning at 2 o'clock. To our world such a practice sounds appalling; it would have been severe but not so unusual in Tudor times. The day started and ended sooner to make full use of the daylight; in summer the London fish market opened at 4 a.m. The Carthusians rose and still rise at night for the chanting of Divine Office and More, having acquired the habit, followed it throughout his life. The modern Trappists observe the same programme. The day starts for them at 2 a.m. and, after the vigil, they do not return to bed. They assure me that, as do night nurses in hospital, they gradually grow used to the regime.

Undoubtedly More prayed at times in the style laid down by Picus and described already in some detail by himself. But it is also clear that he was greatly attracted by the monastic recitation of the Divine Office though he himself, who loved music, had an indifferent singing voice.[2] He derived great assistance from vocal prayer, especially from the psalms. "Following the example of St Jerome and others, he selected certain psalms of which he made, so to say, a Psalter or compendium of psalms.... He recited, each day, morning and evening prayers to which he added the seven penitential psalms and the litanies. Often, too, he said in addition the Gradual Psalms and the *Beati Immaculati* (Psalm 118)." Such a disciplined pattern of prayer, recited regularly at fixed

[1] Nichols, 3, p. 389.   [2] *Ibid.*, p. 399.

hours, bears the imprint of the Charterhouse. He must have compiled his compendium there.[3]

After his prayers, More, following the monks, began the work of the day. He concludes a letter to Erasmus: "London; in haste before daylight, All Saints Eve", and tells Peter Giles in the introduction to *Utopia*: "I therefore do win and get only that time which I steal from sleep and meat." In the early hours of the morning, he studied and wrote his letters before setting off for Mass.

He seems to have assisted at Mass daily, often to have served at the altar, and he went to confession frequently. Colet, his spiritual director, greatly encouraged this practice in his penitents and More seems to have followed his advice. More himself advocates frequent confession, liked to receive encouragement "from some virtuous ghostly father" and admits that the devil is often troublesome before confession as he was also in the Gospel when Christ looked like casting him out.[4]

He gives us a glimpse of himself in the following general description of a Christian, for we know that the litany of the saints was among his favourite prayers:

> The final fight is by invocation of help unto God, both praying for himself and desiring others also to pray for him, both poor folk for his alms and other good folk for their charity, especially good priests in that Holy, Sacred service of the Mass, and not only them but also his own good angel and other holy saints such as his devotion specially stands unto; or, if he be learned, use then the litany with the holy suffrages that follow which is a prayer in the Church of marvellous antiquity. . . . And the holy Saint Bernard gives counsel that every man should make suit unto the angels and saints to pray for him to God in the things that he would have sped at his holy hand. If anyone will not stick at this . . . I will not dispute with him. But yet for my own part I will as well trust to the counsel of St Bernard and reckon him for as good and as well learned in scripture as any man that I hear say the contrary. And better dare I jeopard

[3] Roper, pp. 14, 25; Harpsfield, pp. 88–89; Stapleton, pp. 9, 67, 75.
[4] *Dialogue of Comfort*, pp. 277, 287.

my soul with the soul of St Bernard than with his that findeth fault in his doctrine.[5]

So More was confessed often, heard Mass daily, recited his litanies, prayed to his good angel and then set off for another day with his clients at Westminster.

More was to praise the Utopians for following an order of the day which was, in fact, monastic and there is reason to think that he kept the same pattern himself. His household probably retired to bed at 8 p.m. Copying, again, the Carthusian way of life, he himself, for a time at least, used a block of wood for a pillow and slept on planks. As he lived in an age which knew nothing of bed springs or foam rubber, his may not have been so hard a choice. It seems unlikely that the use of these boards could have been a regular practice after he was married, or when he was travelling abroad. More permanent was his hair-shirt, to which reference has already been made. He wore this all his life with his secular clothes above. Meg washed it for him and he sent it to her from the Tower of London on the day before his death. For us, again, the use of haircloth may seem eccentric, even morbid, but, in those simpler days of smocks and homespun, poor men were less fussy and fastidious. More praised the Utopians for using coarse woven material, for not being too concerned about outward appearance and stressing in their dress only whiteness and cleanliness.

More could see only vanity in the behaviour of the rich who, though they can only wear one garment, keep ten others hanging in a cupboard, profiting them not at all. The Utopians, if one studies their behaviour carefully, not only kept monastic hours but followed the clothing habits of the monks. "When they go forth abroad, they cast upon them a cloak which hideth the other homely apparel . . . one garment will serve a man most commonly two years." To finish with his shirt of hair, the use of such rough material for penance was, in origin, biblical. Monks normally wore them and also many pious laymen; Queen Catherine of Aragon is said to have used one for a time. As always, More was

[5] *Ibid.*, pp. 279–280.

methodical, wearing a hairshirt all his life. At a guess, the brothers
at the Charterhouse would have woven their own material and no
doubt would have been proud to supply so dear a friend.[6]

One final touching incident, mentioned only by Stapleton,
shows how deeply the monastic practice attracted More throughout his life:

> He wore silk indeed when his official position demanded it;
> otherwise he wore the simplest garments and thought so little
> about the matter that he would always wear the same clothes
> unless his servant reminded him. For he had among his servants
> one whom he called his tutor, whose duty it was to buy him
> boots, shoes and other necessary things. Once it happened that
> he went out with badly torn boots. His secretary, Harris, re-
> monstrated with him. "Ask my tutor to buy me a new pair,"
> was his only reply. In short, as to what regarded the body, this
> man in his deep holiness wished, like a monk, to be under the
> authority of others and to obey their commands, either that
> his mind—noble and lofty as it was—might not be disturbed by
> such trivial details or, as I prefer to think, that he might exercise
> the fundamental Christian virtue of humility. For this reason,
> although he was a man of the soundest judgment in many
> points of business or of study, he would ask the advice of Harris,
> his amanuensis, and beg him to warn him of any mistake he
> might make.[7]

2. HE LEASES THE BARGE IN BUCKLERSBURY

For some unaccountable reason Thomas More's life has been so
often linked to Chelsea that few can now see him as a City man.
At most he lived in Chelsea for his last ten years. Before 1524 his
home was in central London, first with his father in the neighbourhood of Milk Street and then in Bucklersbury, at a house
which was called the Barge. More leased this house from the
hospital of St Thomas of Acon, a City foundation, established to
honour the place where St Thomas of Canterbury was born.
Here the Mercers had their chapel and young More, who conducted most of the Mercers' legal business, was admitted in 1509

[6] *Utopia*, pp. 64, 68.   [7] Stapleton, p. 74.

to the freedom of the company. He may have obtained the lease
of the Barge through the Mercers' influence. Dates and details
are now hazy but the evidence suggests that More lived in Bucklersbury from early in his married life.

One may say, for the sake of those unfamiliar with London,
that the Barge stood very close to the present Mansion House.
The Lord Mayor's official residence was built on the site of the
old stock market past which the Walbrook flowed south to join
the Thames. At one time boats came up the Walbrook and
moored outside the Barge. In More's day the brook had been
covered over and there were houses with fine gardens along its
bank. We read of More walking with his daughter Meg in his
garden and here he kept all his pets. Reynolds suggests that More's
garden covered the spot on which an ancient Temple of Mithras
was found in 1954. Directly opposite to More's house stood the
little parish church of St Stephen, Walbrook, destroyed in the
fire of London and rebuilt, damaged in the Blitz and now re-
decorated, marking for us the place where More came daily to
pray.

The Barge at Bucklersbury was a large and roomy house but
in a noisy locality. Bucklersbury itself is a narrow lane running
from Cheapside to Walbrook and now cut in half by Queen
Victoria Street. It derived its name from a worthy citizen called
Buckle who once owned property there. Stowe tells us that the
furriers plied their trade in Bucklersbury. Indeed, if we follow
Stowe, we recapture some of the bustle and excitement of the
medieval city, even if some of his facts belong to other dates.

The mercers, goldsmiths and haberdashers owned the smart
shops in West Chepe near St Paul's Cathedral, the equivalent of
our modern West End. The pepperers and grocers lived in
Soper's Lane, the drapers in Lombard Street, the skinners in St
Mary Axe, the fishmongers in Thames Street, while herrings, sprats,
mackerel and shell-fish could be bought from the boats at Billings-
gate. Further down the Walbrook, the Bordeaux vintners were
unloading their casks of wine.

In 1509 a cart damaged the water conduit in the Stock Market and the citizens of the ward were ordered to attend to the repairs. Traffic jams were common and certain streets were banned to traffic without a permit, nor could drays use any streets unless the front horse was led. Foreigners lived in national colonies, caused endless friction and were cordially disliked. After the riots of Evil May-day, gallows were set up at Aldgate, Blanchapleton, Gracechurch Street, Leadenhall, Newgate, Aldersgate and Bishopsgate.

There was dancing at Smithfield, water regattas on the Thames, especially at Easter, and shooting contests between citizens and courtiers at Mile End. Barlo, a citizen of Shoreditch, won a shooting trophy and was proclaimed Duke of Shoreditch amid much laughter and buffoonery. Cheapside was decorated on all royal occasions and for three years running King Henry VIII rode a-Maying from Greenwich to Shooters Hill. Wine cost a penny a pint at the "Cardinal's Hat" and at the "Pope's Head" in Cornhill. This sketch is trivial but, perhaps, sufficient to provide the setting in which More achieved sanctity.

After leaving the Charterhouse, presumably for his father's house in Milk Street, young More seems to have decided to marry at once. For a time he strikes one as not quite himself. The four years at the Charterhouse had not only matured him but made him painfully earnest and serious. This experience is not uncommon with those who are forced to leave a religious community; time is needed to adjust oneself to the tempo of everyday life. In the light of this, we may forgive his rather humourless behaviour and feel some sympathy for Jane Colt.

3. NETHERHALL: MARRIAGE WITH JANE COLT

The Mores and the Colts were well known to one another and young More went frequently to Netherhall, the Colts' country house in Essex, a red-brick mansion with a drawbridge and a moat. John Colt, the father, was a rollicking, prosperous man who married twice, had eighteen children, loved both hunting and a joke. Socially the Mores and Colts were upper middle-class. Money, apparently, was not mentioned and More certainly had no intention of marrying to promote himself socially. After the Charterhouse he was very serious.

Roper it is who tells us the celebrated story of his courtship, how he was first attracted to a younger daughter, "for that he thought her the fairest and best favoured, yet when he considered that it would be both grief and shame also to the eldest to see her younger sister in marriage preferred before her, he, then, of a certain pity framed his fancy towards her and soon after married her". It should be said at once that More's life is dogged with such stories and it is not easy to decide how much of them to believe. A great many originated with Erasmus who in his private correspondence liked to relate anonymous yarns about his friends. Most of such tales are friendly and partly based on truth.

In some cases we cannot be sure that the stories refer to More himself. Erasmus is simply telling an anonymous yarn, many years later, to amuse a correspondent or to illustrate a point. More uses the same device himself. Occasionally such a story has a true basis but has been exaggerated and it would be dangerous to accept it as it has come down to us. Again, in the case of More, biographers sometimes take such a tale told by Erasmus and add to it. Knowing that More was a saint, they are pleased to lay hands on any edifying item to show his sanctity. These stories have their value, contributing as they do to the colour of More's early manhood but they need to be checked against the facts.

This particular yarn about More marrying the eldest girl Jane out of pity is, at best, unfortunate. The very word pity has now changed its meaning and may easily be misunderstood. As used by Roper and his contemporaries it had no note of patronage. More describes his cheerful and vigorous old father as "a pitiful man". A wrong understanding of pity led to the impression that poor Jane was ugly and ill-favoured and this, in turn, changes More's charity into an odious form of priggishness. From it, biographers have deduced that More married without any love for Jane.

Jane, in fact, was charming and Erasmus himself describes her as one who "would have been a delightful companion for his whole life". As he also informs us that More, when he had decided to marry, "chose a very young girl", we may doubt if Thomas seriously thought first of her sister, who would have been younger still. From all that we know of More's views on the solemnity of marriage, from all that he says in *Utopia* about the care needed in choosing a life-long companion, we may judge it unlikely that he allowed any false sentiment to sway him at Netherhall.

Any statement about More's affection must be conditional. In the first place he was painfully shy. The confidence and poise of his professional life seemed to desert him when he turned to more personal affairs. Then, there was a natural diffidence. More complicated still are the reactions of one with so deep a spiritual vision, for whom human love could only be a means to an end. Young More was ten years older than Jane. Mentally the gap between them was even greater and it seems astonishing that he should ever have thought of marriage with a girl of her age. For the only time in his life he assumes the role of a Dutch uncle deliberately. He who, throughout his youth, had always been happiest with friends far older than himself, suddenly embarked on marriage with a girl of whom Erasmus says "her character was still unformed". More's action was deliberate. "He wanted to fashion her according to his own habits," and these habits, to say the least, were peculiar.

When all these unusual features have been weighed and counted, we may still assert that More loved Jane. He loved her with an ardour which was tongue-tied, inhibited, donnish and, superficially, pedantic but which few other girls will ever know. More was too scrupulous, too earnest, too holy to provide the teenage love which a girl as young as Jane would normally expect. Erasmus was right in his verdict, "she would have been a delightful companion for his whole life". The astonishing love between Meg and her father, a love based on More's spiritual capacity for devotion, would have been Jane's. She was young and he was old beyond his years and they enjoyed together a period of intense suffering and frustration for which neither was to blame. One must feel sorry for Jane. After spending all her life in the country with young brothers and sisters, she found herself installed at the Barge with a husband who was a scholar, a promising lawyer, a member of parliament, who always wore a hairshirt and began his day each morning at 2 o'clock.

Of the troubles of their early life we must rely once more on a story by Erasmus which undoubtedly deals with the More household but need not be taken in all details as accurate.

I am intimate with a gentleman of good family, learned and of particularly keen wit. He married a young woman, a maiden of seventeen, who had been brought up entirely in the country at her father's house, as men in his position prefer to live in the country most of the time for the sake of hunting and fowling. My friend wished to have a simple, unaffected maid so that he might the more easily train her in his own tastes. He began by instructing her in literature and music and to accustom her by degrees to repeat the discourses she heard and to teach her other things that would afterwards be of use to her. Now all this was completely new to the girl who had been brought up at home to do nothing but chatter and amuse herself; she soon grew weary of this life and would no longer submit to her husband's wishes. When he expostulated with her, she would weep, day after day, and, sometimes, throw herself flat on the ground, beating her head as if she wished for death.

As there seemed to be no way of ending this, he concealed his annoyance and invited his wife to spend a holiday with him in his father-in-law's house in the country; to this she most willingly agreed. When they got there, the husband left his wife with her mother and sisters and went hunting with his father-in-law; he took the opportunity of taking him apart from any witnesses and of telling him that whereas he had hoped his daughter would prove an agreeable companion for life, he now had one who was always weeping and moaning, nor could she be cured by scolding; he begged his father-in-law to help him in curing this distemper.[8]

[8] Erasmus, *Colloquies*. Quoted here from Reynolds, *Margaret Roper*, p. 6. See also Chambers, p. 89.

The story ends happily. Colt, a Tudor man of the world, suggests to the timid husband that he should beat her, as most Tudor husbands would have done. More, if so the husband be, admits his rights but will not exercise them: he begs the father to put his daughter in a better frame of mind. Old Colt gave Jane such a talking to that she came to her senses, found her husband kinder than her father, begged his forgiveness and together, joyfully, they rode off home.

Some of the details of this story are unusual but there is little doubt that Erasmus is writing about More. He must have had the facts from More himself. It was not like More to go off hunting; maybe, he had no other way of getting John Colt by himself. Nor is it like More to be both so timid and heavy-handed with the young. When we recall his relations with his children, it is the more surprising that he should seem to fail with Jane. She was, in fact, the first young person with whom he tried to deal.

After this initial trouble, Thomas and Jane settled down happily. Jane not only picked up a little Latin but she studied to play the viol, the spinet and the flute. She was successful with his friends and, between guests and lessons, she bore him four babies, Meg, probably in 1505, Elizabeth in 1506, Cecily in 1507 and John in 1509.

When Erasmus came to England, as he did on two occasions, he found all happy and peaceful at the Barge. In 1509 he stayed with the Mores for several months. Jane coped with this famous visitor who was never easy! Erasmus spoke no English, was always fussy, worried either about his luggage or his health.

Living at the Barge, Erasmus wrote his witty but irreverent *Encomium Moriae* or *Praise of Folly* which he dedicated to Thomas More. Heaven knows how Jane, with four small children, managed also to nurse her ailing guest. Erasmus describes his visit thus:

I was staying with More after my return from Italy when I was kept several days in the house with lumbago. My library had not arrived; and if it had, my illness forbade exertion in more serious studies. So, for want of employment, I began to amuse myself with the Praise of Folly, not with any intention of publishing the result but to relieve the discomfort of sickness by this sort of distraction. I showed the specimen of the unfinished work to some friends in order to heighten the enjoyment of the ridiculous by sharing it. They were mightily pleased and insisted on my going on. I complied and spent some seven days upon the work.

Jane More saw all this. She must have supervised the nursing of Erasmus while possibly herself with child. Mountjoy, Colet, Grocyn and how many others would have come to see Erasmus in her house. After a secluded life chattering with her brothers and sisters in the country, here was a change indeed.[9]

Erasmus has given us his verdict that "she would have been a delightful companion for his whole life". Jane also gave hers of Erasmus; Ammonio wrote to the Dutchman some months later, 19th May, 1511: "Our dear and beloved More and his kind wife who never thinks of you without a blessing upon you, are well, together with their children and the whole household." Within a month or two Jane was dead. Erasmus, writing to Ammonio in September, remarks without much feeling, "I would be to blame if I did not forgive More, considering how pressed he is just now."

Jane vanishes almost unnoticed; there is no record of her death, of mourners at her funeral, of many tears. The parish priest of St Stephen's, Walbrook, writes in a letter that he buried her and that is all that we hear of her for many years. More is silent; her children, as they grow up, do not refer to her. It is probable that she died in childbirth after no more than six years of married life. If More says nothing about Jane, he remains silent as to his own suffering and the sudden crisis which enveloped him. Here he was, a busy and successful professional man, with four small babies, the eldest five years old. In any other case the complete silence would be abnormal but with More silence is all that we may expect.

---

[9] Erasmus, *In Praise of Folly*, Dedication.

No doubt should be maintained about his love for Jane. On a short-term view, he may have been too controlled, too philosophic as a husband and he must have nursed grave misgivings about himself. He knew that his experiment had both succeeded and failed. His love for her was expressed twenty years later when he moved her body to Chelsea to rest in the grave in the parish church which he had planned for himself. Here in stone he calls her "dear Jane, his little wife," which, from so great and loving a saint, is praise enough. What did she look like? I stand before the Holbein portraits and try to work out just how far his children took after More himself. It could well be that in the deep affection between More and his eldest daughter we have some faint clue to all that Jane could have meant to him. Surely it was also a moving tribute to her that he could not face the same experiment again? She certainly has a place in history as the wife, the dear little wife, of a very great and holy man.

4. DAME ALICE ARRIVES AT THE BARGE

The portrait of Thomas More by Holbein—calm, dignified and peaceful—begins to assume a fuller meaning as we look back over More's life. Here was the boy who listened to Mother Maud, who played funerals in the street, who studied so earnestly with Colet, Grocyn, Linacre, Colet and Erasmus, who met Eliza and then departed for the Charterhouse. There for four years he prayed, read Augustine and the Fathers, translated the life of Picus, lived a solitary life. Next, he is back consulting Colet, visiting the Colts, proposing to Jane, marrying her, trying to stop her weeping, trying to stop himself weeping as her body rests in its coffin before the altar in St Stephen's, and he is left with four lusty babies on his hands. In this extraordinary situation, More kept his own counsel and, as Erasmus tells us, did not follow his friends' advice.

For once More acted with bewildering haste. We have unusual evidence for this from Fr John Bouge, parish priest of St Stephen's, Walbrook, who later was to enter the Carthusian monastery at Axholme in Lincolnshire. Writing to console a devout Catholic laywoman, Dame Catherine Mann, after the execution of More and Fisher, Fr Bouge gives us an intimate picture of his former penitent:

> He was my parishioner at London. I christened him two goodly children. I buried his first wife. And within a month after, he came to me on a Sunday at night late, and there he brought me a dispensation to be married the next Monday without any banns asking; and as I understand, she is yet alive.
> This Mr. More was my ghostly child; in his confession to be so pure, so clean, with great study, deliberation and devotion, I never heard many such. A gentleman of learning, both in law, art and divinity, having no man like him now alive of a layman. Item, a gentleman of great soberness and gravity, one chief of the King's Council. Item, a gentleman of little refection and marvellous diet.[10]

Fr Bouge was a simple man and his evidence is clear and precise; More came to a decision in a hurry and acted in a hurry; he must have made up his mind within a fortnight of Jane's death. The future Dame Alice must also have reached a grave decision quickly for she moved to the Barge with three weeks' notice and no trace of romance. The incident is so extraordinary that it deserves careful consideration, throwing, as it does, new light on the character of More.

Times and conditions change and, in the Tudor world, with its high mortality rate, especially at childbirth, it was common for men to marry many times. We need look no further than John More as an example of this. The sudden death of a young wife was not as exceptional as now. That Thomas More would marry again must have been taken for granted, especially as he had a busy practice and four small children who needed care. It is not his second marriage but the speed of it which has us puzzled; it was not like More to seek a sudden dispensation and to disturb the priest late on a Sunday night. The care of his children cannot explain his hurry for he was surrounded by friends and relations who would have helped. He had his stepmother with whom he was on excellent terms, his brother and two sisters, while

[10] Cf. Chambers, pp. 102–103.

Jane's parents, brothers and sisters could have come up from Netherhall.

If More was to marry again, surely two other points would have required due attention, for another young wife would have borne him other children or a rich and influential wife would have helped him in his career. In Tudor days, as in our own, weddings were socially important and carefully planned. At the time of Jane's death, More's prospects were rapidly improving; she may just have lived long enough to see him elected Under-Sheriff while negotiations were afoot for his first journey to the Continent. More certainly longed for children and later filled his house with them. He also needed money and social influence. He had wanted a young wife that he might fashion her to his habits but, now, in almost indecent haste, he obtained a dispensation and had the priest up late on a Sunday evening to arrange a wedding with an undistinguished widow well into middle age. Such an unusual marriage in such a hurry may have been More's last, incomparable tribute to his Jane.

There was no trace of romance about this second marriage and no mention of Alice Middleton in any of More's letters until Fr Bouge heard of her late on that Sunday night. We now know that she was the widow of an established London Mercer who had died two years previously. More's professional links with the Mercers make it likely that he had known the Middletons for some years. If Alice had had other children by her first husband, only her daughter Alice was young enough to join the More household when her mother moved to the Barge. Dame Alice was forty at the time of her second marriage and More was thirty-two. His new wife was a thrifty, middle-class matron with few pretensions; she was practical, amusing and motherly. After one experiment with youth, More had reverted to his former practice; he was happier with people older than himself.

A great many unkind remarks have been passed about Dame Alice, few of them justified. There can be no doubt that More himself was devoted to her and knew well how much he stood in her debt. Only a woman of her uninhibited tastes could have faced such a situation and played a notable part in the building of a household, one of the most distinguished in history. Dame Alice was set in her habits, without much interest in the new or in any kind of learning, not partial to Erasmus and his pernickety ways.

Erasmus and Ammonio, who had both loved Jane, could not easily take to her successor, a middle-aged dame. Ammonio ended one visit to More and moved to another dwelling; he wrote to Erasmus that it was a relief to get away "from the hooked beak of the harpy" and this unkind phrase is now generally applied to More's second wife. Some years later, Erasmus also moved from the Barge and wrote in a letter, "I feel myself becoming a stale guest to More's wife". Harpsfield calls her "aged, blunt and rude". Erasmus ungallantly quotes More's own comment on her, "*Nec bella, nec puella*", an expression far less hurtful in the Latin than in the oft-quoted English version of it, "Neither a girl nor a pearl". The one certain fact, grudgingly admitted by all the biographers, is that More loved Dame Alice very much.[11]

On the credit side stands an inexhaustible fund of merry stories told by More about his second wife. As most of these stories are anonymous, we cannot be certain that all of them apply to Dame Alice, but if even half the facts are true, she appears amusing and lovable. We see her penny wise, pound foolish, charmingly vain about her hair style, squeezing her portly waist into slim, fashionable dresses, at night bolting both the door and the windows of her room. Certainly she enjoyed very much her husband's rise in status and was understandably proud to be the Lord Chancellor's wife. She was over sixty when they took him to the Tower and she made no pretence of understanding what his famous scruple was about. She suffered much poverty and humiliation through him without ever grasping why.

In the end, she made great friends even with Erasmus. He wrote kindly of her in praising the skill and tact of More:

> More did not however long remain single but, contrary to his friends' advice, a few months after his wife's death, he mar-

11 Nichols, 2, pp. 31, 320; 3, p. 394.

ried a widow, more for the sake of the management of his household than to please his own fancy, as she is no great beauty nor yet young, "nec bella admodum nec puella", as he sometimes laughingly says, but a sharp and watchful housewife; with whom, nevertheless, he lives on as sweet and pleasant terms as if she were as young and lovely as anyone could desire; and scarcely any husband obtains from his wife by masterfulness and severity as much compliance as he does by blandishments and jests. Indeed, what more compliance could he have, when he has induced a woman who is already elderly, who is not naturally of a yielding character and whose mind is occupied with business, to learn to play on the harp, the viol, the spinet and the flute and to give up every day a prescribed time to practice.

So far Erasmus, but Dame Alice herself was not beyond joking with him; More ends a letter to Erasmus: "My wife desires to send a million compliments, especially for your careful wish that she may live for many years. She says she is the more anxious for this as she will then live the longer to plague me."[12]

Erasmus has the last word. Writing to Meg Roper after he had seen the Holbein family portrait, he adds: "Convey my respectful and affectionate salutations to the honoured Lady Alice, your mother; since I cannot kiss her, I kiss her picture."[13]

During the twenty-four years of their life together, Dame Alice proved, as Erasmus has said, a sharp and watchful housewife with a practical head for details which More himself might have overlooked. She saw to it that the children carried out the small family duties assigned to them. More, writing from the Court to their tutor, mentions her maternal love for her stepchildren "which has been proved to me in so many ways". She certainly made a great effort with her music and reached the stage that she could play a duet with him. More was less successful in trying to teach her the elements of science; "while a certain worshipful man was trying to teach his good woman the elements of science, she nothing went about to consider his words, but, as she was wont

---

[12] *Ibid.*, 2, p. 448.   [13] Cf. Reynolds, *Margaret Roper*, p. 54.

to do in all things, studied all the while nothing else but what she might say to the contrary".

Harpsfield tells us one of her "merry conceited talks" which More liked very well. She said one day to her husband after confession, "You can be merry for I have finished with my past nagging and now intend to start afresh."[14]

A little may be said, later, about their marital relations but, in public at least, More's second marriage proved a considerable success. A man of More's temperament, inclined to scrupulosity and often prone to worry, urgently needed a companion who enjoyed teasing and was happy to be the butt for his jests. These were always kindly, as well she knew. More was completely at ease with her, trusted her with his children, wrote her a most practical business letter when, in his absence, some of the barns caught fire and were destroyed. Her presence in the house was a safeguard for, with More so spiritual, her cheerful lack of deep devotion prevented him from turning Chelsea into a semi-monastery. She knew little of his spiritual exercises, and when she discovered about his hairshirt, she asked Fr Bouge to order More to stop wearing it.

Dame Alice deserves her proud place in the Holbein portrait. If she was not by his side, as, perhaps, one might have expected, she enjoys a very prominent position with the monkey by her side.

More paid a sincere and graceful tribute to her, still to be seen in Chelsea, in the verses which he wrote above what should have been their grave.

> Within this tomb Jane, wife of More reclines;
> This for himself and Alice More designs.
> The first—dear object of my youthful vow,
> Gave me three daughters and a son to know.
> The next—ah virtue in a step-dame rare,
> Nursed my sweet infants with a mother's care.
> With both my years so happily have passed,
> Which the more dear, I know not—first or last.

[14] For Dame Alice, see Stapleton, p. 94; Roper, p. 40; Harpsfield, pp. 105–108.

O! had religion: destiny allowed,
How smoothly, mixed, had our three fortunes flowed.
But be we in the tomb—in heaven allied;
So kinder death shall grant what life denied.[15]

5. THE BEST YEARS OF HIS LIFE

From the human viewpoint, the first six years after his second marriage were the most regular and peaceful in More's life. Like many of us, he did not see this at the time. Frequently he complains of being too busy, of neglecting his studies, but he was unworried and contented as he would never be again. One recalls the words of Picus: "The golden mediocrity, the mean estate is to be desired ... my little house ... my study ... the pleasure of my books ... the rest and peace of my mind." More moved in a steady circle, Westminster, Lincoln's Inn, the Compter in the Poultry, St Stephen's and the Barge.

This was the period in which, with the example of the Carthusians and Picus before him, More could adjust his spiritual programme to the requirements of a busy professional life.

First, he had a large and increasing legal practice and we are told that there was hardly a famous case in which he was not briefed by one of the litigants. He would not accept a brief unless he had studied the details carefully. Next, he would try to get the contestants to come to terms. If he failed in this, he would warn his clients "that they should not in a single detail turn aside from the truth". He would, then, give them a private opinion: "If your case is as you have stated it, it seems to me that you will win." Where he had any doubts about the honesty of a case, he would refuse to continue but would direct the client to another man. More was often pleading in court. Erasmus knew no one better than More at extempore speaking, "the happiest thoughts being attended by the happiest language while a mind that catches and anticipates all that passes and a ready memory, having everything as it were in stock, promptly supply whatever the time or the occasion demands". More's voice was penetrating though he did

[15] Wrangham's translation, cf. *Philomorus*, p. 58.

not speak loudly. It was not very melodious, but "is simply suitable for speech" with excellent articulation and neither hurried nor hesitant. During these early years he was beginning to earn good money, £400 a year by Tudor reckoning might be £10,000 a year in our own.[16]

In the same period of years, More gained a great reputation as a lecturer and at least twice was appointed a reader at Lincoln's Inn. The old hall still stands in which his lectures were heard. The office of reader, as Stapleton points out, "is one of the most illustrious in England and only given to seniors and never exercised except by the most skilful, the rest, who feel themselves unfit, purchasing their liberty at a great expense". More was first a reader in 1511; he held the office again in 1516.

During that critical time when Jane More was dying, and Dame Alice was worrying Ammonio, More was not only reader at Lincoln's Inn but Under-Sheriff of London, an office which he held for several years. He admitted to liking this post "better than many others of higher rank". The Under-Sheriff fulfilled the duties of our police court magistrate. The three chief magistrates of the City, the Lord Mayor and two Sheriffs, were elected yearly and were normally merchants or business men, unskilled in law. The custom had been established for a distinguished lawyer to act in their place and administer justice inside the City boundaries. More sat in his court in the Compter in the Poultry, near to the site of the present Bank of England and barely five minutes' walk from the Barge. He was in court each Thursday morning and told Erasmus that he liked the office because it afforded him a practical opportunity for showing his affection for his fellow citizens. As always, he made every effort to prevent litigation and was generous in remitting fees.[17]

It was as Under-Sheriff that he acquired his intimate know-

[16] Cf. Stapleton, p. 17; Nichols, 3, pp. 390, 398. Erasmus often spoke of More's skill, e.g.: "I do not think, unless the vehemence of my love leads me astray, that nature ever formed a mind more present, ready, sharp-sighted and subtle . . . add to this a power of expression equal to his intellect . . . a singular cheerfulness . . . an abundance of wit and you miss nothing that should be found in a perfect advocate" (Nichols, 1, p. 406).

[17] Stapleton, p. 17.

ledge of London, all the sorrow, cruelty and suffering that was hidden by London's impressive façade. While West Chepe dazzled all foreign visitors with the golden display of fifty goldsmiths, much poverty and evil germinated in the warren of small streets behind the main roads. More lists the bawds, queans, whores, harlots, strumpets, brothel-houses, stews, tippling-houses which caused poor men to go stealing when their money had gone. He tells many tales of Newgate prison and its inmates, some of them full of pity, as the one of the poor fellow who was to be hanged as a cutpurse and reckoned death worthwhile for the pleasure of having the purse for one night.[18]

More was involved in the scandal of Richard Hunne which shook London; this prosperous merchant, imprisoned for heresy, was found hanged in the bishop's prison while awaiting trial. The Under-Sheriff went with the Lords of the Council to Baynard's Castle to examine witnesses. More played a significant part in the notorious "Evil May Day" riots, started by two apprentices. More met the rioters and his eloquence "almost brought them to a stay". Unfortunately a sergeant standing with him was hit by a stone, lost his temper, attacked the rioters and thus caused the tumult to start again. Thirteen young men were hanged publicly by the King's orders and More went with a civic deputation to the King and to Wolsey to plead for clemency. More was well aware that the two ringleaders were never punished and that the Evil May Day riots were in part caused by the idle and worthless servants kept by men like Wolsey in their palaces and mansions round Westminster.

It is extraordinary to watch this busy, practical man dealing with the day-to-day problems of a city when one knows that he will be praying half the night. No other saint in history attempted a vocation quite like this.

When More came back to the Barge after his long round of professional duties, he could not turn at once to study and prayer. In the introduction to *Utopia*, he himself sets out his programme in a letter to Peter Giles.

[18] *Utopia*, pp. 22, 28 seq.; *English Works*, 2, pp. 232–242 seq.

Howbeit, to the dispatching of this so little business, my other cares and troubles did leave me almost less than no leisure. While I daily bestow my time on law matters, some to plead, some to hear, some as an arbitrator with my judgement to determine, some as an umpire or judge with my sentence to discuss, while I go one way to see and visit a friend, another way about my private affairs; while I spend almost all day away from home with others and the remainder at home among my own; I leave to myself, I mean to my book, no time. For when I am come home, I must commune with my wife, chat with my children and talk with my servants. All the which things I reckon and account among business, forasmuch as they must of necessity be done and done must they needs be, unless a man will be a stranger in his own house. And in any wise, a man must so fashion and order his conditions and so appoint and dispose himself that he be merry, jocund and pleasant with those whom either nature hath provided or chance hath made or he himself hath chosen to be the fellows and companions of his life; so that with too much gentle behaviour he does not mar them and by too much sufferance of his servants make them his masters. Among these things now rehearsed stealeth away the day, the month and the year.[19]

So, at this stage of his career, More gave Dame Alice her music lesson and slowly brought her to the point where she could play her famous duet with him on the flute. Stapleton tells us that in these early years he taught his children their first lessons himself. Surely Erasmus is also describing the More household when he speaks of children whom he knows, learning the Greek alphabet by shooting with their bows and arrows at the letters?

In his letter to Peter Giles, More mentions one of his many kindnesses, the frequent visits he made to his relatives and friends. Erasmus in describing More to Hutten devotes a whole paragraph to this: "It would be difficult to find anyone living on such terms with his mother as he [More] does with his stepmother. For his father had brought in one stepmother after another and he has been as affectionate with each of them as with his mother.

19 Preface to *Utopia.*

He has lately introduced a third and More swears that he never saw anything better. His affection for his parents, children and sisters is such that he neither wearies them with his love nor ever fails in any kindly attention." It would be impossible to compile an accurate list of all More's relatives living around London; he was in constant touch with the Rastells, the Heywoods, the Stavertons. Frances Staverton, his niece, came for a time to live at the Barge to join More's children at their work. More once rode to Coventry to see his sister but we have no record of any later visits to the Colts at Netherhall.[20]

Had his family been his one concern, More would have been busy, but to the circle of his relations was added the endless demands of his many friends. Erasmus, who was, in fact, the most exacting of all his correspondents, paid a gracious tribute to More's never-ending charity.

> He seems to be born and made for friendship, of which he is the sincerest and most persistent devotee. Neither is he afraid of that multiplicity of friends of which Hesiod disapproves. Accessible to every tender of intimacy, he is by no means fastidious in choosing his acquaintance, while he is most accommodating in keeping it on foot and constant in retaining it. If he has fallen in with anyone whose faults he cannot cure, he finds some opportunity of parting with him, untying the knot of intimacy without tearing it; but when he has found any sincere friends, whose characters are suited to his own, he is so delighted with their society and conversation, that he seems to find in these the chief pleasure of life, having an absolute distaste for tennis and dice and cards and the other games with which the mass of gentlemen beguile the tediousness of time. It should be added that, while he is somewhat neglectful of his own interest, no one takes more pains in attending to the concerns of his friends. What more need I say? If anyone requires a perfect example of true friendship, it is in More that he will best find it.

The concerns of his friends, as one reads through More's correspondence, the demands of his friends grow more exacting

[20] Nichols, 3, pp. 391, 395.

and oppressive, with the endless needs of Erasmus well to the top of the list. Erasmus, when abroad, used More as his man of business and the busy lawyer was for ever running errands for his friend's sake. We find him going by boat to Lambeth to interview Archbishop Warham about the Dutch scholar's need for cash. Then a cask of wine has been mislaid, then Erasmus wants a horse, or a secretary or wants to send a boy to be trained in England or has had all his money stolen while waiting for the channel boat. Of this inspired circle of scholars, More alone was a professional business-man with outside work. Colet, Erasmus and the others were priests or students who did not scruple to pester More. It is all "I sent More a letter for the bishop of Rochester but I do not know whether he has delivered it; arrange with More for giving it [the Manuscript] to his brother to be copied; I do not wish to obtrude the bearer upon you; but if you want a clerk, he writes correctly and legibly in Greek as well as Latin." There is one amusing note to Erasmus from Bishop Fisher. "The Cabalistical Book which you say was presented to me by Reuchlin has not yet reached me. Your friend More has sent the letter but still detains the book in his old way; as he did before with the Oculare Speculum." It is bewildering to see how much work More fitted to each day.[21]

As More had told Peter Giles, he could only find time for writing and for study by cutting down on his sleep and on his meals. Yet he wrote much in these most fruitful years. His life of Picus, his history of King Richard III, his epigrams and several lengthy and controversial letters were published in book form. Finally came *Utopia* itself. More is very agitated, very anxious, very uncertain about this. He wants to know from Erasmus what Giles thinks of it, what is Tunstall's reaction, whether Busleiden is pleased. He has doubts about its reception, as to whether it should be published, but is prepared to follow the advice of his friends. In the end he was genuinely excited and could write to Erasmus: "Your letter has excited my expectations and I now look every day for our Utopia with the feelings with which a mother awaits the return of her boy from foreign parts."[22]

At dead of night, with his wife and family fast asleep around him, More began to fashion his own peculiar lay version of the contemplative life. As in a monastery, this was regular and methodical, for behind all the friendliness and joking, More was a very purposeful man. We may already have noted in his letter to Peter Giles how he treated his loving relationships with his family as part of his business, carefully planned and exactly carried out. The order of the day at the Barge and later at Chelsea was to be monastic, so much time for work, so much for leisure, so much for meals. Even in the Tower of London his precious interviews with Meg always began with the litanies. This disciplined life was not natural to More who was, we know, somewhat careless and untidy, but he had learned the value of routine in the Charterhouse and had discovered that this is essential for a life of prayer.

As usual More says nothing about his interior life; we have to rely on the reminiscences of others, bearing in mind those deep fears, worries, scruples about which he wrote in the *Dialogue of Comfort*, which he must have endured and mastered during these earlier years.

Little is said either way by any author on More's private relations with his second wife. Harpsfield records that he married her more "for the ruling and governing of his children, house and family than for any bodily pleasure" and this is all that we are told. It seems to me at least likely that More now slept alone. It is hard to see how he could have risen at 2 a.m., slept on boards with a block of wood for a pillow if Dame Alice and the family were about. That she only discovered about his hairshirt after more than a year and wondered how he washed it, suggests that he had virtually returned to a single life. True, on one occasion

[22] Nichols, 2, p. 447. Earlier More has invited Erasmus to visit him in Utopia where More would be king. He promises Erasmus great honour. He ends: "I was proceeding further with this most delightful dream when the break of day dispersed the vision, deposing poor me from my sovereignty and recalling me to prison, that is to my legal work." (Nichols, 2, p. 443.)

at least he refers to her in a letter as "my good bedfellow", but such an expression might possibly be conventional. Once, in the Tower of London, when Meg wondered whether he had given his position enough thought, More made a most moving declaration which certainly seems to imply that he lived alone:

> Yet since nothing is impossible, I forgot not in this matter the counsel of Christ in the Gospels, that ere I should begin to build this castle for the safeguard of mine own soul, I should sit and reckon what the charge would be. I counted Margaret, full surely, many a restless, weary night, while my wife slept and thought I slept too, what peril were possible to fall to me; and in devising I had a full heavy heart. But yet, I thank Our Lord for all that, I never thought to change, though the very uttermost should happen to me that my fear ran upon.[23]

Later, at Chelsea, More was to have his new building, his private oratory, to which he could retire alone. In the Barge, he must have had his own room. One imagines that his astonishing haste after Jane's death, his choice of a widow so much older than himself, of no great physical attraction, represents a firm decision taken directly Jane died. Those poems on love written to the theme proposed by Picus were certainly not forgotten now that More was a busy professional man. His routine of prayer was designed to keep them before his mind. The emptiness of this world, the reality of God's love, the need to safeguard one's singleness of purpose, alone can explain his ruthless programme of austerities. He married Jane because he was advised that God wanted him to do so; after her death, he was certain that he should reach for God alone.

After More was dead, certain prayers collected by him and arranged by him for his own private devotion came into the hands of his children and were piously preserved. Reynolds rightly describes one of them as "the sum of his life's devotion", and this offers some clue to those nights at the Barge. We have to fit Dame Alice, Jane, the children, Erasmus, *Utopia*, stepmothers, apprentices, cutpurses, kings and clients to the theme of this:

[23] Rogers, p. 530; Bridgett, p. 373.

Give me Thy Grace good Lord to set the world at nought.
To set my mind fast upon thee,
And not to hang upon the blast of men's mouths.
To be content to be solitary.
Not to long for worldly company,
Little and little utterly to cast off the world
And rid my mind of all the business thereof.
Not to long to hear of any worldly things,
But that the hearing of worldly fantasies may be to me displeasant,
Gladly to be thinking of God.
Piteously to call for his help.
To lean unto the comfort of God.
Busily to labour to love him.
To know my own vility and wretchedness.
To humble and meeken myself under the mighty hand of God.
To bewail my sins passed,
For the purging of them, patiently to suffer adversity.
Gladly to bear my purgatory here.
To be joyful of tribulations.
To walk the narrow way that leadeth to life.
To bear the cross with Christ.
To have the last things in remembrance.
To have ever before mine eye, my death,
A death that is ever at hand.
To make death no stranger to me.
To foresee and consider the everlasting fire of hell.
To pray for pardon before the judge comes.
To have continually in mind the passion that Christ suffered for me.
For his benefits incessantly to give him thanks.
To buy the time again that I before have lost.
To abstain from vain confabulations.
To eschew light foolish mirth and gladness.
Recreations not necessary, to cut off.
Of worldly substance, friends, liberty, life and all, to set the loss at right nought, for the winning of Christ.[24]

[24] These prayers were published by the Catholic Truth Society, 1929. Cf. also Reynolds, pp. 337–338.

CHAPTER FIVE

The School of Sir Thomas More

I. MORE'S VIEW OF HIS POSITION

ONE OF THE first and greatest of More's modern biographers raises a significant point. Fr Bridgett rightly remarks that More's popular attraction across the centuries has turned on his family life. Without Dame Alice and the children, would he have won the hearts of friend and foe alike? Writes Fr Bridgett: "Had he been all that he was in life and death with only one exception—an ecclesiastic instead of the father of a family—he would still have been great, amiable, holy, but Macaulay would probably not have selected him as 'a choice specimen of human wisdom and virtue'." Bridgett goes on to say that the very circumstances by which, in his own eyes, More was placed on a lower level than his unmarried and consecrated fellow martyrs, have raised him to a higher estimation in the minds of modern Englishmen. This, I believe, is fair. Without his family, he would have appeared, at best, as a Tudor version of Picus, Earl of Mirandola, learned, saintly but almost too good to be true. Somehow, the letters and lessons to his children, the family portrait, Dame Alice, the monkey, the merry jests at Chelsea, have made More appear very much more human than most of his fellow saints. We may see him as humorist, writer, statesman, father of a family where other holy people look like saints and nothing more.

Because More, without knowing it, presented holiness to us outside the conventional pattern, it is so much easier to know him and to admire him in a straightforward, human way. Yet in this very fact lurks the danger of a grave misunderstanding, the misunderstanding into which King Henry fell; Henry had laughed and joked with More, had met his children and walked with him

in his garden, had read the bold views on divorce expressed in
More's *Utopia* and must have thought that here was a man,
broad and tolerant, who would accept the ways of the world.
Henry proved wrong. More was as determined and as ruthless
as any saint before or since his day. His cocked hat and fur tippet
made him no more compromising than Ignatius of Loyola,
Fisher, Teresa of Avila, Francis Xavier and the other saints of his
age. Bacon, Swift, Macaulay and his other admirers, had they
lived in Tudor Chelsea, might well have discovered this point.
We have already quoted the opinion of Erasmus that More
loosened the bond of intimacy with those friends whose vices
admitted no correction; such an attitude would prove disconcerting
in any age. Erasmus also tells us, "He talks with his friends
about a future life in such a way as to make you feel that he be-
lieves what he says".

As More grew older, he had fewer and fewer intimate friends.
By the time that he went to the Tower, Cuthbert Tunstall, bishop
of Durham, was perhaps the one whom he loved and trusted best.
Antonio Bonvisi, the Italian banker who had known him intimately since boyhood, was faithful to the very end. Fisher, his
fellow martyr, always admired, now was closer to him though
never in that profound, personal way. More sincerely respected
Queen Catherine of Aragon and she loved him. They spoke the
same language, shared the same spiritual approach. They could
not be friends in the accepted way but the bond between them was
profoundly strengthened through the sufferings of those final years.
Except for these few, More, as he grew older and more holy,
found his true friendships among the young. Meg, his eldest
daughter, knew him most fully but his affection extended to his
whole household and to all the inmates of his school. His love
was not purely natural; it derived from a common motive and
united purpose, for, in all his lessons to them from their childhood, More's chief theme had been the love of God.

His views on education and his approach to his school are so
much part of his personal religion that they must not be treated as
accidental or studied outside the general pattern of his holiness.

To understand More better, we may consider his attitude to his children under four heads.

Fr Bridgett, in the quotation given above, touched on a central problem, for More, in his own eyes, saw himself on a lower level than those who had chosen the contemplative life. Those early poems on the love of God as well as the prayers quoted at the end of the previous chapter express his profound conviction that God must be loved exclusively. This was no pious or passing sentiment.

When he left the Charterhouse and married Jane Colt, More was certain that God had not called him to the highest expression of the contemplative life. He recognized that for him this solitary life would be a form of escape, that he was temperamentally unsuited to it, that he had other talents, that a scrupulous form of cowardice was tempting him to leave the world. His decision was painful to him but he forced himself to follow Colet's or another's advice. He entertained no false, narrow, Jansenist views on marriage and recognized it as a holy and sacramental state. He was not afraid of marriage but he was always afraid of himself. Further, though he knew that it was not for him, he envied the contemplatives. Twice in his life he seems to have thought seriously of retiring from public business, and on the tragic occasion in the Tower of London when he stood with Meg to watch the Carthusian priors starting out for their martyrdom at Tyburn, he expressed most fully those interior yearnings so long fostered in his heart. His words are so vivid that we ought to read and consider them.

> Lo, dost thou not see, Meg, that these blessed fathers be now as cheerfully going to their deaths as bridegrooms to their marriage? Wherefore, thereby mayest thou see, mine own good daughter, what a great difference there is between such as have in effect spent all their days in a strait and penitential and painful life religiously, and such as have in this world like worldly wretches, as thy poor father hath done, consumed all their time in pleasure and ease licentiously. For God, considering their

long-continued life in most sore and grievous penance, will no longer suffer them to remain here in this vale of misery, but speedily hence taketh them to the fruition of His everlasting Deity. Whereas thy silly father, Meg, that like a wicked caitiff hath passed forth the whole course of his miserable life most sinfully, God, thinking him not worthy so soon to come to that eternal felicity, leaveth him here still in this world further to be plagued and turmoiled with misery.[1]

The Carthusian priors were executed just two months before More himself. When they died, he had as yet no certain knowledge that he would follow them and, for all his fear, he regretted this. More, as a man and still more as a married man, held an abject view of himself.

This same humility he expressed on another occasion but in a setting which shows how completely his humility was matched by hope. He wrote in the *Dialogue of Comfort* of the glory that will come to those who have left home and wealth for Christ's sake but adds, almost as an afterthought: "There are, as our Saviour says, in the house of His Father many mansions. And happy shall he be that shall have the grace to dwell even in the lowest."[2]

2. VOCATION AS A FATHER

Because More's inclination was to Godward, his duty towards his children became the chief purpose of his life. His books, his career, his friends, his money were of secondary importance: his home was, for him, the road to salvation, his alternative to the contemplative way of life. He could never have assumed the role of so many fathers who see their task completed when they have earned the cash. He wrote to Meg on one occasion: "I beg you, Margaret, tell me about the progress you are making in your studies. For I assure you that, rather than allow my children to be idle and slothful, I would make a sacrifice of wealth, and bid adieu to other cares and business to attend to my children and

---

[1] Roper, p. 39; Harpsfield, p. 153. Bridgett's version is given here.
[2] *Dialogue of Comfort*, p. 297.

my family, among whom none is more dear to me than yourself, my beloved daughter."[3]

So simple was More's view of life and so methodic its development, that one may study his theory of education easily. First one visits Utopia to learn how these good pagans educate their children and then, at the Barge in Bucklersbury, or in the fine new house in Chelsea, one sees how More put into practice the theories which the Utopians employed. *Utopia* is a fascinating book. More may be said to have hoaxed Europe, presenting his own deep, spiritual principles wrapped in a pagan disguise. Here were the results of his days and nights of study, the conclusions which he had reached not only from his reading of the pagan classics but after four years at the Charterhouse. In his intriguing, fictional style, he so cunningly portrayed the charm of these imaginary pagan people that priests of his own period were ready to set off at once to evangelize Utopia.[4]

More makes every effort to maintain his pretence, to base the Utopian State entirely on unaided and purely natural reason, but his own deep faith seeps through the veneer. The Utopians do not know it but their life is virtually monastic, even in their pagan liturgy. The principles on which they base their education are the principles used by More himself. He wrote *Utopia* when Meg, his eldest, was about ten years old. She was to be the first Utopian.

More was quick to see the full possibilities of a setting in which good pagans could preach religion by example to bad Christians who were living a pagan life. The contrasts are brilliant, and

[3] Stapleton, p. 103.
[4] Small effort has been made here to examine the influence of the Greek philosophers on Thomas More's thought. The subject has been treated adequately in many books. *Utopia* owes much to More's classical training but this theme may have been too much stressed by students who admired More's scholarship while paying less attention to his deep religious views. He may well have wanted the Utopians to be pagan, even Greek, but he was quite unable to disguise his profoundly Christian view of life. Hence Utopia is in many ways monastic, as Professor Chambers saw. Indeed Chambers argues from *Utopia* to the effect of the Franciscan spirituality on More. This view does not exclude the classical influence but shows *Utopia* as one of More's truly spiritual works. Cf. Chambers, pp. 345 seq.

to preserve the hoax, More introduces with the Utopians one or two alarming practices based on reason to shock the theologians and to startle the devout. Though he was praying half the night, he was merry enough to provide his pagan Utopians with several advanced opinions so that solemn critics, themselves very far from holy, could throw doubts on his orthodoxy.

The skill of More's book is seen in the care with which he builds up the character of Hythloday. This devout Christian man, who knows Europe well and admires England, is forced to admit in conversation that he has discovered a far wiser form of government in foreign parts. His detailed account of Utopia, charmingly told, serves as a powerful admonition, contrasting as it does with the abuses which he has noticed since returning to the West. Hythloday's criticisms are More's criticisms while More permits himself the added fun of intervening to argue against Hythloday. No one can hope to grasp More's educational theory who does not study the views exposed by Hythloday.

One must read the first part of the book for a full picture of the abuses which force the traveller to prefer Utopia. Only one point may be touched on here. Hythloday's attack on contemporary England is not directed against the poor, the thieves, the vagrants but to the deceits and selfishness of the Establishment. The rich, for all their talk of Christian principles, "wink at the most part of all those things which Christ taught". They are utterly irresponsible, using poor men like cattle, manipulating the lives of thousands to serve their selfish ends. Hythloday is not afraid to attack More's own profession, "a justice more beautiful in appearance and more flourishing in display than it is just or profitable".

When we reach the kernel of Hythloday's complaint, we find that he, after watching the Utopians, must attribute all the ills of Christendom to worldliness. From this false principle, so widely held, comes the flattery of kings, rivalry between states, monopolies and other dishonest practices, idleness, vanity and all ostentatious display. To acquire wealth, to show it off, to enjoy its corrupting power, Christian men will stoop to any deceit.

Hythloday is especially severe on idleness: "First, there are a great number of gentlemen who are not only content to live idle like drones on money for which others have laboured but they must also carry about with them at their tails a great flock or train of serving-men, who have acquired no craft whereby they may earn their living honourably." His grudge is not against the poor but against the wealthy who from conceit are ready to create a proletariat. He sees these poor serving men, insecure, unskilled, pampered, aping the conceit of their masters, lacking that pride of achievement proper to men. They are no longer able to do an honest day's work for an honest wage. Hythloday has been convinced by the example of the Utopians that full human happiness will never be achieved by money but by honourable pride in human skill. He ends this part of his commentary with a telling verdict, applicable even in our day.

"For by suffering your youth wantonly and viciously to be brought up and to be infected, even from their tender age, by little and little with vice, then in God's name, to be punished when they commit in manhood the faults which they acquired in childhood; what are you doing but making thieves and then punishing them?"

Turning to the Utopians, nominally a pagan people, Hythloday shows how such a vicious circle has been broken, chiefly through the cultivation of a true family life. Clan life it is, for one of More's most treasured principles prevented him from making his family exclusive; it embraced old and young, natural and adopted children, tutors, secretaries, servants and friends. So, the Utopians judged it "a great point of cruelty that anyone in their need of comfort and help should be cast off and forsaken or that old age which both brings sickness with it and is in itself a sickness, should be treated unkindly or unfaithfully"! These wise pagans had seen that old and young should mix together, for the old may contribute much to the young and the young to the old.

The Utopians, even in church, made the children kneel with their parents and families so that they might learn to pray together and, further, learn to behave. At meals, as in a monastery, young and old were carefully mixed. The wisdom of the old was thus passed on to the young ones but, because old people can be garrulous, great care was taken that the young should have a chance to speak.

In a Utopian hall, a special nursery was set aside so that the very babies should feel themselves part of the family life. In this crèche, the babies slept, were fed and fondled and held before the fire to give them a little extra fun. More thought of everything. At meals the men sat with their backs to the wall with the women in the inside places so that they could slip off without embarrassment to attend to their babes. One further and courteous point, all delicacies at meals were placed before the elders that the dignity of these might thus be honoured while they might also teach the young a lesson by serving young and old impartially. The Utopians never guessed it, but they were reared on the courtesy of monastic life.

As one might have expected in so reasonable a State, no idleness was ever permitted and all the citizens, men, women and children, not only studied but were taught a trade. The Utopians would have been shocked by some of our modern views on education in which the cramming of information to pass exams, and so to earn one's living, seems to be the primary end. For More as for the Greeks, learning was in itself the end. Adult education in this pagan State was not the fad of a few blue-stockings but an essential ingredient of human happiness. Here was another of More's basic principles in the education of his children and he made the Utopians select not those subjects which would prove financially useful later, but the subjects which would turn the children into balanced and educated citizens. From their tender years, the little ones were taught languages, music, astronomy. They practised various crafts adapted to their age. In the meantime the adults also attended lectures, not from compulsion but of choice. The Utopians had learned to think, had discovered that intellectual development is not just a means of making money, but a joy in itself. It was for this reason that they were taught to love music and drama, earnestly tended their gardens, condemned all foolish games like dice, which achieved no purpose other than the utterly crazy one of killing time. The Utopians had two games, both very popular and most exciting, which Hythloday described as "not unlike chess".

The Utopians were no kill-joys, indeed by Christian standards they were hedonists. Pleasure was the end of their lives but always intelligent and thoughtful pleasure, in the arts or in the flesh. They could not bring themselves to follow any fashion for no other motive than snobbery. Hence in their dress they wore what was convenient and becoming, unlike Dame Alice who was pinching her massive middle to fit it into a fashionable dress. The women saw no point in painting their faces because they knew that true love was an attitude of mind.

As worldliness to Hythloday seemed to be the basic weakness of the Christian countries, we might suppose that the Utopians, by their manner of living, would teach us a lesson about this. Indeed they do. Hythloday tells us over many pages how much they guarded against counterfeit pleasure of any kind. For More worldliness is exactly translated by counterfeit. So the Utopians despised the hoarding of gold or precious stones. Hythloday is so moved by their example that he suddenly breaks off to put a rhetorical question: "What shall I say of those who keep superficial riches to take pleasure only in the looking at them, not in their use?"

It was their distrust of the counterfeit that led the Utopians to collect pearls, diamonds, carbuncles, to polish them and give them as playthings to the children in their early years. The little ones were at first attracted by their sparkle but, as they grew older, like all children, came to despise the trinkets with which as babies they had played. The Utopians were more severe with gold:

> For whereas they eat and drink from earthen or glass vessels, which, indeed, are curiously and properly made but without much value, of gold and silver they commonly make chamber pots and other vessels that serve for the most vile uses both in the community halls and in private homes. Furthermore, of

the same metals, they make great chains, fetters and gyves with which to tie their prisoners. Finally, whosoever is disgraced for any offence, by their ears hang gold rings, upon their fingers they must wear rings of gold, about their necks chains of gold and, in conclusion, their heads be tied about with gold. Thus, by every possible means, they procure to have gold and silver regarded among them with reproach and infamy.

How much fun was caused to these reasonable people when a foreign embassy arrived on their shores. The wretched ambassadors had not been warned of the quirks of these strange people and, taking them to be the same as Europeans, decked themselves out in their very best in order to impress. "Yea," says Hythloday, "you should have seen the children that had thrown away their own pearls and precious stones, when they saw the like sticking upon the ambassadors' caps; they dig and push their mothers under the sides, saying thus to them, 'Look, mother, how great a lubber that is who wears pearls and precious stones as though he were still a little child'. But the mother answers in good earnest, 'Peace, son, I think he be one of the ambassador's fools'."

So much, then, about the Utopians' education of children, the learning of languages and crafts, pearls used as playthings for the babies, the mixing of old and young, the careful guarding against all that is counterfeit. We may finish with Hythloday's description of a meal. "They begin every dinner and supper by reading something that pertains to good manners and virtue but it is short so that no man may be grieved therewith. Afterwards the elders take occasion of honest communication but this is neither sad nor unpleasant. However, they do not spend the whole of the dinner on such long and tedious talk but they are glad to listen to the young men also and provoke them deliberately to talk that they may have proof of everyone's wit and boldness of disposition to virtue, which commonly in the freedom of feasting is expressed easily. Their dinners are very short but their suppers last somewhat longer because, while after dinner they have to work, after supper sleep and natural rest will follow which is more healthful and wholesome for the digestion. No supper passes without music nor do their banquets lack conceits and junkets . . . for they be much inclined to this opinion that no pleasure should be forbidden whereof cometh no harm."[5]

Professor Chambers, who ranks with Fr Bridgett as More's greatest biographer, sums up *Utopia* in these words:

> We shall find, I think, that few books have been more misunderstood than *Utopia*. It has given the English language a word "Utopian" to signify something visionary and unpractical. Yet the remarkable thing about *Utopia* is the extent to which it adumbrates social and political reforms which either have been carried into practice or have come to be regarded as very practical politics. Utopia is depicted as a sternly righteous and puritanical state where few of us would feel quite happy, yet we go on using the word Utopia to signify an easy-going paradise whose only fault is that it is too happy an ideal to be realized.

The extraordinary fact is that More in *Utopia*, allowing for certain fictional devices, in the main set out what he proposed to do himself. It was always his contention that reason was the handmaid of faith.

The careful mixture of ages insisted on by the Utopians was also, in the More household, most strictly observed. The Mores were a clan, not a family. Perhaps for the very fact that, after Jane's death, there were no more children, More welcomed as equals any number of guests. Only his own peculiar and sanctified sense could have balanced protocol and charity so perfectly. So Meg remained his eldest and dearest child without favouritism or any trace of exclusion for the rest.

Dame Alice had her place and his full affection without intervening between More and his children or upsetting his relations with the staff. His old father on the Utopian model was the honoured patriarch. In his private affections, the children were all equal but he is always careful to give John due honour as his son and heir. In the Holbein portrait Dame Alice and the girls give place to John and his fiancée, Anne Cresacre.

---

[5] The Utopian views on education are found in *Utopia*, pp. 64–66, 74, 79–82, 100.

But his school was very much larger than his family and though he preserved a deep intimacy with his son and daughters, this was never to the exclusion of the rest. He was devoted to his step-daughter Alice Middleton. He loved her and when he was a prisoner in the Tower, she, poor dear, did all that she possibly could to win the help of Lord Audley, his successor as Chancellor. Even Meg would hardly have dared to claim that he loved her more than he loved Margaret Giggs, an adopted daughter, possibly a distant cousin, possibly the child of Meg's nurse. When More wrote to the whole family, he inserted a special clause in the title: "Thomas More to his dearest children and to Margaret Giggs whom he numbers among his own", or: "Thomas More to Margaret, Elizabeth, Cecily, his dear daughters and to Margaret Giggs as dear as though she was his daughter". She was one of his dearest and one who proved herself in her later fidelity. She was his almoner and administered his charity in the village of Chelsea and, yet, between the Holbein sketch and the finished portrait, he moved her position to place his daughter Elizabeth nearer to himself.

The More household was for ever increasing until he was taken to the Tower of London and this happy little world was shattered for good. In the Holbein paintings, again between the sketch and the finished portrait, John Harris, his devoted secretary, was introduced. Patenson, the fool, had his appointed place. The long line of tutors were also regarded as part of the family, as was Dorothy Colley, Meg Roper's personal maid. As his daughters came to marrying age, More included their fiancés in his household, William Roper living with More for sixteen years. Giles Heron, who married Cecily and who later died at Tyburn, lived with More at Chelsea and managed the estate.

Eleven grandchildren were born during More's lifetime and the final total came to twenty-three. Such figures do not include the marriage of John Harris to Dorothy Colley and of Margaret Giggs to John Clements, the first of the tutors, who was with More in Antwerp when he began to write *Utopia*.

Erasmus, who never came to England after 1517 so who never

saw the house at Chelsea, describes the spirit of the household thus: "With the same address he guides his whole household in which there is no disturbance or strife. If such arise, he immediately appeases it and sets all aright again, never conceiving enmity himself or making an enemy. Indeed there seems to be a kind of fateful happiness in this house so that no one has ever lived in it without rising to higher fortune; no member of it has ever incurred any stain on his reputation."[6]

Most readers will feel a certain interest in the financial arrangements for maintaining so large a household: by the end of his time as Chancellor, More may have been supporting as many as forty, his family, in-laws, grandchildren, stepchildren, foster children, tutors, domestic and outside servants, secretaries, watermen. More began his career with next to nothing; if we accept the story of his early clash with Henry VII, John More, his father, had to pay the fine of £100. True to his Utopian principles, he hoarded nothing, lived in the present moment and bought land where he could. As a lawyer he was very careful to refuse all presents and on two occasions would not accept financial gifts. Early in his career, he told Erasmus that the King had offered him a pension for a service rendered, but that he would refuse it lest the citizens of London would think that he was in the pay of the Crown. Later, in desperate straits, he returned a large gift offered by a group of bishops, as he did not want it to appear that he was being paid for his defence of the Church. When he was arrested, he was back to where he had started and had little left.

Yet so great were his earnings as a lawyer and at Court, earnings that were honestly earned in thirty years of devoted service, that he was able in the time of his prosperity to support all those who lived at his house. Reynolds thinks it likely that he paid the board of all his in-laws while they were lodging with him. He had enough to lease the Barge and when he moved to Chelsea, the old home was still retained. The Ropers may have lived there and it then passed to John Clements when he married

---

[6] Stapleton, pp. 94–97. Stapleton quotes Erasmus. He is wrong in saying that Erasmus had seen the house in Chelsea.

Margaret Giggs. Bucklersbury was very much part of the More circle for the Rastells came to live next door. It used to be held that More once lived at Crosby Hall in Bishopsgate. In June 1523 More leased this "sumptious building" but, six months later, sold it to Antonio Bonvisi, his Italian friend. This may have been no more than a professional transaction or More may have wished to remain in the City when the Barge proved too small for his clan.

At about the same time, he purchased 34 acres at Chelsea and began to build his new home. He had a farm, an orchard, a spacious garden and also purchased other small parcels of land. As his father had married four times, his son inherited none of his property. All More's money had been earned. He had enough to build the Lady chapel and to purchase his future tomb in Chelsea parish church. As Chancellor he acquired certain official emoluments: £200 per annum for attending at the Star Chamber, £64 p.a. for 12 tuns of wine and £16 p.a. for wax. He never worried about money or troubled to save it; the land which he acquired was intended for the family.[7]

When he resigned the Lord Chancellorship, he found himself in dire financial straits. Not only had he lost his official salary and payments but the lucrative legal practice which he had abandoned when he entered the service of the King. We know from Roper that he called the whole family together and put the position before them in one of the most touching passages recorded of him:

> After he had thus given over the chancellorship and placed all his gentlemen and yeomen with bishops and noblemen and his eight watermen with the Lord Audley, that in the same office succeeded him, to whom also he gave his great barge, then, calling us all that were his children unto him and asking our advice how we might now in this decay of his ability ... from henceforth be able to live and continue together as he wished we should. When he saw us silent, and in that case not ready to shew our opinion to him, "Then will I", said he, "shew my

[7] *Letters and Papers*, Vol. 4, Part 3, N. 6079.

poor mind unto you. I have been brought up", quoth he, "at Oxford, at an Inn of Chancery, at Lincoln's Inn and also, in the King's Court and so forth from the lowest degree to the highest, and yet have I in yearly revenues at present left me little above an hundred pounds by the year so that now must we, hereafter, if we like to live together, be contented to become contributories together. But, by my counsel, it shall not be best for us to fall to the lowest fare first. We will not therefore descend to Oxford fare, nor to the fare of New Inn, but we will begin with Lincoln's Inn diet, where many right worshipful and of good years do live full well. Which, if we find not ourselves the first year able to maintain, then will we, the next year, go one step down to New Inn fare wherewith many an honest man is well contented. If that exceed our ability too, then will we, the next year after, descend to Oxford fare where many grave, learned, and ancient fathers be continually conversant, which if our power stretch not to maintain neither, then may we yet with bags and wallets go a begging together and hoping that for pity some good folk will give us of their charity, at every man's door to sing Salve Regina, and so still keep company and be merry together."[8]

When, on his arrest, the Government immediately searched his house to confiscate his money, none could be found. In the Tower, More, as a prisoner, was deeply distressed at this. He feared that his family would again be molested with a second search. Knowing too well his former colleagues in the King's service, he was certain that they would never believe that a former Government official had not, in his heyday, feathered his nest. More alone had laboured for every penny of his earnings and had spent every penny in maintaining his Utopian and patriarchal home. For him there could be no life without his home.

So far has our world drifted from the Utopian ideals on which More established the happiness of his huge household that the programme at the Barge may sound dull enough today. Drinking, betting, trivial talk and trivial reading are now so much taken for granted that few could imagine a happy home without such

[8] Roper, pp. 26–27.

diversions as these. Where would we be without fashions and the talk about fashions, without schemes for making money on the cheap? Yet, in the More household, history presents us with unshakeable evidence of a happiness which few know today. More kept his family together for just thirty years. After he was dead, his children struggled not only to preserve his memory but to conduct their lives and train their children according to his principles. The school of More became famous throughout Europe and deserves to be copied today. He himself certainly saw this as his vocation and it was his unique achievement thus to express his love for God as a husband and as a family man.

No idleness was tolerated at the Barge. Children and servants alike were given chores, tended the garden, cared for the menagerie. Meals were conducted on the Utopian plan, first with a short reading, then ordered conversation, finally a merry interlude begun by More himself and with Patenson, the jester, taking part. Almost certainly, music followed the evening meal. We do not know if, in More's house, there was a nursery for the babies in the hall. Nor do we have any record of the family playing the two games used by the Utopians which Hythloday described as similar to chess. There were no punishments at the Barge, other than a nagging from Dame Alice and an occasional rebuke from More himself. Margaret Giggs recalled that this was so kindly given that she did things wrong to be rebuked by him. In an age when it was fashionable to beat children for trivial offences, punishment at the Barge was administered with a peacock's feather.

Yet, from their tenderest years the children had to work. They did not study to make their names, to make money, to make an impact on the world about them, but simply because study was a reward and pleasure in itself. For More, intellectual development according to the capacity of the individual meant self-completion, self-expression and lasting happiness. For him study was a God-given talent which would invariably lead man to God. The children applied themselves to Latin every day, translating from Latin into English and then, later, turning their English version back to Latin again. No distinction was made between the boys and the girls. More, who was a pioneer in the education of women, while admitting that girls might have certain initial problems, treated each child individually. His method was rewarded and both Meg and Margaret Giggs became accomplished scholars, two of the best educated women of their day. Margaret Giggs had the distinction of becoming one of the first women to study medicine; she married John Clements, a very distinguished doctor, and later was able to help him with his work.

After Latin came Greek and, possibly, French. The children studied some elementary science and when Bishop Tunstall published his arithmetic book, he dedicated it to More, knowing, as he says in the preface, that he, More, will pass it on to his school. The children also studied astronomy under the expert guidance of Nicholas Kratzer, who later became astronomer to the King.

Part of the reason why the children did not find their studies dull rests in More's own approach to learning and the care that he took to encourage the adults to study as well. It was probably this desire to have adult co-operation in the studies of the children that led More not only to marry a very young wife whom he could fashion but to go too fast with poor Jane. For the same reason Dame Alice found herself busily practising the flute. Lessons were never set or undertaken in that hopeless spirit: "This may be boring but, one day, it will be useful to you". More saw learning as a pleasure in the present moment, never as a chore. As the scholars of his school grew up, they continued with their studies so that Meg and her husband were once rivalling each other, with More egging his daughter on. The tutors joined in many of the exercises and More, though always busy, often found the time to compete. His *Four Last Things* was written as an exercise. Meg and her father were both to write an essay to the same text.

Above all, More taught his children through the daily letters which he urged them to send to him. He read these with genuine excitement and answered them in Latin most punctiliously. To please him, the children took great trouble with their letters, but not as much as this busy man put into each reply. Once, when riding miserably through the rain on King's business, he composed a letter to them in Latin verse. Let me quote from one letter to Meg which is typical:

> It would be a delight to me, my dear Margaret, to converse long with you on these matters but I have just been interrupted and called away by the servants who have brought the supper. I must have regard to others, else to sup is not so sweet as to talk with you. Farewell, my dearest child, and salute for me my most gentle son, your husband. I am extremely glad that he is following the same course of study as yourself. I am ever wont to persuade you to yield in everything to your husband but now, on the contrary, I give you full leave to strive to get before him in the knowledge of the celestial system. Farewell again. Salute the whole company but especially your tutor.[9]

The work of More's school was not impeded by examinations or restricted to subjects which might prove useful afterwards. Living, as he always did, in the present moment, More judged study on its immediate value as a pleasurable exercise. Often in his own youth he had written poems "for his pastime" and he conducted his school on the same lively and original lines. If he placed great emphasis on language and on grace of expression, he was also deeply attached to music and drama and to all methods of stimulating thought. Later in their lives, his daughters were to debate philosophic subjects before the King, but their own discussions were often very practical.[10] Vives, the distinguished Spanish scholar, brought from Spain by Queen Catherine for the education of her daughter Mary, describes one incident thus:

> More had told the story of Quintilian's first declamation to his little boy John and to his daughters Margaret, Elizabeth and Cecily, the worthy offspring of such a father. He had discoursed

[9] Stapleton, pp. 118–119.
[10] Palgrave to More, Rogers, p. 403. Palgrave ends his letter: "whan your dowghters disputyd in philosophie afore the kyngis Grace, I wold yt hadde bene my fortune to be present."

in such a way as to lead them all by his eloquence the more easily to the study of wisdom. He then begged me to write an answer to the declamation which he had expounded, so that the art of writing might be disclosed more openly by contradiction and, as it were, by conflict.

Reynolds, to whom I am very much indebted here, turned up Quintilian's first declamation to see the subject on which More, Vives and the children were to debate. The case for discussion is of a blind boy who, on his father's second marriage, is given a room in a remote part of the house. The father is murdered in the night. His body is found in bed the next morning with his son's sword through it and bloodstains along the walls from the scene of the murder to the boy's room. Had the father been killed by his wife or by his son?

Stapleton quotes another case in which Quintilian defended a poor man whose bees had been poisoned by a spray which a rich neighbour used on his flower-beds. Margaret Roper was set to expound the case for the rich neighbour and she completed her task with so much grace that Stapleton, no mean scholar, was prepared to print her essay next to Quintilian's.[11]

One final hilarious incident should be reported to mirror the many happy moods of More's school. Walter Smyth, an educated man, who served for nine years in the More household, was then promoted sword-bearer to the Lord Mayor. The Lord Chancellor went in person to the Court of Aldermen to speak for his man. Smyth published an amusing book called *Twelve Merry Jests of One Edith, the Lying Widow which still liveth*, purporting to give the story of this naughty old girl. Edith left her husband in Exeter. Pretending to be a woman of means, out of cash for the moment, she wheedled her way into twelve distinguished homes. Not only did famous people give her cash but there was much flirtation in the servants' hall. Who would want to miss a widow with so much brass? After calling at many famous houses and hoaxing the staff of the Earls of Wiltshire and Oxford, Cardinal Wolsey and Bishop Fisher, Edith came to Battersea.

[11] Cf. *Margaret Roper*, pp. 25–26; Stapleton, p. 116.

And when she saw her time, on an holy day,
She walked to a thorp called Battersea;
And, on the next day after, she took a wherry,
And over the Thames she was rowed full merry.
At Chelsea was her arrival,
Where she had best cheer of all,
In the house of Sir Thomas More.

Edith, the lying widow, is unimportant and we may leave her enjoying the merriest time of her whole trip in the house of Sir Thomas More. She told the same old yarn, changing the place names; she had a farm, fifteen male servants, seven female servants and a mill. Her property was at Eltham and the More household fell for it. Each one thought her a suitable match for one of their servants while one or two of the servants, including Walter Smyth, decided to propose to her direct. Margaret Giggs, who married John Clements and later risked her life to solace the Carthusians, reports in the poem that there was a "general bumming about" and that everybody laughed.

The story of Edith, the lying widow—they medicated her ale in the final stages—may be true, or partially true, or false. Her only importance rests in this that the story could never have appeared in verse, mentioning names and sponsored by a devoted servant, unless it had had the approval of the More school. Professors Chambers and Reed do little more than tell the story with approval, Reynolds goes so far as to risk the obvious deduction: "It is tempting to suggest that this rough ballad was a kind of family production, and, as it was printed by John Rastell, would certainly have had More's approval." No more is known of the merry widow who, at least, proves that the house at Chelsea was more merry than those of the Earls of Wiltshire and Oxford, Cardinal Wolsey and Bishop Fisher; not surprising if the More clan helped in the compilation of Walter Smyth's merry tale.[12]

More managed his home with so much charm and persuasion that it flourished both in charity and laughter for thirty years. Erasmus has already been quoted as witness that More ruled his

[12] Reed, *Early Tudor Drama*, Ch. 6, pp. 148 seq.

household so that there were no tragic incidents or quarrels: "If anything of the kind should be likely, he either calms it down or applies a remedy at once". We have no record of his method but we know the custom of the Utopians. "Before they come to church, the wives fall down prostrate before their husbands' feet at home and the children before the feet of their parents, confessing and acknowledging themselves offenders either by some actual deed or by the omission of their duty and desire pardon of their offence. Thus if any cloud of privy displeasure was risen at home, by this satisfaction it is overblown and they may be present at the sacrifices with pure and charitable minds." The Utopians were pagans but reason itself seems to demand such humility. More may have had sacramental confession in mind, to which, as we have seen, he was himself devoted, when he thus provided his Utopians with a substitute. Again, he may have copied the custom from the monastic chapter at which public transgressions were duly admitted and confessed. Three incidents, already mentioned, afford a faint hint of a similar practice in his own home. We have Dame Alice admitting after confession that she has finished with her past nagging, Margaret Giggs committing small faults for the pleasure of receiving his correction, and More himself kneeling before his old father for his blessing before passing to the Chancellor's court.[13] Beyond the world of speculation stands the verdict of Erasmus that More's home was "a school for the knowledge and practice of the Christian faith".

3. WHAT MORE TAUGHT HIS CHILDREN AND HOW HE TAUGHT THEM

Greek, Latin, Astronomy, Music, Declamations, the jests of the widow Edith "which still liveth", provide but a superficial view of More's plan. For him, study was a spiritual weapon and we would miss much of his message if we neglected this essential fact. "More avers," writes Erasmus, "that he is indebted to literature both for better health, for the favour and affection he meets with from his excellent prince, as well as from his countrymen and

[13] *Utopia*, pp. 127–128.

foreigners, for an increase in wealth, for becoming more agreeable both to himself and his friends, more useful to his country and his relatives, more fitted for the life of court and intercourse with nobles, as well for society and social life, and lastly, more dear to heaven." More truly believed this and he saw it as a duty to offer the same opportunity to his family.[14]

Vives, the Spaniard, recognized and reported this. In his book on the education of women he writes:

> Now if a man may be suffered among Queens to speak of more mean folks, I would reckon among this sort the daughters of Sir Thomas More, Knight—Margaret, Elizabeth, Cecilia and, with them, their kinswoman, Margaret Giggs—whom their father, not content only to have them good and very chaste, would also they should be well learned, supposing that by that means they should be more truly and surely chaste. Wherein neither that great, wise man is deceived, nor none other that are of the same opinion. For the study of learning is such a thing that it occupieth one's mind wholly and lifteth it up into the knowledge of most good matters, and plucketh it from the remembrance of such things as be foul.[15]

It is interesting to note from this that More saw in study a safeguard to chastity. He went a great deal further and was to assert that study was essential both for human happiness in this world and for our spiritual progress towards the next. He was wholly opposed to the attitude of those who remain satisfied with blind observance, making no corresponding effort to deepen their knowledge of God. More is, in effect, the patron of spiritual reading, without which prayer lacks content and fails to expand the capacity of the soul in its craving for God.

Study for More was the adjunct both to prayer and holiness. Yet he was far from the position of those who would limit study to the reading of so-called spiritual books. Thus, he was vigorous in his condemnation of those scholastic theologians who confined their attention to the jargon of the schools. He disliked the scholastic manuals and chided Dorpius for preferring "these kitchen

[14] Erasmus to Budé, cf. Bridgett, pp. 115-116.   [15] Cf. *Margaret Roper*, p. 26.

maids to the most Holy Bible, the Queen of all books". The friar at Coventry catches it for basing his devotional promises about the rosary on "a Mariale and from other books of that kind". More lays in to those preachers who borrow their sermons from the standard sermon manuals, for the sermon thus borrowed "is foolish in itself and when declaimed by a man more foolish still, how dull and stupid the whole affair becomes". More was not pious in the false, conventional way. He shocked many in his lifetime and would still shock many today.

Study for More began with the Scriptures, about which he wrote with so much respect and feeling, repeatedly. His order of priorities was set out in his letter to Dorpius. "I do not think that you will contest with me that whatever is necessary for salvation is communicated to us in the first place from the sacred Scriptures, then, from the ancient Fathers from hand to hand, and, in fine, by the sacred definitions of the Church." More went back to these sources himself and offered the same to his children after he had taught them to think. He disliked potted text-books, manuals, summaries and Summas which prevented men from studying the sources for themselves. His own knowledge of the Scriptures is astonishing when one recalls that he was a busy professional man.[16]

Yet More did not confine his attention to spiritual studies, rather he thought of all genuine study as leading to God. In his celebrated defence of the Classics written for the University of Oxford, he aptly sets out his views. "Although no one denies that a man may be saved without a knowledge of Latin and Greek or of any literature at all, yet learning, yes, even worldly learning, prepares the mind for virtue ... there are even some who make the knowledge of things natural a road to heavenly contemplation and so pass from philosophy and the natural arts—which this man condemns under the general name of worldly literature—to theology, dispoiling the women of Egypt to adorn the Queen."[17]

[16] More to Dorpius, Rogers, p. 115; Bridgett's translation, pp. 93–94.
[17] More to Oxford University, Rogers, p. 115. Hallett's translation; Stapleton, p. 41.

We know that More gave his long letter to the University as an exercise to his children and they translated it. There they were able to learn what, no doubt, they had already guessed, that their father saw in all forms of study a means of reaching God. For a man with a mind to Godward, all branches of learning prove to be spiritual. As we study More's letters, our amazement grows, for his reactions are always spiritual and the most trivial incidents lead him towards God. When Tunstall sends him a fly, pickled in amber, More is absorbed with the depth of colour, more lovely than a precious stone. Erasmus and Giles present him with their portraits and he regrets that the pictures will not survive the ravages of time. Meg studies astronomy and her father hopes that she will see in the heavens the genius of God. Even the famous monkey whom Erasmus watched defending a rabbit from a weazel, seems to have led More to the spiritual life. "Whosoever will mark the devil and his temptations shall find him therein much like an ape. For like as an ape, not well looked unto, will be busy and bold to do shrewd turns, and contrariwise, being spied, will suddenly leap back and adventure no further, so the devil, finding a man idle, slothful and without resistance, ready to receive his temptations, waxeth so hardy that he will not fail still to continue with him until to his purpose he hath thoroughly brought him."[18]

More was to express himself most fully on his educational ideals to William Gonnell, one of the most devoted of the tutors, who cared for his children while More was at Court. It would seem from the context that Gonnell had written to More suggesting that Meg should be more encouraged and before answering the question, More sets out his principles.

> Though I prefer learning joined to virtue to all the treasures of Kings, yet renown for learning when it is not united with a good life, is nothing else than manifest and notorious infamy ... among all the outstanding benefits that learning bestows on men, none is more excellent than this, that, by the study of books, we are taught in that very study, to seek not praise but

[18] Nichols, 3, p. 93; Roper, p. 15.

usefulness. Such has been the teaching of the most learned men, especially the philosophers, who are the guides of human life, although some may have abused learning, like other good things, simply to court empty glory and popular renown.

In his education of his children, More's motives were typical of his whole approach to life. He wanted his children to study and grow wise "because the reward of wisdom is too solid to be lost like riches or to decay like beauty, since it depends on the consciousness of what is right, not on the talk of men than which nothing is more foolish or mischievous".

Two more quotations must be given from the letter to Gonnell because we have in this the best expression of More's ideals. Gonnell wants to praise Meg more and her father, though agreeing about her merit, is plainly worried, so great is his fear of human vanity and pride. At Court, he saw this danger, on every side. In *Utopia*, he was to single out love of wealth and love of praise as the two greatest threats to good living and lasting happiness. If these extracts seem long, they still deserve most careful attention, for More was both a saint and a father and his advice is highly practical.

I have dwelt so much on the craving for glory, my dear Gonnell, because you say in your letter that Margaret's high-minded disposition should not be impaired. In this judgement I quite agree with you but to me, and no doubt to you also, that man would seem to ruin a generous character who should accustom it to admire what is vain and low. He, on the contrary, enhances the character who rises to what is virtuous and good and who, in contemplating the sublime, despises those shadows of the good which almost all mortals, through ignorance of truth, greedily snatch at as if they were the good.

Therefore, my dear Gonnell, since we must walk by this road, I have often begged not only of you, who out of affection for my children would do it of your own accord, but my wife who is sufficiently induced by her maternal love for them which has been proved to me in so many ways, and also all my friends, to warn my children to beware the dangers of pride and haughtiness and rather to walk in the pleasant meadows of modesty; not to be dazzled by the sight of gold; not to lament that they do not possess what they erroneously admire in others, not to think more of themselves for gaudy trappings nor less for the want of them; neither to deform the beauty that nature has given to them by neglect, nor to try to heighten it by artifice; to put virtue in the first place, learning in the second and in their studies to esteem most whatever may teach them piety towards God, charity to all and Christian humility in themselves. By such means they will receive from God the reward of an innocent life, and in the assured expectation of it, will view death without horror and meanwhile possessing solid joy will neither be puffed up by the empty praise of men, nor dejected by evil tongues. These I consider the genuine fruits of learning and though I admit that not all scholars possess them, I would maintain that those who give themselves to study with such views will easily attain their end and become perfect.

More reveals much of himself in this letter, describing his own aspirations at the same time as his desire for his children's holiness. When he talks of a man contemplating the sublime or condemns empty praise or mentions the horror of death, the gift of solid joy, the genuine fruits of learning, he is betraying his own yearnings and his own struggles over many years. He wants his children to be perfect, not just good. His seeming preoccupation with praise and the danger of it stems from his own painful experience. He must have needed all his vigils, all his austerities, his many meditations on the Four Last Things and the emptiness of this world, to prevent the praise of men from turning his head. From early childhood he had always been loved and always praised.

Erasmus not only wrote sweet flattery in letters but published such letters for all the civilized world to read. At the time when he wrote this letter to Gonnell, More was the favourite of both King and Queen. We are told by Erasmus that some stupid man started the fashion and wore his gown awry in imitation of More's carelessness of dress. Years of study and prayer had saved More from self-conceit but he was aware of the danger when he set his children on the same studious path.

These fears come out very clearly in another part of the long letter and should be noted here. He writes to Gonnell:

I fancy that I hear you object that these precepts, though true, are beyond the capacity of my young children, since you will scarcely find a man, however old and advanced, whose mind is so firmly set as not to be tempted sometimes by the desire of glory. But, my dear Gonnell, the more I see the difficulty of getting rid of this pest of pride, the more do I see the necessity of dealing with it from childhood. For I find no other reason for evil clinging so to our hearts, than that, almost as soon as we are born, it is sown in the tender minds of children by their nurses, is cultivated by their teachers, and brought to its full growth by their parents; no one teaching even what is good without, at the same time, awakening the expectation of praise as the proper reward of virtue. Thus we grow accustomed to make so much of praise, that while we study how to please the majority, who will always be the worst, we grow ashamed of being good with the minority. So that this plague of vainglory may be banished far from my children, I do desire you, my dear Gonnell, and their mother and all their friends to harp on the theme, reiterate it and pound away at it, that vainglory is a vile thing and to be treated with contempt and that there is nothing more sublime than that humble modesty so often praised by Christ and this your prudent charity will so enforce as to teach virtue rather than reprove vice and make them love good advice instead of hating it. To this purpose nothing will more conduce than to read to them the lessons of the ancient Fathers, who, they know, cannot be angry with them; and, as they honour them for their sanctity, they must needs be much moved by their authority.

If you will teach something of this sort, in addition to their lesson in Sallust, to Margaret and Elizabeth, as being more advanced than John and Cecily, you will bind them and me still more to you. And thus you will bring about that my children who are dear to me by nature and still more dear by learning and

virtue will become most dear by their advance in knowledge and good conduct.
From the Court on the Vigil of Pentecost.[19]

It would be difficult to find in the writings of any of the saints a letter so practical, so entirely in the spirit of the gospels, so wise and affectionate on the education of the young to a full Christian life; a very severe letter by modern standards and one which most parents would hesitate to follow, not knowing how to command the obedience of their children without threats or promises. More is right in suggesting that one of the most tedious and painful habits of middle age is sown in most children young. How, then, did he cope with such a situation and did he never reward or praise his children for their virtue, for their obedience, for the efforts which they made and for the results that they achieved?

In the first place the bond between More and his children was woven from so many years of love. This was never a moody or sentimental love but a constant devotion which compelled More out of his very love for them to share their lives. He had to make no effort for he was on their level or raised them to his at every age. It was physical pain to him to be away from them and they knew it, "The fervent desire that I had to see my native country, my wife and my children whom I did much long and covet to see, because, at that time, I had been more than four months from them."[20] The care that he took to answer their letters, to correct their work, to partake in their exercises continued until they had reached maturity. Busy as he was, it was his idea that they should write to him every day.

If he was afraid of vainglory in his children, he was never averse to praise which was honest and justified. He wanted them to work for no other motive than love of study and love of himself. His praise, he knew, was the reward they loved best. The model answer to their letters, the one that teaches, encourages and conveys the most unbounded affection is the letter he wrote praising the youngest, his little son John.

[19] More to Gonnell, Rogers, pp. 120–123; *Margaret Roper*, pp. 15–18.
[20] *Utopia*, p. 14.

Thomas More to his dearest children and to Margaret Giggs whom he numbers among his own.

The Bristol merchant brought me your letters the day after he left you, with which I was extremely delighted. Nothing can come from your workshop, however rude and unfinished, that will not give me more pleasure than the most accurate thing another can write. So much does my affection for you recommend whatever you write to me. Indeed without any recommendation, your letters are capable of pleasing by their own merits, their wit and pure Latinity. There was not one of your letters that did not please me extremely; but to confess frankly what I feel, the letter of my son John pleased me best, both because it was longer than the others and because he seems to have given to it more labour and study. For he not only put out his matter prettily and composed in fairly polished language but he plays with me both pleasantly and cleverly, and turns my jokes on myself wittily enough. And this he does not only merrily, but with due moderation, showing that he does not forget that he is joking with his father, and that he is cautious not to give offence at the same time that he is eager to give delight . . . etc.[21]

His letters to his children should be read and read again as indeed they were by these same children in middle age and when their father had gone. They, the letters, were falling to pieces with such affectionate scanning when Stapleton finally gained possession of them and printed them. More could say to Margaret, "To a father, even a blemish will seem beautiful in the face of his child", and to the school together, "If I did not love you so much, I should be really envious of your happiness in having so many and such excellent tutors"; or again, "I am so longing to return home"; or again, "I cannot put down on paper, indeed I can hardly express in my mind the deep pleasure that I received from your very well expressed letter, my dearest Margaret". More certainly gave his children presents, indeed in his celebrated letter

[21] All the surviving letters of More to his children are given in Rogers. Hallett's translations are found in Stapleton, pp. 101 seq.; Reynolds also gives the letters in *Margaret Roper*, pp. 20 seq.

written in verse while riding on horseback, he recalls that he brought them always cakes, fruit and silk. But these were not bribes to encourage them to study but marks of his love. He tells them that though he has, by nature, a tender and loving heart towards his children, their progress in virtue has made it still more loving and he begs them to go on in the same way until even his present love may seem as nothing by comparison with what he will then feel.

Out of so much incomparable material, so often quoted and reprinted, one small incident remains to be mentioned here. Once when Meg timidly wrote to ask for money, More was delighted, telling her that she asked too bashfully, "since you are asking from a father who is longing to give". He assures her that there is more where this money came from, "so the sooner you spend this money well, as you are wont to do and the sooner that you ask for more, the more you will be sure of pleasing your father." Here he was giving money to show his love.

On another occasion, however, the bishop of Exeter gave More money to send to his daughter and, though he duly accepted it and forwarded it to her, he was more embarrassed than proud. The letter is a revealing one and well worth quoting for it expresses his love, his delight in her accomplishments but his dislike of money when used as a reward for work. He writes:

> I will refrain from telling you, my dearest daughter, the extreme pleasure your letter gave me. You will be able to judge better how much it pleased your father when you learn what delight it caused to a stranger. I happened this evening to be in the company of his Lordship, John, bishop of Exeter, a man of deep learning and of a wide reputation for holiness. Whilst we were talking, I took out of my desk a paper that bore on our business and by accident your letter appeared. He took it into his hand with pleasure and examined it. When he saw from the signature that it was a letter from a lady, he read it the more eagerly because it was such a novelty to him. When he had finished, he said he would hardly have believed it to have been your work unless I had assured him of the fact and he

began to praise it in the highest terms (why should I hide what he said?) for its latinity, its correctness, its erudition and its expressions of tender affection. Seeing how delighted he was, I showed him your declamation. He read it and your poems as well, with a pleasure so far beyond what he had hoped that although he praised you most effusively, yet his expression showed that his words were all too poor to express what he felt. He took out at once from his pocket a gold coin which you will find enclosed in this letter. I tried in every possible way to decline it but was unable to refuse to send it to you as a pledge and token of his goodwill towards you. This hindered me from showing him the letters of your sisters, for I feared that it would seem as though I had shown them to obtain for the others, too, a gift which it annoyed me to have to accept for you. But, as I have said, he is so good that it is a happiness to be able to please him. Write to thank him with the greatest care and delicacy. You will one day be glad to have given pleasure to such a man. From the Court, just before midnight. September 11th.

Few letters equal this one in revealing the character of the writer; indeed More's letters to his children are about the best comment we will find on the quality and extent of his love for God.

4. FAREWELL TO HOME

Seebohm, so often wrong, makes full amends with a bold and moving sentence, as true at the end of More's life as in its early years. He writes: "Along with great intellectual gifts was combined in the young student a gentle and loving disposition which threw itself into the bosom of a friend with so guileless and pure an affection that, when men came under the power of its unconscious enchantment, they literally fell in love with More." With any other historic figure allowance would have to be made for exaggeration but not, I think, in this exceptional case. To read in Stapleton's account the letters passing between More and Tunstall, Giles, Grinaeus, Dorpius, Budé, Bonvisi and Erasmus, is to savour a style of human friendship not paralleled outside the Gospel text. Many, no doubt, have felt such love for friends but few are sufficiently unselfconscious to express the ardour which More reveals. Such complete devotion to all his friends is the more unusual for, with More, no friendship was exclusive or founded on any form of self-help. Nor were these friends young or emotional people, but tough old cynics, scholars, bishops, ambassadors and businessmen.[22]

Let two examples stand for all; the one, More's remarkable answer to Bishop Tunstall when this good friend had sent him the piece of amber in which was embalmed a common fly. More writes:

> The amber which you sent to me—a rich and noble tomb for flies—was most acceptable on many grounds. As for the material, in colour and brightness it can challenge comparison with any precious stone and, as for the form, it is all the more excellent in that it represents a heart—a symbol of your love for me. For thus do I interpret your meaning. As the fly, winged like Cupid and as fickle as he, is so shut up and enclosed in the substance of the amber that it cannot fly away, so embalmed in the aromatic juice that it cannot perish, so your love will always remain constant and unchanged. That I have nothing to give you in return does not greatly trouble me. For I know that you do not look for gifts in exchange and, moreover, I am willing to remain under an obligation to you. But yet I am somewhat distressed that my capabilities are so poor, for do what I will, I must ever seem unworthy of such proofs of your friendship. Wherefore, since I cannot hope to win the approval of others, I must be content that you know, as well as I do myself, the depth of my affection for you.[23]

There are many such passages to many friends in More's private letters but our second example is very different, a letter written to young John More by a great German scholar, Simon Grinaeus, a Lutheran, when More was in disgrace. This letter is the more touching because More did not agree with Grinaeus, warned him not to teach his heretical opinions and sent John Harris with him

[22] Seebohm, p. 25.   [23] Stapleton, p. 50.

to Oxford, partly to watch him, partly to aid him in his work. Grinaeus writes to John:

> Your father at that time held the highest rank, but apart from that, by his many excellent qualities, he was already marked out as the chief man of the realm whilst I was obscure and unknown. Yet for the love of learning in the midst of public and private business, he found time to converse much with me; he, the Chancellor of the Kingdom made me sit at his table; going to and from the court, he took me with him and kept me ever at his side. He had no difficulty in seeing that my religious opinions were on many points different from his own but his goodness and courtesy was unchanged. Though he differed so much from my views, yet he helped us in word and deed and carried through my business at his own expense. He gave us a young man, of considerable literary attainments, John Harris, to accompany us on our journey, and, to the authorities of the University of Oxford, he sent a letter couched in such terms that at once not only were the libraries of all the colleges thrown open to us but the students, as if they had been touched by the rod of Mercury, showed us the greatest favour. .... I returned to my country overjoyed at the treasures I had discovered, laden with your father's generous gifts and almost overwhelmed by his kindness.[24]

This extraordinary generosity and love, offered to all, becomes almost painful in intensity when we visit More in his own home. His deep affection extended to all, servants, secretaries, tutors as well as to his children, grandchildren, stepchild, foster child, sons-and daughters-in-law. Again, it was a love which spurned flattery, bribes, emoluments, compromise of any sort. Nor was the household an easy one to manage: William Roper was a Lutheran for a time; John Rastell, More's brother in-law, became a heretic; Giles Heron asked for some judicial favour and was refused. As for Dame Alice, More with his tongue in his cheek could write to his friend Francis Cranevelt: "As to what you write ... about ill-tempered wives, I am so far of your opinion that I do not think it possible to live with the best of wives without some discomfort.

[24] *Ibid.*, p. 63.

... this I would say with all the more confidence were it not that generally we make our wives worse by our own fault." More loved and was loved by all. Two years before his arrest Erasmus could report More as living happily in his new house at Chelsea with his wife, his four children and eleven grandchildren.[25]

Nothing is recorded of the trek from the Barge; for More, surely, a poignant occasion after twenty happy years. Some time in 1523 or 1524 the furniture, the menagerie, the library were shifted and the clan moved to Chelsea, a village on the river, some distance from the town. More himself says nothing, though to most men would come a sense of great achievement in buying property and building a fine house. He remained silent and entirely indifferent; the move, as Roper hints, was for the sake of the family. More expressed himself comfortable and contented even in the Tower. He remained unmoved when Dame Alice tried to persuade him to return to "your right fair house, your library, your books, your gallery, your orchard and all other necessaries so handsome about you".[26]

Nothing now remains of More's house. Reynolds provides a plan and many facts about it; it stood six hundred feet back from the river, its centre directly in line with the present Battersea Bridge. The convent in Beaufort Street stands on the site of its east wing. More's estate, if we may use such a term for thirty-four acres, was bounded by the present Milman's Street, Old Church Street and the King's Road. The garden extended to the river and More had his landing stage by the northern end of Battersea Bridge.

The house was reached most easily by river; there were few roads in the Chelsea of Tudor times. More had his barge and watermen. With the family waving him off, he would be rowed down the river to Westminster or Greenwich and upstream to Richmond and Hampton Court. He often took Roper with him on his journeys and on one occasion, at least, we find him reading a book.

Holbein has given us a glimpse of the house in the family

---

[25] *Ibid.*, p. 60.   [26] Roper, pp. 37–40.

portrait and, when in Chelsea, we may still visit the parish church. This alone, beautifully restored, and with the names of the household cleverly woven on the hassocks, helps to remind us of the Mores. Sir Thomas never maintained a private chaplain but preferred to go daily to the parish church. Here he attended Mass, often assisted at the altar, acted as verger, sang in the choir and carried the processional cross on Rogation days. He moved Jane's body to the tomb which he had bought on the south side of the high altar and built the small Lady chapel which alone survived the air raid of 16th April, 1941.[27] When the Mores arrived at Chelsea the parish priest was Father Robert Dandie; in 1530 More presented the living to Father John Larke, later to die at Tyburn, who declared himself proud to follow in the footsteps of his great parishioner.[28]

Roper it is who gives us the details of the New Building which More erected on his property, near to the parish church. Reynolds places this building where Danvers Street meets Cheyne Walk.

Says Roper: "And because he was desirous for Godly purposes sometimes to be solitary and sequester himself from worldly company, a good distance from his mansion house built he a place called the New Building, wherein there was a chapel, a library, a gallery, in which as his use was upon other days to occupy himself in prayer and study together, so on the Friday

[27] As the epitaph and tomb of Thomas More in Chelsea parish church has had frequent mention, the following kind and instructive note from E. E. Reynolds is of special interest. Reynolds writes: "The so-called tomb is not a tomb, the stone-work is purely decorative and what looks like a tomb is empty. The monument originally stood on a wall of the More chapel but when this wall was pierced in the late 17th century to turn the chapel into an aisle, the monument was removed to the chancel. The present stone-work is not the original and the lettering on the tablet was recut. Probably the only original part now left is the tablet, shattered in the blitz but skilfully pieced together. The More vault lies under the chapel; therein are the remains of Jane Colt, Margaret Roper, and, probably, of Dame Alice and son John who seems to have died in Chelsea about 1547. I saw the ruins the morning after the blitz. Some years ago I had a talk with one of the fire-watchers on duty that night who later worked on the clearance. He told me that the bomb melted some coffins just in front of the More chapel but not of the actual vault. The explosion also revealed that there was another vault (full of coffins) under the chancel."

[28] *Margaret Roper*, pp. 44–47; Stapleton, p. 68.

there usually continued he from morning to evening, spending his time only in devout prayers and spiritual exercises."[29] This New Building in the last few years became the centre of More's life. For many years he was often away from home as the Court moved from one palace to another but, when he became Lord Chancellor, More resided in the capital. Here in this New Building he prayed at night. Here the household joined him, morning and evening, to recite "certain psalms and collects" on their knees. More wrote many of his controversial books in the New Building, scourged himself, pondered and prayed about those pressing problems which were to lead him to the scaffold in the end.

If the years at Chelsea were a strain for More—and who can doubt this?—he kept his worries strictly to himself. Superficially, his professional career was highly successful and the house at Chelsea was filled with important guests. The King would drop in unexpectedly and here it was that he walked after dinner in the garden with his arm around More's neck. Holbein, too, came to Chelsea with a letter of introduction from Erasmus and it would seem that More, to help him, decided on the family group. Stanley Morison in his magnificent study, *The Likeness of Thomas More*, tells the full story: the rough sketches, the alterations made, the final portrait, the fate of the original copies, all that we can now hope to know of this historic event. It was surely More's decision not to be painted alone but to have the family with him and to be one of the first in Europe to sponsor such an informal family group.[30]

Though More himself was worried and saddened throughout his stay in Chelsea, this did not check his merriment and laughter or the activities of the school. Indeed Chelsea gave full expression to the ideals put forward in *Utopia* or, as Erasmus saw it, "You would say that Plato's academy had come to life again".

It is now no longer easy to be certain about dates, to distinguish between grandchildren born at the Barge and those born in

---

[29] Roper, p. 14.
[30] Cf. Stanley Morison, *The Likeness of Thomas More*, pp. 20 seq.

Chelsea, to determine who belonged to the school in any particular year. What is certain is that the life of the school continued unbroken to the end. Servants and family trimmed the gardens, fed the animals, went to the parish church together, practised their music, laughed at the widow Edith, waved to their devoted father as he set off for London in his barge. Stapleton gives us some of the names.

More had no children by his second wife who was a widow when he married her but by his first he had one son, John, and three daughters, Margaret, Elizabeth and Cecily. Margaret was married to William Roper and bore him two sons, Thomas and Antony, and three daughters, Elizabeth, Mary and Margaret. . . . More's second daughter, Elizabeth, married John Dauncy and bore him five sons, John, Thomas, Bartholomew, William and Germain, and two daughters, Alice and Elizabeth. Cecily, More's third daughter, became the wife of Giles Heron and had two sons, John and Thomas, and one daughter, Anne. John More, Sir Thomas's only son, took to wife Anne Cresacre and had five sons, Thomas, Augustine, Edward, Bartholomew and another Thomas, and one daughter, Anne. This numerous progeny recalls the verse of the psalmist, "Thy children as olive plants, round about thy table". Of those just mentioned, More's own four children and eleven of his grandchildren were instructed in his school during his lifetime. Of his twenty-one grandchildren, ten were born after his martyrdom. Margaret Giggs, afterwards the wife of John Clements, was educated with his children.[31]

"It would be difficult," wrote Erasmus, "to find a man more fond of children than he." Here is no exaggeration; children fascinated More as he, in turn, fascinated them. To the extraordinary love and sympathy which he invariably showed to all around him was added, when he dealt with children, that sense of wonder which kept him young. We have already considered his partiality for strange and unusual objects, flies in amber, monkeys, peacock feathers, glass-blowing, ancient coins. In every room of

---

[31] Stapleton, p. 100.

the house he was placing some strange object "which will catch your eye as you enter", and, as Erasmus has already told us, "More's own pleasure is renewed every time he sees others interested". This most pleasing trait explains why there never was a dull moment at Chelsea and how it was that a busy statesman riding in the rain on horseback could settle down to write to his children in Latin verse. Roper tells us how More was fretting when Court business allowed him home for only two days in a month.[32]

Quotations have already been given from *The Four Last Things*. Here, this remarkable treatise need only be considered as an example of More's methods with the young. Quite as much as *Utopia*, published a year or two before, *The Four Last Things* reveals More's personal convictions with the added interest of his approach to Margaret, Elizabeth, Cecily and John.

At the time when he wrote this for them, Meg had probably just been married to William Roper at the early age of sixteen. Elizabeth was, therefore, fifteen, Cecily fourteen and John about twelve. The ages of the children are not exactly certain but, from More's treatise, we may see the standard that they had reached in their early teens. Other unusual features mark this work. More wrote it at Court and in a hurry and certainly never intended it to see the light of print. Because it was meant for his school only, he dropped his favourite fictional setting and dialogue form. Where he was reticent with adult friends, here, in the adolescent world, he was far more willing to commit himself. Again, we note that More avoided lecturing his children but, as an effective means of teaching them a lesson, he was humble enough to join with them in a common exercise. A text was chosen on which he and they would write. We cannot be sure of the younger children, but Meg certainly completed her attempt. I can see no trace of More talking down to children; in a wonderful way he lifts them up to himself.

There is much that is crude in *The Four Last Things*, a vividness and vulgarity not normally expected in a scholar nor to

[32] *English Works*, I, pp. 459–460.

be found in *Utopia*. Yet this treatise is genuine More. It is the work of one who is utterly unconcerned about his reputation, wholly concerned with the salvation of his children and their approach to God. He had written to William Gonnell: "I do desire you, my dear Gonnell, to harp on the theme, reiterate it, pound away at it that vainglory is a vile thing and to be treated with contempt." More, in his *Four Last Things*, is attempting just this. Where Gonnell might have produced a polished lecture, More with almost undergraduate zest and sometimes with fourth-form humour, ardently commits himself.

More makes a delightful start in a chemist's shop. While the ordinary doctor prescribes a medicine "of many strange herbs and roots, fetched out of far countries", the prescription written in the Scriptures is much more simple, "containing only four herbs, common and well-known, that is, to wit, death, doom, pain and joy". More writes happily about the swallowing of unpleasant medicine; his medicine need not be swallowed, one has only to think about it to be cured.

His treatise, so cunningly begun, makes no effort to be pious; throughout it is based on facts. He preserves the topical note, quoting Plato, Pliny and Plutarch, the authors whom they had studied, *Aesop's Fables*, our Lord in the Gospel and David in the Psalms. He mentions the execution of the Duke of Buckingham, an event which had shocked the country, pokes gentle fun at Dame Alice and digs out examples and illustrations from every part of the world. From the laws of duelling in Spain, we skip to the method of eating butter in Iceland, then to the prisoners in Newgate, last to a sow "content with dirt and hogwash, caring neither for better meat or better bed". How the children must have laughed at the extraordinary image of a glutton's overloaded stomach, so heavy that if it had been put on his back, he could scarcely have carried it. More so often reverts to one of his favourite illustrations, seeing death as a raging lion ready to pounce while two misers argue over money like boys fighting for cherry stones.[33]

[33] Cf. Introduction to *Four Last Things*, Professor Reed; *English Works*, I, p. 20.

While the essay on the Four Last Things is vivid, amusing, grim, the lessons taught are simple and essential, those principles which More himself applied throughout his life. Again and again he returns to the immediate threat of death. He emphasizes for his children the difference between the genuine and the counterfeit. He tells them of the joy of spiritual pleasure and the deep satisfaction to be had in penance and sorrow for one's sins. He warns them, on the other hand, of the misery to be reaped through carnal pleasure, through envy, jealousy and pride. In one short, unexpected passage he speaks of the danger of mooning, thinking it better for them to speak foolishly of trivial subjects than to seem so wise in keeping silence, while imagining filthy, sinful devices "of which their tongues, if they were set on babbling, could not for shame utter and speak the like".

So much is said today of the need for sex instruction; here is More speaking of the subject to Margaret, Elizabeth, Cecily and John:

> The eye is also a bawd to bring the heart to the desire of the foul, beastly pleasure beneath the belly. For when the eye immoderately delights in long gazing at a lovely face, with a white neck and round paps and so forth as far as it findeth no let, the devil helps the heart to frame and form in the fantasy, by foul imaginations, all that ever the clothes cover. And that in such excellent fashion that the mind is more excited by this feigned figure of his own making than it would probably be if the eye saw the naked belly itself. That is why the prophet warns us, "Turn your eyes away from gazing at vanities".[34]

The treatise on the Four Last Things, factual, reasonable, so sincerely written, would serve as a powerful medicine even in our day. Reading its salutary lessons, so frankly stated, we grasp not only the spiritual capacity of More's four children but also the ruthless realism of a father who could write to them in such a way. How much they knew of his danger, we cannot tell, but they had had warnings in plenty of the suddenness of death. One senses as one reads his words that More himself was not only ready to die

[34] *English Works*, I, p. 493.

at any moment but had an inkling of the future, twelve years before his violent death. Here in *The Four Last Things* he reveals his thoughts and worries about the upkeep of his children, the need to part at death from all that one loves dearest, which for More meant his school.

Typical of More, on the last free day of his life he went from Chelsea to the City with William Roper that he might hear the sermon at St Paul's. Together they walked down Cheapside and More spent the day with John and Margaret Clements, now living at the Barge. It was Low Sunday, 14th April, 1534. There at the Barge he received the summons to appear, next day, before the Commissioners at Lambeth to take the oath.

More said nothing to the family, so it is unlikely that they fully grasped the danger or the pain of the sacrifice which, secretly, he was prepared to make. On the Monday morning he walked to the parish church, went to confession, heard Mass, received Holy Communion, following exactly the pattern of so many years. He broke his routine only in the manner of his parting from his school. Roper writes:

> And whereas he evermore used at his departure from his wife and children that he tenderly loved, to have them bring him to his boat and there to kiss them all and bid them farewell, then would he suffer none of them forth of the gate to follow him but pulled the wicket after him and shut them all from him and with heavy heart, as by his countenance appeared, with me and our four servants there took he his boat towards Lambeth. Wherein sitting still sadly a while, at last he suddenly rounded me in the ear and said, "Son Roper, I thank Our Lord the field is won". What he meant thereby I then wist not, yet loath to seem ignorant, I answered, "Sir I am thereof glad". But, as I conjectured afterwards, it was that the love he had to God wrought in him so effectually that it conquered all his carnal affections utterly.[35]

[35] Roper, p. 36.

CHAPTER SIX

The Court

1. WHY MORE WENT TO COURT

IT MAY SEEM unusual to dismiss to a short chapter the spectacular series of Court promotions which crown More's professional career. The offices which he held—Privy Councillor, Master of Requests, Speaker of the House of Commons, Under-Treasurer, Chancellor of the Duchy of Lancaster and Lord High Chancellor —still cause in our hearts a responsive thrill. To the Catholic apologists—and who will blame them?—here was proof both of More's greatness and of his loyalty. To men like Harpsfield and Roper, living under persecution, such high offices held by a martyr were honours worthy to be proclaimed. The majority of the Catholic martyrs were little people while here was a Lord High Chancellor who was ready to lay down his life for the papal claims.

Fr Bridgett had his doubts but he too was naturally proud of More's promotion, writing as he did at the turn of the nineteenth century when the status of the martyr could add respectability to the resurgent Catholic cause. It fell to Professor Chambers, himself never a Roman Catholic, to see More's life in perspective and to gauge the mounting tragedy of the last fifteen years. Chambers puts it very well:

> For twelve years More served the King before his career was crowned by his succeeding Wolsey in the Chancellorship. To all appearances his life during these years was one of steadily increasing distinction and power. In reality these years saw the hopes which More had cherished for his country and for Christendom, one after another overthrown. And as each blow falls we can see More's destruction brought one stage nearer.

The Chancellorship, which to the world may have looked like
the culmination of a successful career, was in reality, the last
of the many successive strokes of doom.[1]

This view, fully confirmed by the facts but not widely appre-
ciated, adds poignancy and great courage to More's last fifteen
years. During those very years in which he was writing his
loving letters to his children, he was watching the slow deprecia-
tion of English public life. While Wolsey survived, More could
shelter behind the pretentious bulk of the great Cardinal and Tudor
statesman; when Wolsey fell and More was invited to assume his
office, he found himself face to face with the overwhelming men-
ace of the King. While we must admire his defence both of the
Church and of the papacy, secretly we may regret that More
appeared to die for a partisan issue when, in fact, he laid down his
life for justice, honour and sanity.

As the schoolmen so rightly put it, every comparison limps.
Yet it is worth the risk to refer to the dilemma facing the honourable Germans of Hitler's early days. A German citizen of the
calibre of More, urged to participate in the new administration,
would have undertaken such service in the vague hope of achiev-
ing some good but with grave misgivings and at considerable
personal risk. Despotism has appeared in history under many
disguises but at heart all despots are the same. King Henry VIII,
bluff, handsome, debonair, may now seem preferable to Hitler
but he posed the same problems, used the same methods, proved no
less treacherous and unstable in his small, sixteenth-century way.
Royal service under Henry may have seemed honourable and
hopeful at the beginning but in the end it led inevitably to a
choice between death or compromise.

Why, then, did More decide to go to Court? The choice, which
saddened Erasmus and his friends, though they were partly responsible, is now more easy to explain. One point is certain,
More knew very well the risks that he was taking when he threw
up his studies and his legal practice and accepted a career at Court.

[1] Cf. Chambers, p. 149.

By temperament, training and inclination More was wholly unsuited to the life at Court. He lacked both the ambition and the toughness needed to gain promotion in so stupid, arrogant and unscrupulous a world. A scholar who prayed at night, who never drank or diced or flirted, who hated war and intrigue, who had already set out on paper the sane rules for reasonable government, was out of place in the silly circle of the young King's courtier friends. That More saw the situation clearly is proved by his introduction to *Utopia*. We hardly need Erasmus to tell us that *Utopia* is based entirely on the laws and behaviour of the English and that the savage criticisms expressed by Hythloday were aimed at the English Court.

More was already under pressure when he wrote *Utopia*. Though he had travelled to Antwerp as negotiator of the London merchants, he was already a lawyer of distinction, an obvious choice for a government post. More writes to Erasmus on his return from the Netherlands:

> Nevertheless on my own return, I had a yearly pension offered me by the King, which whether one looked to the profit or the honour of it, was not to be despised. This, however, I have hitherto refused, and shall, I think, continue to do so, because, if I took it, the place I now hold in the City which I prefer to a higher office, would either have to be given up, or retained— much to my regret—with some offence to the citizens, who, if they had any question with the Government, as sometimes happens, about their privileges, would have less confidence in me, as a paid pensioner of the King.[2]

Here, then, was More's dilemma, with *Utopia* half-written, and it was typical of him to argue the question publicly. He has Hythloday, his fictitious friend, deploying all the arguments against accepting royal service while More himself argues, against his natural inclinations, the uncongenial course which, in fact, he was going to choose. Hythloday asserts with considerable vigour that service at any Court would be an utter waste of time. Kings are preoccupied with war to gain new possessions though

[2] Nichols, 2, p. 260.

they do not trouble to rule those which they already hold. All Courts thrive on envy; each courtier so admiring himself that his only aim is to tear his neighbour down. Law is administered to the King's advantage; any judge who resists will be silenced either by money or by threats. Hythloday ends with a remarkable outburst which More was brave to publish: "All that I should be able to do would be to preserve my sanity while I strived to cure the madness of the rest."[3]

Hythloday does not win in this debate. More himself, in reply to the traveller, sets out the valid arguments on which his own decision was to rest. He says:

I perceive, Raphael, that you neither desire wealth or greatness; and, indeed, I value and admire such a man much more than I do any of the great men of the world. Yet I think you would do what would well become so generous and philosophical a soul as yours is, if you would apply your time and thoughts to public affairs, even though you may happen to find it a little uneasy to yourself. And this you can never do without so much advantage as being taken into the Council of some great prince and putting him on noble and worthy actions which I know that you would do if you were in such a post. *For the springs both of good and evil flow from the Prince over a nation as from a lasting fountain.*[4]

This italicized sentence expresses the view not only of More himself but of most honourable statesmen and politicians in a despotic State. That it was a crazy and irrational system More knew very well—he did not hesitate to say so—but as a realist he saw no present alternative. To the question as to why he went to Court, More would have answered us as he answered Hythloday:

It is even so in a commonwealth and in the council of princes; if ill opinions cannot be quite rooted out and you cannot cure some accepted vice according to your wishes, you must not therefore abandon the commonwealth any more than you should abandon a ship in a storm because you cannot command the winds ... you ought rather to cast about and to manage

[3] *Utopia*, pp. 20–21, 48.   [4] *Ibid.*, p. 20; Bridgett, p. 154 (Burnett's version).

things with all the dexterity in your power, so that, if you are not able to make them go well, they may be as little ill as possible; for, except all men were good, everything cannot be right and that is a blessing that I do not at present hope to see.[5]

One last point should be made—in a book of this size it must, alas, be made superficially and briefly—and then we may follow Thomas More to the Royal Court. The painful decision which led to his death was not taken on small domestic issues; if we fail to grasp the acuteness of his vision, we must also miss the greatness of the man.

We who, in our present age, are threatened with the disastrous spread of nuclear weapons may better appreciate More's sense of urgency. Both he and Erasmus, looking towards the future, could foresee the tragic outcome of national selfishness. More certainly feared the wreck of Europe in Luther's wake. Our desperate efforts today to achieve some sort of unity between Christians, our legacy of bigotry and bitterness, show us clearly all that More hoped to avert. In the same way, the growth of the modern states, bolstered by national pride and professional armies, gave Europe four centuries of useless, savage, intermittent war. The very ills that we now try to cure derive in large measure from the errors of Renaissance days.

"In some ways the task of statesmen seemed perhaps easier in More's days than it does now; the humanists had only to teach three young men to be reasonable. Maximilian's death in 1519 followed by Charles' election to the Empire placed the sovereignty of Western and central Europe in the hands of three young men, who were chivalrous and impressionable, Henry, Francis and Charles; only the year before they had been treating for Universal peace. If they would really act in concord, it seemed as though the Golden Age might return."[6]

To More the risk was worth taking for so great a good. To achieve universal peace and to safeguard the unity of Europe, he

---

[5] Bridgett, p. 162.
[6] Cf. Chambers, p. 375. Chambers is commenting on a passage from Allen's *Age of Erasmus*; here the two are fused.

was prepared to go to Court. There was some hope of success, for the young King of England sought the advice of wise counsellors at the start of his reign. Erasmus was loud in the praise of the English monarch; More, though he presented the King with a few flattering verses, remained more cynical. His remark to Roper, so often quoted, shows us exactly how he felt.

"I thank our Lord, son," quoth he, "I find his Grace my very good Lord indeed and I believe he doth as singularly favour me as any subject within this realm. Howbeit, son Roper, I may tell thee, I have no cause to be proud thereof, for if my head could win him a castle in France (for then there was war between us) it should not fail to go."[7]

At about the same time More was to give advice to one of the King's new servants, the man who played so active a part in destroying the Chancellor's work. "Master Cromwell, you are now entering into the service of a most noble, wise and liberal Prince. If you will follow my poor advice, you shall, in your counsel-giving unto His Grace, ever tell him what he ought to do but never what he is able to do . . . for if a lion knew his own strength, hard were it for any man to rule him."[8]

More failed. Professor Chambers was to sum it up: "Henry VIII destroyed more things of beauty and more things of promise than any other man in European history. And yet our historians continue to admire Henry, because he helped to break such European unity as he found, although in doing it, he had to break all the most beautiful things in England. But he is called 'the founder of England's religious independence' because he made every man's religion depend upon the King, claiming to pronounce ex cathedra from the English throne what every Englishman must believe on pain of death." Perhaps Chambers would have changed his verdict slightly after Hitler had had his day.

The decision to go to Court was a grave one and, typically, More hesitated for at least a year. The pressure on him was considerable. The King made the first move, "to cause Cardinal Wolsey, then lord chancellor, to procure him for his service".

[7] Roper, p. 12.   [8] Roper, p. 28.

Next, the Cardinal, "according to the King's request, earnestly laboured to persuade him", but More, "loath to change his estate", put up such arguments against the move that the Cardinal was for the time satisfied. Later when More successfully pleaded the case for a papal ship, impounded by the King at Southampton, "by no entreaty would the King from henceforth be induced any longer to forbear his service". No certain date can be given for More's final decision but he seems to have worked for the Crown at least from 1518.[9]

Dame Alice was certainly delighted. If Roper's satisfaction is typical of the rest of the family, More by his promotion may have brought great pride and pleasure to the Barge. Old Sir John would also have approved, for one may sense in More's epitaph the pride that his father was to feel when his son became Chancellor. On the other hand More's scholarly friends were far less satisfied. "You are lost to us and to learning," wrote Erasmus, who later qualified this verdict in a letter to Tunstall. "I should regret what has happened to More who has been drawn into court life, were it not for such a King. . . . Still we shall get no more news from Utopia to make us laugh and I know that More would rather laugh than be carried in official state." Ammonio is slightly more cynical in his comment: "More is returned from his friends in Flanders . . . he now haunts with us the smoky chambers of the palace; no one is more punctual in carrying his morning salutation to My Lord of York." In another letter Erasmus remarks: "I see More too, who has hitherto remained unconquered, is being snatched away by the same hurricane."[10]

It was in answer to a kind letter from Bishop Fisher of Rochester, congratulating him on his knighthood and asking him to use his power with the King in favour of Cambridge, that More expresses how he feels about the change:

> It was with the greatest unwillingness that I came to court as everyone knows, and as the King himself in joke often throws up in my face. I am as uncomfortable there as is a bad rider in the saddle. I am far from enjoying the special favour of

<hr>

[9] Roper, p. 6.   [10] Nichols, 3, p. 361; 2, p. 243; 2, p. 524.

the King but he is so courteous and kindly to all that everyone who is in any way hopeful finds ground for imagining that he is in the King's good graces; like the London wives who, as they pray before the image of the Virgin Mother of God which stands near the Tower, gaze upon it so fixedly that they imagine it smiles upon them. But I am not so happy as to perceive signs of favour or so hopeful as to imagine them. But the King has virtue and learning and makes great progress in both with daily renewed zeal, so that the more I see His Majesty advance in all the qualities that befit a good monarch, the less burdensome do I feel this life of court.[11]

At the start of his career More was not without many friends at Court. Erasmus rejoices at the number of distinguished men whom the King admits "into his household and into his chamber": Mountjoy, Linacre, Pace, Colet, Stokesley, Latimer, More, Tunstall, Clerk and others like them, any one of whose names signifies at once a world of virtues and accomplishments.[12]

2. MORE AT COURT

It is no longer easy for us to comprehend the Tudor setting in which More was to play a forlorn hand. Titles and institutions have so changed that such words as King, Parliament, People convey to us subtle shades of meaning which no Tudor Englishman would have understood. In theory and on paper, men had their rights in Tudor England; in fact, there was small chance of redress against the Crown. Not all the kings were bad, not all their acts were cruel or their intentions selfish but, as in the case of Henry, they could govern as they liked. Such rule by whim did not long survive—a system too crazy to be suffered—it declined from the absolutism of Henry VIII to that moment a century later when King Charles was beheaded outside Cardinal Wolsey's ill-fated palace at Whitehall.

The medieval kings had, in theory, enjoyed similar powers but the exercise of their despotic rights had been more carefully controlled. Inside the feudal system, powerful barons could

[11] Rogers, p. 111; Stapleton, p. 77.   [12] Nichols, 3, p. 399.

check the Crown. Above the monarchy was the spiritual authority of the Church. When More went to Court, the ancient system was collapsing; the labels and titles and checks were in existence but the substance of power had gone. The old aristocracy was exhausted and bankrupt after a century of war. The churchmen had become the senior civil servants, bolstering the monarch as the chief guarantor of ecclesiastical rights. How different Wolsey from Becket or the Tudor bishops from their predecessors who had wrested Magna Carta from King John. Henry VIII was absolute master as no English monarch has been, before or since.

It would be foolish here to attempt even an outline of the political situation; the shelves of libraries are overweighted with historical research. Few periods of history have attracted more attention than the Tudor and every detail of Henry's reign has been weighed and analysed. But while the historians tie themselves up in the web of Reformation details, certain salient facts are not made very clear. How refreshing it always is to return to the works of the great Professor Brewer, first Editor of "Letters and Papers of the Reign of Henry VIII". This expert historian, reared on the State Papers, is able to place a precise finger on the essential points.

First, the Tudor kings owed their immediate power to the Crown lands. However obtained, these lands belonged to the King personally and afforded to him gigantic opportunities for patronage. The lives of thousands in every class of society were in his hands. "He had at his disposal the stewardships of forests, manors, chaces, castles, fisheries and mines," the collectorships of customs in various ports, nominations to churches on his estates, not to mention his ancient right of wardship and marriage, which now sank into an insignificant item compared with the more splendid and lucrative offices at his disposal. Appointments of ambassadors, commissions in the armed forces, stewardships of royal farms, the leasehold of lands acquired through the courts by act of attainder were all in the free gift of the Tudor King. He had, as Brewer suggests, the nucleus of a standing army, the beginnings of a spy system, the requirements for establishing a police State.

Next, the documents of the period make it clear that "scarcely any man holds any office of importance who is not familiarly known to the King". The exclusive road to promotion is through personal service. No minister dispenses or even shares the patronage of the Crown. Men like Wolsey might recommend, might for a time appear to promote their friends with the King's tacit approval but, in the long run, those only raised themselves who served the personal wishes of the King. Ministers were often taken from the lower ranks, looked only to the King for promotion and worked for the extension of the royal power as the only way of profiting themselves. Says Brewer, "They are the servants of the Crown, an epithet which the ancient nobility of a past age would have rejected with disdain as they would have rejected that subordination which it signified."

"It is scarcely necessary for me," says Brewer, "to point the moral suggested by these remarks. The ecclesiastics who surrounded the throne of Henry VII and Henry VIII and sanctioned with their presence and authority the acts of both these monarchs, invested royalty with a spiritual influence in the minds of the people which could not be disintegrated from it or resumed when the Kings changed their religious principles and dismissed their spiritual ministers. Their royal supremacy was now triumphant ... fools could raise objections, the wisest could hardly catch a glimpse of its profound significance."[13]

More was one of those few wise men who saw such a significance and who went to Court highly critical of the monarchy. This was not a question of loyalty. Of More's deep love for his country there can be no doubt. For one so European in thought, on such friendly terms with Dutch, French, Spanish and German scholars, More's touchiness about the prestige of his own country is surprisingly quick to show itself. He could not entertain the thought that Louvain was better than Oxford, that French sailors were as good as the English sailors, that the clergy and

[13] Brewer, I, pp. 69–73.

faithful in other countries surpassed the fervour of the English Church. More was devoted to England but without shutting his eyes to her defects.

By birth and training he was a monarchist. As a lawyer he stood for law and order, and was, in this sense, a strict conservative. His dislike of the early heretics was based on their secret mischief, midnight meetings, clandestine intrigues. Never for a moment would he tolerate plotting or hidden treachery. It is not surprising that Henry wanted so honourable a man in his service; the King could feel safe with More.

Yet, surprisingly enough, More, for all his loyalty and devotion, was a man of astonishing independence, with a pronounced radical streak. Throughout his life a series of small revolts are recorded which should have made Henry think. If we accept the story given only by Roper, More in his first session as a member of parliament fell foul of King Henry VII by opposing a royal money Bill. He, More, was in some danger and thought of going to the Continent. This was at the time of his first marriage and soon after he had left the Charterhouse. As speaker of the Commons he withstood the pretensions of Cardinal Wolsey and so far annoyed the powerful minister that Wolsey tried to despatch him on an embassy to Spain. Again, it was recorded that More would not leave Mass before the end when summoned by the King. Nor would he abandon the custom of serving Mass though the Duke of Norfolk thought it, for a man of his position, undignified. Finally, when he published *Utopia* he wrote a scathing attack on Christian Kings. Hythloday ends his story with this bold statement:[14]

"When I consider all these commonwealths which nowadays anywhere do flourish, so God help me, I can perceive nothing but a conspiracy of rich men, procuring their own commodities under the name and title of the commonwealth."[15]

It says much for More's reputation and charm and for Henry's goodwill and tolerance that the King should so much have wanted a man of More's independence at his side. For More directed his

[14] Roper, pp. 4–5, 10–13; Stapleton, pp. 66–68.   [15] *Utopia*, p. 132.

most scathing attacks at the official royal policy, the silly European
wars, the leagues and anti-leagues, the crossing and double-
crossing which marked all Henry's diplomacy. He felt and
asserted that the poor, simple people were being used as cattle,
that the wealth of England was being squandered that kings and
nobles might play their stupid games. More had his own priorities, in which reform of the Church, reform of the law, the spread
of scholarship, an honest deal for honest people took pride of
place. Instead, all that the people received from the Court was
war, shortage of food, high prices, loss of trade, heavy taxation
and the endless sight of idle courtiers enjoying themselves. With
Erasmus, More was bitterly opposed to the papal policy of a
whole series of warlike popes. It was galling, later, for him to
recall how he had warned Henry that the Pope, acting as an
Italian monarch, should not be encouraged too much. More
failed—not because he was wrong; history has proved him right
in everything.

When set beside his life at home with his wife and children,
with his intimate circle of friends and scholars, his years at Court
seem painfully jejune. How did he spend his days?

The question would take too long to answer unless we cover it
briefly under different heads.

When Erasmus foretold "we shall get no more news from
Utopia to make us laugh" he hit on the truth. More spent hours
at his desk. He had the letters from his children in the drawer to
entertain him in the dull round of office chores. He was away from
home whenever the Court left London and his letters carry the
names of the various towns and palaces from which he wrote to
friends. From 1519 onwards we find him at Woking, Greenwich,
Canterbury, Calais, Newhall, London, Easthampstead, Woking
again, Guildford, Woodstock, Hertford, Stony Stratford, Richmond, Windsor and Cambrai. Only when he became Lord
Chancellor in 1529 is he able to write from Chelsea again.

Among his letters, the few truly happy ones are those written
to his children about which much has been said in another place.
He maintains a regular correspondence with Erasmus but it

soon becomes clear that official business is preventing the same intimacy with his scholarly friends. Chambers points out that, in the year after *Utopia* was published, the three best-known names among European scholars were Erasmus, the Dutchman, Budé, the Frenchman, and More, the Englishman. As More became more involved in the King's business, he gradually gave way in this triumvirate of learning and Vives, the Spaniard, took his place. "Never does More betray the slightest touch of jealousy or disappointment at seeing himself outstripped by one so much his junior."[16]

Mixed up with these months at Court, transcribing endless letters to Wolsey on official business, were the tedious journeys to the Continent on official embassies. The King himself intervened to arrange this. He wrote to Wolsey: "Whereas old men do now decay greatly within this his realm, his mind is to acquaint other young men with his great affairs and therefore he desireth Your Grace to make Sir William Sandys and Sir Thomas More privy to all such matters as your Grace shall treat at Calais." Wolsey, in a restricted, worldly way, was a very great statesman, quite unable to share his work or to delegate. It is Brewer's opinion that the true cause of his fall was his age. The King was aware of his minister's weakness and marked off More as the type of man who might one day take his place.[17]

More seems to have assisted on six such embassies. He went on three to Bruges, one to Calais, Amiens and Cambrai. On all such diplomatic missions More was mainly concerned with trade. When he wrote his epitaph, though he mentions the other journeys in general terms, he singles out the mission to Cambrai. He found most of them tedious. During the first of them, undertaken for the City of London, he wrote the first part of *Utopia*. More gives us a glimpse of himself abroad, for "upon a certain day when I had heard the divine service in Our Lady's Church— which is the fairest, the most gorgeous and curious church in all the city and also the most frequented of people—and the service being done, was ready to go home to my lodging, I chanced to

---

[16] Cf. Chambers, p. 207.   [17] Bridgett, p. 190.

espy this aforesaid Peter talking with a certain stranger".[18] So it
is that we first meet Hythloday. Our only other detailed record
of More abroad, one which reveals something of his style in
negotiations, also opens with his coming out of church. Gasparo
Contarini, at the time Venetian Ambassador to the Emperor, met
More in Bruges. "On coming away from the solemn Mass of the
Holy Ghost in St James' church (celebrated in the presence of the
Emperor, the Cardinal and the resident ambassadors) I invited an
English gentleman, by name Master Thomas More, a very learned
man, to dine with me. He had accompanied Wolsey to Bruges.
During dinner we discussed the business negotiated with the
Emperor but More did not drop the slightest hint of any other
treaty than that of peace between the King of France and His
Imperial Majesty." More must have known that another, more
secret and more important matter was under discussion, the
betrothal of the Emperor to Princess Mary of England.[19]

These frequent embassies were frustrating, tedious and pro-
longed. We read of the Commissioners, More among them,
running short of money, having trouble with boats, meeting with
stiff opposition, journeying from one town to another on the
Cardinal's business. Once More is sent back suddenly to England
by the Cardinal to carry an urgent message to the King. Once
Tunstall fell from his horse while returning with More from the
Continent. The bishop hurt himself sufficiently to remain in
bed for some days. More, therefore, went alone before the King
and Council to report the outcome of the embassy.

More attended the Field of the Cloth of Gold in the King's
company but leaves us no description of these juvenile junketings
which cost a fortune, achieved very little and lasted for twenty-
one days. He seems to have slipped away to negotiate a trade
agreement for the City with the Hanseatic League. He had the
joy of seeing Erasmus, who came to Bruges in the Emperor's train.
The two great friends met for the last time in Bruges in 1521.

The last of his embassies, the one which was particularly praised
by the King when More was installed as Chancellor, brought

---

[18] *Utopia*, p. 14.   [19] *Venetian State Papers*, Contarini to the Signory, N. 302.

peace to Europe for thirteen years through the treaty of Cambrai. This was his most difficult assignment for, by then, the policy of the Cardinal had disintegrated and Wolsey, on the very verge of disgrace, decided to remain at home. Tunstall and More were negotiating from great weakness and their moderate success was not expected by the King. In his epitaph More wrote: "And last of all at Cambrai ... where he both joyfully saw and was present ambassador when the leagues between the chief princes of Christendom were renewed again and peace, so long looked for, restored to Christendom. Which peace our Lord stable and make perpetual."

The sad, melancholy note of the following letter reveals something of the inner conflict which More underwent throughout these years.

l approve of your plan in not wishing to be involved in the busy trifles of Princes; and you show your love for me by desiring that I may be disentangled from such matters in which you can scarcely believe how unwillingly I am engaged. Nothing can be more hateful to me than my present mission. I am sent to stay at a little seaport, with a disagreeable soil and climate and, whereas at home, I have naturally a great abhorrence of litigation, even when it brings me profit, you may imagine what annoyance it must cause one here, when it is accompanied with loss. But my Lord promises that the King shall reimburse the whole; when I receive it, I will let you know. Keep your health till then and you can hardly wish for more.[20]

There is, perhaps, some value in thus considering More as courtier and senior civil servant, especially for the encouragement of those who are tied to a desk themselves. For More, the glorious days of liberty had gone. As part of his civic duty and in an effort to lead his country in a wise and Christian manner, he had sacrificed his studies and his home. He took with him only his prayers. Nor are these mentioned at all in his official letters or referred to by those who dealt with him on routine tasks. The point that is mentioned and that shows how prayer works itself out in strange and uncongenial settings, is his astonishing charity. Not a word of complaint against More is to be found in any official letter of the time; no scandal is breathed against him, no accusation of ill-temper or impatience, no faintest hint that he is feathering his nest. Erasmus puts the position neatly, at least for the early days of More's career.

He had made up his mind to be contented with this position which was sufficiently dignified without being exposed to serious dangers. He has been thrust more than once into an embassy in the conduct of which he has shown great ability; and King Henry in consequence would never rest until he had dragged him into court. "Dragged him" I say, "and with reason" for no one was ever more ambitious of being admitted to court than he was anxious to escape it. But as this excellent monarch was resolved to pack his household with learned, serious, intelligent and honest men, he especially insisted upon having More among them with whom he is on such terms of intimacy that he cannot bear to let him go; if serious affairs are in hand, no one gives wiser counsel; if it pleases the King to relax his mind with agreeable conversation, no man is better company. Difficult questions are often arising which require a grave and prudent judge; and these questions are resolved by More in such a way that both sides are satisfied. And yet no one has ever induced him to receive a present. What a blessing it would be for the world if magistrates like More were everywhere put in office by sovereigns.

Meantime there is no assumption of superiority. In the midst of so great a pressure of business, he remembers his humble friends; and from time to time he returns to his beloved studies. Whatever authority he derives from his rank or whatever influence he enjoys by the favour of a powerful sovereign are employed in the service of the public or that of his friends. It has always been part of his character to be most obliging to everybody and marvellously ready with his sympathy; and this disposition is more conspicuous than ever, now that his power of doing so is greater. Some he relieves with money, some he protects with his authority, some he promotes by his recommendation, while those whom he cannot otherwise assist are benefited by his advice. No one is ever sent away in distress and you might call him the general patron of all poor people. He counts it a great gain to himself if he has relieved some oppressed person, made the path clear for one who was in difficulties or brought back into favour one who was in disgrace. No man more readily confers a benefit, no man expects less in return. And successful as he is in so many ways; while success is generally accompanied by self-conceit, I have never seen any mortal more free from this failing.[21]

3. MORE AND THE KING

Erasmus in this moving eulogy, surely the best description ever penned of sanctity in a layman, leads us to More's greatest act of charity, his love for the King. How hard it is to recall a parallel friendship in history. Here is the story of a scholar and saint, a man of European reputation, who was ready to sacrifice both convenience and career not only for the sake of his country but from a deep and lasting affection for the King. That More could read Henry through and through and yet allow the King to triumph over him is the final proof of his extraordinary charity. More loved Henry, and the King, in a brittle, self-centred way, returned this love.

More was twelve years older than the King. He was already a student at Lincoln's Inn when he collected Erasmus from Lord Mountjoy's house in Greenwich and went with him and another student, Edward Arnold, to Eltham palace to visit the royal children in their nursery. Who had the influence and how they gained admittance is not told. Erasmus, at least, was taken by surprise. He found himself greeting the royal children; "in the midst stood Prince Henry, then nine years old, and having already something of royalty in his demeanour, in which there was a certain dignity combined with singular courtesy." More had verses ready while Erasmus, wholly unprepared, was annoyed with his friend for not warning him.[22]

When More and the King met again in Greenwich and Richmond, the former would have been forty, the latter twenty-

[21] Nichols, 3, p. 397. [22] Erasmus, *Catalogue of Lucubrations*; Nichols, 1, p. 201.

eight. Catherine of Aragon, whom More had described so charmingly when he saw her arriving at St Paul's for her wedding with Prince Arthur, was now thirty-three.

If More was a distinguished man, Henry also enjoyed a considerable reputation as the model renaissance prince. He had reigned for nine years. All the available evidence goes to show that he was handsome, debonair, good-humoured, with sudden bursts of uncontrollable temper which were passing and did little to detract from his predominant courtesy. Physically, Henry towered above his courtiers. He was fair, thin-skinned, with impressive biceps and the blush of a girl. For all the emphasis on his more manly virtues, the records cannot conceal a certain effeminacy. Henry was exceptionally vain, loved dressing up, longed to be admired, in many ways showed himself spoilt, even babyish. Always he looked for praise and encouragement. He needed to be mothered and Catherine held her position because of her motherliness.

It is now not easy to distinguish flattery from fact. Henry wanted to excel and it cost the courtiers little to arrange for this. They did him no good service; his undoubted talents needed no such artificial help. The King sang well and rehearsed his music daily; he further taught himself four languages. Painfully pious, he liked to attend five Masses daily, three only on hunting days. Professor Brewer with the State Papers before him is loud in praise of Henry's industry. In these early years, the King read every report, was actively interested in the well-being of the country, gave personal attention to the humblest requests. Though the French ambassador could describe Henry in a report as "a youngster who cared for nothing but girls and hunting and wasted his father's patrimony", the verdict is almost certainly prejudiced. Henry was genuinely devoted to Catherine and his infidelities were passing and do not seem to have affected his married life. He had liaisons with at least three women, and his illegitimate son by Bessie Blount was born soon after Thomas More arrived at court.[23]

[23] Cf. Brewer, I, p. 231.

In Catherine, More met one of the noblest women ever to occupy the English throne. A Spaniard, heroic daughter of a most noble mother, the Queen enjoyed in England an extraordinary popularity. She had taught herself English and both spoke and wrote it fluently. She retained a delightful sense of humour which survived all her sufferings. To the very end, she loved Henry and believed in him. She blamed his advisers, never the King. Catherine is probably the only person in the Court circle whose integrity could be compared to More's. Sadly enough, More's position with the King seems to have made it difficult for him to deal much with the Queen during those last, painful days. In happier times they were close friends. The Queen read *Utopia* and loved it; she enjoyed More's conversation and tried to persuade him to make an English translation of Vives' book. In the end, the two noblest characters of the century were ruined by the King whom they served so well.[24]

The King's fatal weakness was not sexual; he was destroyed by his craving for praise. He thought of nothing but his own excellence. He yearned for display, for pageantry, for a dazzling Court, a circle of learned friends, popular applause, those acts of military prowess which would match up to the idealized image that he entertained of himself. All that More was struggling to avoid for his children, he found in this lovable, generous and wilfully conceited young man. Henry was counterfeit. He played at grandeur, bonhomie, friendship and theology. Reading the papers of the period, one still feels ashamed. Henry's childish behaviour at the Field of the Cloth of Gold, the folly of his wars, the near buffoonery of his Court pageants, match the cowardice of his panic at the time of the plague. The King ran for his life, moved from place to place, concocted special pills and potions, worried himself sick. Wrote the French ambassador sarcastically: "The King has at last stopped twenty miles from here at a house built by Wolsey, finding removals useless. I hear that he has made his will and taken the sacraments for fear of sudden death. However he is not ill."[25]

[24] Cf. Mattingly, pp. 138, 142.   [25] Cf. Brewer, 2, p. 273.

The craving for praise, harmless when he was young, led in middle age to touchiness, suspicion and jealousy. Wolsey, in the days of his ascendancy, knew how to manage the King. He supplied pageantry, flattery, military glory on a nauseating scale. If the King seemed jealous, Wolsey would present him with what he wanted, be it a palace or a choirboy. Courtiers and bishops followed the lead with disastrous results. Henry became increasingly suspicious, more and more sure of his own superiority, less willing to tolerate opposition in any form. In the end, he was, to all intents and purposes, deranged. Yet beneath the surface he was a simple, frightened and very lovable man. For all his conceit, he tended to follow the advice of the last person to whom he had been speaking, to cling in a pathetic way to old friends. The new nobility, who discovered how to use him, had to take great care to arrange his company. With Wolsey, with More, and with Catherine, Henry, if left to himself, would certainly have changed. To the end Catherine, who knew and loved him best, was clear about this.

When More came to Court, the King's Council was still a vague, irregular body, summoned when the King wanted, composed of those whom the King chose to consult. The honorary offices of State remained in the hands of the hereditary aristocracy but the authority reposed in Wolsey, and the day-to-day administration was committed to those whom the King happened to like. It was the King, rather than Wolsey, who took an immediate fancy to More. More had all those qualities which the King lacked. He was honest, free of all ambition and spontaneous in his sympathy. Henry so reformed his Council that More should be always in residence. The document runs: "And because, per case, it may chance some of these aforenamed persons to be absent, be it always provided that the Bishop of Bath, the Secretary, Sir Thomas More and the Dean of the Chapel or two of them at least always be present, being every day in the forenoon by 10 of the clock at the furthest and at afternoon by 2 of the clock in the King's dining chamber, or in such other place as shall fortune to be appointed for the Council Chamber."[26]

[26] *Ibid.*, I, p. 54.

At the start at least, this was the arrangement and More was little more than the King's private secretary. In his many letters to Wolsey, More drops hints about the situation with which he had to cope. On one occasion the King tells More to commend the Cardinal for the excellence of his letters which must have taken him much labour since they took the King two hours to read. On another occasion when Wolsey had sent urgent letters requiring the royal approval, Henry exclaimed laughing, "Nay by my soul, that shall not be, I will read the remnant at night". Later that night, More gained access to the royal rooms and managed to get a letter to the Emperor signed. He had no sooner left the royal apartments when a letter from the Lord High Admiral arrived. Back he went with it, to find the King in the Queen's apartment. The King brought him in and read the letter to Catherine who was, More tells Wolsey, very delighted with the news. For many years, Henry conducted business in the Queen's apartments and interviewed ambassadors there. Even when he was carrying on with Anne Boleyn and had initiated his appeal to Rome to have his marriage terminated, he still sat with the Queen in the evening while she sewed for him. Such small scenes as these, especially with More and the Queen alone with Henry in the royal apartments, help to emphasize the sense of tragedy.[27]

Such day and night intimacy with the royal pair led to the very situation which Erasmus has described. More was a councillor by day but he served the King and Queen for recreation when official work was done. Often he supped with the King. He went with the King to the leads to discuss and explain the movements of the heavenly bodies; Henry knew as much as More about astronomy. On other occasions theology was the subject for dispute and the royal theologian held forth on the duties of a layman to recite vocal prayers. Once when More had been absent for some days, Henry wrote to Wolsey to demand his presence and the Cardinal answered that More was essential at the treasury

[27] Letters between More and Wolsey, Rogers, pp. 279 seq., especially pp. 263, 281, 311.

for four or five more days. He begged the King not to call More to Court until the accounts were complete.

More, we know, loathed the life at Court. After a time he assumed a more melancholy mood so as to get away. He had his children's letters on his desk, as he told Meg on one occasion, already quoted, and for them in these early years at Court he composed *The Four Last Things*. He tells us nothing of his prayers. At one period he wrote in Latin a savage answer to Luther and must certainly have been engaged in preparing the material for his controversial books. Most of his collected letters from the time he went to Court are business letters, letters to his children or letters to old friends. Erasmus was right, and in these years we miss some of the laughter of the Utopian days.[28]

Though he disliked the life at Court, Stapleton admits that More in these early years derived some satisfaction in that the spirit of the Court was good. Erasmus, less well informed and probably less holy, is eloquent in its praise. He writes: "The high reputation for virtue that the English court continues to enjoy, possessing as it does, besides a King richly endowed with all the qualities of a perfect monarch and a Queen worthy of him, so many men of unimpeachable character, of learning and of piety, has moved the Prince of Bergen to send his son Anthony to no other school."[29]

More, though no less charitable, was less naïve. Already in *Utopia* he had forecast the lines of deterioration along which a counterfeit world must run. The deep and intimate friendship of the King had not put him off his guard.

Neither was there any man that the King used more familiarly, nor with whom he more debated, not only for public affairs but in matters of learning, withal taking great comfort besides in his merry and pleasantly conceited wit. And took such pleasure in his company that he would sometimes, upon a sudden, come to his house in Chelsea to be merry with him. . . . Of all the which favours, he made no more account than a deep, wise man should do and as the nature and disposition of the King (which he deeply and thoroughly perceived) did

[28] Roper, pp. 6–7.   [29] Stapleton, p. 77.

require, and as, indeed, he afterwards in himself most of all
men experienced. Wherefore, even at this time when flattering
fortune seemed most pleasantly to smile on him and all things
seemed as beautiful as the lustre of a bright diamond, he well
thought as well upon the disposition and inclination of the
said Prince as upon the frail, instable and brittle state of such as
seem to be in high favour of the Princes.[30]

4. HUMILIATIONS

The legendary picture of King Henry VIII as a jovial, good-
natured Bluebeard has earned for him a sneaking popularity
which he never deserved. Much is forgiven in history to the big-
hearted philanderer. How different are the facts, and we may now
see the King's marital excesses as no more than minor symptoms
of that moral degeneracy which was to ruin the last two decades
of his reign. Henry ended as a tyrant in the fullest sense. We do
well to remember that he was feared and detested, not only by
those whose lives were directly threatened, but by the normally
jovial London mob. All the lampoons and jokes were directed
against himself. We need only recall that he was waiting at Richmond for the gun from the Tower to proclaim Anne Boleyn's
execution and that he immediately rode off to Wiltshire to marry
Jane Seymour on the following day. He was mad. During the
divorce proceedings, Queen Catherine was so popular with the
crowds and so widely applauded that the Privy Council had to ask
her not to show herself. Revolt was in the air and would certainly
have succeeded had Catherine been ready to give a lead. Henry
survived, along with other despots, by the use of scapegoats and
the organization of what now looks very like a police State.[31]

Comparisons are always dangerous. So much divides the two
men that one hesitates to write their names in the same sentence;
yet it is of Hitler that one thinks when reading the story of King
Henry VIII. No need to push the likeness further; the Tudor
King was the smaller and more respectable operator with the
same lunatic opinion of himself.

[30] Harpsfield, p. 67.
[31] Strickland, *Lives of the Queens of England*, IV, p. 314; Mattingly, pp. 282–290.

The story of the King's "Great Affair" has been told so often from every viewpoint and with so much nauseating detail that it would be foolish to repeat it here. Few emerged from the ordeal with any credit for, by the finish, Catherine, Fisher and More were dead. Wolsey deserved to die in shame, Cromwell, Cranmer and Anne Boleyn perished on the scaffold with many far more humble, innocent people—Father Larke and Giles Heron among them—whose lives were forfeited pointlessly to satisfy a tyrant's whim.

The timidity of the Pope looks no better today than the compliancy of Cranmer; men like Tunstall lived long to regret their panic[32]: Henry survived, physically a wreck, morally corrupt enough still to entertain the highest opinion of himself. Here is one of the most discreditable events in English history, and reunion between Christians will come the more quickly when both sides are ready to hang their heads in shame.

Chambers, here as always, expresses the matter well. Writing of the Reformation, he says:

> The real differences lie, not between Catholic and Protestant but between Catholic and Protestant on the one side, and on the other the tools of Henry, the Norfolks and the Riches and the Southwells and the Paulets. The creeds of Catholic and Anabaptist had more in common with each other than with the creed of these men which contained one simple clause: *The wrath of the King is death*. Or, to put it in terms of Utopia, the difference lies between the men who merely obey the laws of the State, and the men who have, as every citizen of Utopia was bound to have, a belief that there is an ultimate standard of right and wrong, beyond what the State may, at any moment, command.[33]

Fortunately we are here concerned only with More who, of all the participants, suffered death for this one unchanging principle. Suddenly faced both with scandal and dilemma, More did not alter his position from first to last. Yet, in a strange and happy way, he was the least involved. We may dodge the Legatine

[32] Stapleton, p. 51.   [33] Cf. Chambers, p. 380.

court, the endless intrigue, the delays in Rome, the scruples of
Henry and the gout of Campeggio, for Harpsfield, in the quotation
already given, shows how More not only had misgivings as to
Henry but doubts about the men who now clustered around the
King. Henry was weak and easily led. For a man as shrewd as
More, the problem of the divorce lay not so much in the Legatine
court at Blackfriars but in the character of those who were the
King's friends.

The Calendar of State Papers shows us the situation from More's
point of view. The first significant change is seen after the battle
of Pavia when the defeat of France threw the English nobles out
of work.

Until the close of the year 1524 the superabundant activity
of the King himself and of his young courtiers, wasting itself
mainly on muscular amusements or exchanging them for the
less justifiable excitement of dice and card-playing, found more
wholesome occupation in the war with France or the expectation of war. But the defeat of Francis at the battle of Pavia left
them in utter idleness, without the hope of employment. Men
of education, sagacity and experience, generally ecclesiastics,
were at that time engaged in all the diplomatic posts requiring
more than usual tact and ability. For such employments, the
nobility and gentry, who frequented the new court, were either
disqualified by ignorance of their own and still more of the
Latin tongue—the common vehicle of communication—or
declined to qualify themselves by the necessary sacrifices of their
time and amusements.[34]

This point is not new to us for we have met it in More's writings,
in *Utopia*, in his letter to Gonnell, in his warnings to his children
of the urgent danger of idleness. Idleness overthrew the King.
By 1525 Henry, thirty-four years old, was beginning to pay less
attention to business, withdrew himself more and more from the
metropolis and spent his days in the hunting field. By 1526 the
Venetian ambassador could report, "Everything is left to Cardinal
Wolsey who keeps a great court". Clerk was to write, "On my

[34] Brewer, 2, pp. 158–159.

arrival here yesternight, the King was forth a hunting and came not home till nine of the clock". Fitzwilliam tells the same tale: "I received a packet of letters addressed to the King, which I took to His Majesty immediately; but as he was going out to have a shot at a stag, he asked me to keep them till the evening." The same type of report appears often: "The King is merry and in good health . . . the officers of the earl of Northumberland to whom this place belongs, presented the King with six oxen and forty wethers and he had good game for his recreation." More himself gives us no account of the King's behaviour but he was secretly suspicious and his judgement was acute.[35]

In Utopia, idleness was seen as an urgent danger because with it went ostentation and the endless struggle for wealth. More's humiliation would have been the greater when he found himself not merely writing about the extravagance of Christian Courts but living in the midst of almost lunatic luxury. As Brewer puts it: "I have stated before that the King had the entire and exclusive control of the money paid into the Exchequer. He had nothing to do except sign a warrant to John Heron, the treasurer of the Chamber, and whatever sums were in the hands of the receivers of the revenue were instantly paid over to the King's use." Throughout his reign Henry was careless about money, pouring it away on trivialities, pageants, jewellery and presents to his friends. To read his expense accounts and the costly nonsense on which he wasted public money is to form a less favourable opinion even of the early days of his reign. Even in the year when More was writing *Utopia*, the money paid for plate, jewellery, pearls, diamonds, sables is scandalous. More knew well the other side of the picture, dealing, as he had to do, with the poor vagrants, beggars, cutpurses, awaiting execution in Newgate Jail.

About the time when More came to Court, Henry had begun a new habit, helping himself to heavy sums for his own use without accounting for the mode of their expenditure. In May 1515 he took £3,000, in August £3,000 and again in December £6,000; in June 1516 £2,000 and again in October £3,000. In

[35] *Ibid.*, 2, pp. 101–102.

March 1517 £3,000; in December 1518 £2,000. Brewer writes: "How these sums were employed it would be useless to speculate. They were received by Sir William Compton, the chief gentleman of the King's bedchamber 'for the King's use' and formed no part of the regular expenses for the household, the entertainment of ambassadors, secret or public service money, all of which are fully entered."[36]

The mention of Sir William Compton may lead us to enquire about the type of courtier who hunted, gambled and spent this money with the King. It comes as no surprise to learn that the ceaseless round of Court revels cost the King's friends considerable sums of money and left most of them in heavy debt.

> Lands were pawned, estates were wasted in providing the richest arms of the latest fashion, the most dazzling jewels and fantastic disguises without which no young man of any pretensions could hope to distinguish himself from the throng or take part in these courtly amusements ... the minor nobility and gentry of England condescended to various means of recruiting their exhausted finances and thus constituted a large body of royal retainers, grateful for 4d or 6d a day ... to needy men whose incomes had not advanced in proportion to their wants, even small sums of ready money, and inferior employments under the Crown, small fees and offices in the gift of lay patrons and guardians of religious houses were an object of solicitude.

Many of the nobility were deeply in debt to the King. They borrowed from the Crown to float themselves. Others turned to a man like Thomas Cromwell, whose astonishing career, first with Wolsey, then with Henry, began in supplying loans. Few of the nobility could afford to dispute either with Cromwell or the King.

In the very years in which Henry was arguing with Thomas More about vocal prayer or dropping in at Chelsea unexpectedly for supper, he was also wasting his days in idleness and luxury

---

[36] *Letters and Papers*, Vol I, Part 2, The King's Book of Payments, pp. 1441–1480. See also Brewer, I, pp. 226–228.

with a new clique of friends. Chief of these were Sir William
Compton, Sir Francis Bryan, Sir Gilbert Pickering, Sir Henry
Norris and George Boleyn. To these must be added the Duke of
Suffolk, exclusively remarkable for his strength and stature; the
Duke of Norfolk, a small, spare man of dark complexion, cruel
lips and more cruel temper, and Sir Thomas Boleyn, advanced to
the peerage in 1525 as Viscount Rochford.

Of this favoured set, the majority were closely connected with
Anne Bolyn. Sir Thomas was her father, the Duke of Norfolk
her uncle, George Boleyn her brother, Sir Francis Bryan her
cousin, Norris, a near relative and admirer, and Compton, an
intimate friend. Another common failing unites them all, one
which Brewer puts forward as the true reason why More began
to shun the Court. "There was hardly one of them whose character was not seriously tainted with that vice against which the
unsullied purity of More's mind revolted; not one who looked
upon the transgression of the marriage vow as deserving reproba-
tion or censure, or, at least, as worse than a jest." Compton was
cited before the ecclesiastical courts for living in open adultery,
Norris and George Boleyn perished on the scaffold with Anne,
accused of incest, Norfolk lived on scandalous terms with his
Duchess, Suffolk was unfaithful, "Sir Francis Bryan, the chief
companion of the King's amusements and the minister of his
pleasures, was pointed out by common fame as more dissolute
than all the rest".[37] Thomas Cranmer, a little-known scholar,
comes into the story as the protégé of the Boleyns. When More
was summoned to appear before various commissions, he found
himself facing Cromwell, Cranmer, Sir Thomas Boleyn and their
friends. His humiliation was complete.

We almost come to regret that More said so little about this
period or about himself. In the first place, it was dangerous to
commit oneself to writing, next, most of his papers were seized
when he was committed to the Tower; finally, he himself disapproved of uncharitable gossip of any sort. Later he was able to
assert with truth that he had never written against the King or

[37] Brewer, 2, pp. 159-161, 392-393.

spoken about his royal business or sought in any way to upset the conscience or allegiance of any man. Once only does he refer to a topical event which distressed him greatly, the execution of the Duke of Buckingham. He used this in writing to his children as an example of sudden death.

For I suppose, if there were one right far above thee, yet thou wouldst not greatly envy his estate, if thou thoughtst that thou mightst be his equal the next week. And why shouldst thou envy him now, while thou seest that death make you both equals the next night, and shall undoubtedly within few years? If it so were that thou knewest a great Duke, keeping so great estate and princely port in his house that thou, being a right mean man hadst in thine heart a great envy thereat and specially at some special day in which he keepeth for the marriage of his child a great honourable court above other times; if thou being thereat, and at the sight of the royalty and honour shown him, of all the country about resorting to him, while they kneel and crouch to him, and at every word bare-head begrace him, if thou shouldst suddenly be surely adver-tised, that for secret treason, lately detected to the King, he should undoubtedly be taken the morrow, his court all broken up, his goods seized, his wife put out, his children disinherited, himself cast into prison, brought forth and arraigned, the matter out of question, and he should be condemned, his coat armour reversed, his gilt spurs hewn off his heels, himself hanged, drawn and quartered; how thinkest thou, by thy faith, amid thine envy shouldst thou not suddenly change into pity?[38]

Here, except that he was certain of his children's prudence, was the one indiscreet remark that More ever made. We may feel that it served him as a perfect example for his purpose, for Meg was to be married in the July and Buckingham was killed on 17th May. More was wrong on one detail; finally Buckingham was beheaded on Tower Green. His vast estates were divided up, the King taking the major part. Two of his judges, Norfolk and Suffolk, picked up some spoils along with Henry Norris, Sir William Fitzwilliam and others of the King's friends. On the day

[38] *English Works*, 1, pp. 482-483; Introduction, p. 21.

of the execution, Wolsey was with the King at Greenwich and suggested a letter of condolence to the late Duke's widow and son. Such a gesture, which reminds one of Hitler's great wreath at the funeral of Rommel, was not made immediately; on the day of Buckingham's death Henry had a touch of ague and was nursing himself. Wolsey had to remind the King a few days later, "If you think them [the letters of condolence] not convenient to pass, I remit them to you."[39]

Buckingham's execution proved to be the first of many which were to disgrace Henry's name. The charge of treason was based entirely on hearsay acquired in a dishonourable way. More himself was sent to the City to pacify the citizens. Rumours were rife and More must have known well the kind of charges that were being made. Had he heard the story which Francesca de Carceres sent to Don Luiz Caroz that the Duke had been involved in a bitter quarrel with Sir William Compton, having caught Henry's bosom friend in his younger sister's room? Gossip had it that Compton was but a stalking horse for the King himself. We need not believe such stories; the Duke died as a candidate for the succession, the King having no son. Such a style of rumour is, however, not without some significance.[40]

The humiliations of these final years were never-ending and it may puzzle us that a man of More's convictions should have been ready to bear with them. Undoubtedly he saw his service to the King as a duty to be continued despite the difficulties. Further, it was not easy to escape from the royal service, and More had no alternative. The King continued to shower dignities upon him, making him Under-Treasurer in 1521 and Chancellor of the Duchy of Lancaster in 1525. Once the King's scruple about his marriage had been put to him, More could not in safety leave. Later, he was to rejoice that he was out of the country when the marriage rumours broke. He continued to perform his round of duties, delivering an address of welcome to the Emperor or reading aloud the proclamation in the Palace of Bridewell when the

---

[39] Brewer, I, p. 397.
[40] *Cal. of State Papers (Spanish)*, Suppl. to Vol. I and 2. N.8.

King's bastard son, Henry Fitzroy, was raised to the peerage and, at the age of seven, left the chapel as a Duke. One of More's first acts as Chancellor was to go in the company of Norfolk to demand the deeds of York Place from the fallen Cardinal and to hand these to the King in his chancery.[41]

Seen in its rightful setting, More's appointment to the Chancellorship—the highest honour paid to him—was both humiliating and disastrous. He might inscribe in his epitaph the pride of old Sir John More at his son's appointment to the highest legal office but his own misgivings may be guessed. Indeed, guesswork is hardly needed for we have the explicit statement of Rastell, More's nephew, that the King, determined not to give the office to any cleric, "offered it to Sir Thomas More, who refusing it, the King was angry with him and caused him to accept it and laboured to have him persuaded on his side in the matter of his divorce; and because he could not be persuaded, he hated him for it".[42]

The hatred of the King, here mentioned, must be considered later, for Henry did not hate More at the time when he offered him the seals. It seems almost certain that he offered More the Chancellorship as a bribe. Much evidence points to this and More himself must have been well aware of the trap. Again, in the end, he had no alternative to accepting the office unless he wished to incur the royal displeasure immediately. His position was humiliating and dangerous. He must have known as much as the French ambassador who wrote home before More had reached his decision: "The Duke of Norfolk is made head of the Council; in his absence the Duke of Suffolk; over all is Mademoiselle Anne. It is not yet known who will have the seal. I think no priest will touch it and that, in this parliament, the clergy will have terrible alarms." Next morning Chapuys, the Imperial envoy, adds to and complicates the story: "The Chancellor's seal has remained in the hands of the Duke of Norfolk till this morning when it was transferred to Sir Thomas More. Everyone is delighted at his promotion, because he is an upright and learned man and a good

[41] Brewer, 2, p. 103.   [42] Cf. Chambers, p. 228.

servant of the Queen." More himself cannot have been delighted when, on Monday, 25th October, he received the seals from the King at Greenwich, and, next day, flanked by Norfolk and Suffolk, before a great crowd of nobility and prelates, took the oath in Westminster Hall. Poor Erasmus, now hopelessly out of touch, expressed his joy in many letters: "I do not at all congratulate More nor literature; but I do indeed congratulate England, for a better or holier judge could not have been appointed."[43]

The humiliation of More as Lord Chancellor rests partly on the duties of his office, partly on this final attempt of the King to gain his approval in the marriage case. The humiliations of the office were certainly great. In the first place More was now in an ambiguous position, seeming to approve of what was being done in the King's name. Almost his first act as Chancellor was uncharacteristic, a bitter attack on the fallen Cardinal.

The relations between More and Wolsey had at times been strained. More had made much fun of the Cardinal's pretensions and had, as speaker, and on other occasions, resisted him to his face. Yet he had also praised Wolsey as an excellent Chancellor and had worked loyally, even intimately with him for many years. His speech against Wolsey, with the King standing beside him, was ungracious and still comes as a shock to More's friends. Possibly we have a garbled account, possibly More sincerely felt hostility towards the fallen man. Wolsey in his day had done great harm to the cause of peace. He, more than any man, had spoilt the King. Yet More himself was not by nature vindictive and his speech on this occasion was not true to him. The only explanation possible is the one given by Chambers, that More by his very position was compelled now to speak for the Government. As Chancellor, and with the King and Council around him, he found for the first time that he must follow the party line.[44]

He was also most cruelly placed, not only in Parliament itself in which he was forced to support the King's position, but in the smaller details of Chancery routine. We know that he sat in his

---

[43] Erasmus to Tunstall, *Letters and Papers*, N.6179. Cf. Bridgett, pp. 223–225.
[44] Cf. Chambers, p. 230; Stapleton, pp. 20–25.

hall at Chelsea each afternoon to help petitioners and to hear complaints. In the morning he went to Westminster and, after receiving his father's blessing, presided in the Chancellor's court. While he showed his skill and integrity in the more usual cases, he was in many ways powerless. When the Fellows of Wolsey's Oxford College appealed to him, he could only refer them to the King. Similarly, he did what he could to enforce the antiquated laws against heretical propaganda but seems to have lacked support. He had to be very careful in the matter of receiving gifts. Always scrupulous in this, he yet was to be charged later with a trumped up offence. At a meeting with the judges, he dealt with their complaints. All the evidence available points to his popularity and considerable success as Chancellor, but one is aware, all the time, of mounting tension and opposition and the sense that More is not being true to himself. He had, of course, been placed in an impossible position and the King was entirely responsible for this.

So, at the end, we must consider the marriage problem which was the direct cause of More's death. Apologists later were to assert that More died for the Catholic Church, for the papal supremacy, that he was killed by Protestants, that he was dominated by the clerical faction and, given the gift of hindsight, these and other cut-and-dry theories may, no doubt, be justified. There can be no question that by the time he suffered martyrdom, More's challenge to Henry turned on the power and jurisdiction of the Pope. Yet to More, looking ahead, and guiding his course by immediate decisions on practical issues, papal supremacy was not, till the end, the urgent point. He parted company with Henry and his Court on the issue of the marriage, a dispute between Catholics for, when More died, not one of the men who agreed to his execution was a Protestant.

We are fortunate to have More's own detailed account of the controversy for he later wrote a long letter to Cromwell explaining the situation point by point. He more or less admits at the start that he had heard rumours of the King's scruple before these were public news. He could hardly have avoided this. As early as 1525 there was talk. Anne Boleyn came to court in 1522 and in the same and subsequent years her father received extraordinary emoluments. He became treasurer to the household, steward of Tunbridge, bailiff of Brasted, keeper of Penshurst, keeper of Thundersley, steward of Swaffham, and in 1525 he was made a peer. At the same time, stories were told which suggested that Henry was jealous of some of his courtiers, but men like Wolsey did not take these too seriously. Anne Boleyn was a pretty girl and Henry had a roving eye.

It now seems certain that Mary Boleyn, Anne's sister, had been Henry's mistress and, later, an outrageous rumour was to be sponsored by Rastell that Henry had been intimate with Anne's mother and that Anne Boleyn was, in fact, Henry's child. Such revolting and fantastic rumours deserve no credence but they provide an accurate guide to the climate in which the King's doubts about his marriage with Catherine were discussed. Later, blame was evenly distributed between Wolsey, the bishop of Tarbes, and the bishop of Lincoln, Henry's confessor, any one of whom may have raised the question whether or not the King's marriage to Catherine was valid in the eyes of God.

More seems to have heard rumours of some affair before he left for the Continent on a royal mission, and when he returned to England and went at once to report to the King about the negotiations, the King, who loved him, hastily asked for his advice. We know the exact place, in the gallery at Hampton Court.

Sir, upon the time of my coming from beyond the sea, where I had been on the King's business, I repaired, as was my duty, unto the King's Grace, being at that time at Hampton Court. At which time suddenly His Highness, walking in his gallery, broke to me his great matter and showed me that it was now perceived that his marriage was not only against the positive laws of the church and the written law of God but also, in such wise, against the law of nature, so that it could in no wise by the church be dispensed ... the first time that ever I heard that point moved that it should be in such high degree against the law of nature, was the time in which, as I began to tell you, the

King's Grace showed it me himself and laid the Bible open
before me and there read me the words that moved His Highness and many other erudite persons so to think, and asked me
further what I myself thought about it.[45]

More, at the time of writing on the very verge of complete
disaster, tells his story skilfully, slowly, pitifully. He is writing to a
self-made man, not his match in integrity or learning, yet he
writes with great humility. He knows that he is ruined and yet
he is not prepared to vary his tale. He had consulted the men whom
the King had suggested, he had read all the books which they put
forward, he had pondered and prayed about the matter and he
was compelled to report his honest verdict to the King. He would
serve the King in any other way, he would never discuss the
subject, condemn the King, or try to turn others from their
allegiance, but he was unable in conscience to accept the royal
arguments. More does not quote texts or debate the subject; he
informs the King and the Council and ourselves across the
centuries that he cannot accept the validity of the King's proposed
marriage to Anne Boleyn.

As far as we can tell, More bore no grudge against Anne
Boleyn. He is ready to pray for her, he speaks kindly of her, he
wishes her well, is willing to accept her offspring if approved by
the laws of England but he cannot recognize her as Henry's
lawful wife.[46]

It would, I think, be ungenerous to Henry to deny his friendship and true affection for his old and devoted friend. They had
been together for ten years, had shared hours of intimate conversation in happier days. When the King asked More for his opinion,
he certainly wanted More to support him in his scruple and yet
was ready to allow to so honest a counsellor the liberty to speak
as he wished. More's first, unconsidered opinion was hostile but
the King only asked him to consult with Fox and to read a book,
stating the royal case. When More returned after studying the
subject, the King was plainly saddened that the servant whom he

[45] Rogers, pp. 492–500. The spelling has been modernized.
[46] Stapleton, p. 81.

so much admired should decide against his point of view. More tells us clearly that when the King made him Chancellor, he again begged him to consider the King's point. It would seem that the subject was raised between them before More accepted the seals. Yet, still, the King insisted, as he had done on previous occasions, that More must "first look to God and after God to him; which most gracious words were the first lesson also that ever His Grace gave me at my first coming to his noble service. This motion was to me very comfortable." There is little room for doubt that, on all the many occasions in which the King and More discussed the subject, the pattern remained the same. More could see no valid reason for disputing the King's marriage to Catherine and the King agreed that More must be free to follow his conscience in this great affair. No evidence of any sort exists to show that on any occasion More and Henry ever quarrelled face to face. Even when More resigned the Chancellorship, Henry not only praised and thanked him but pledged himself to stand by More in any suit.[47]

It is hardly our business here to analyse Henry's motives and behaviour; in public and in the presence of More he always behaved most courteously. With a man as just and thoughtful as More, it may not have been easy to do otherwise. The same friendliness and consideration is shown throughout his many examinations by Norfolk, Cromwell, Cranmer, Audley and the rest. More had been the friend of all, all of them knew that he was completely honest, few dared withstand him to his face. Such was his charity and virtue, that they could only stab him from behind.

With Henry, the situation was beyond control. In the first place, and though Henry never admitted the fact or showed any repentance, one senses that he never was honest enough to examine himself. After years of flattery and adulation, as with so many tyrants, he had lost this critical faculty. In a twisted way, he admitted his tragic error later by rounding on the Boleyn clique. Within a year of More's death Anne, her brother and her friend,

[47] Cf. Rogers, p. 495; Stapleton, pp. 147–151; Bridgett, p. 244.

followed by Cromwell a little later, died under the axe. As one historian remarked pointedly, the Stuarts took the blame for the misdeeds of all their henchmen, while the Tudors always found a scapegoat and were themselves never to blame.

It is difficult to read the documents of the period without forming the opinion that Henry was guilty and that, in a mad, intolerant way, he was aware of this. In cold blood—his blood was never below boiling point at the time in question—he would have agreed with More. When More was present, he was entirely reasonable, but his madness showed itself when he was by himself. In the first place, he badly needed the moral support of More's name. All the years of prayer and penance and study had given More an integrity which the Norfolks, Cranmers and Cromwells lacked. Henry knew this and the success of his cause turned on the agreement of one man. History, in fact, has supported his contention, for he is condemned today because More was on the opposing side. The execution of Cromwell, Buckingham, Surrey, Wyatt and many others may be taken now as part of the Tudor picture; he will never be forgiven for killing a man of the integrity of More.

Next, we must face the fact that the position of the King in the country at large was very uncertain and that More alone among all his immediate followers decided to resist his will. At a critical moment, the most distinguished man in England preferred to die rather than to follow him. Fisher, the Carthusians, Fr Reynolds of Sion, all made the same decision, but they were priests. Cromwell, in a sense, chose them to break the resistance of the second estate. More was Lord Chancellor, for long a privy councillor, the only Government official who dared to resist a Tudor King. It was for this reason that the various commissions stressed to More that the King had been a good master to him, had showered favours upon him, had, in fact, created him. Tyrants will normally meet a certain opposition but it is rare when a tyrant is opposed by the most distinguished of his own men. Henry, when More was not present, could not stomach this. Indeed, almost to the end, he hoped and believed that More could be won for a price. Never before or since had he met a servant who was adamant. It could well be that God led More from the Charterhouse for this only reason, that a King's servant should put God first.

Finally, we cannot exclude Anne and her clique. The King was a weak man, easily swayed by friends. Had he met More even once after the latter's imprisonment, he probably would have collapsed. With the fallen Wolsey, the Norfolk clique stood in terror lest the King should change his mind. On the one occasion when Henry met the fallen minister, he kept him talking for an hour while the opposing party bit their lips. Catherine always felt that if she could see Henry, he would once again be himself. Poor Anne in the Tower thought the same. More made no move to see Henry for he was too great to play on the generous reactions of a timid man. Anne held complete power for a spell. Henry, without any doubt, doted on her; he was carried away with that curious, middle-aged passion, not uncommon enough to merit unbelief. Middle-aged men are, in fact, overwhelmed by it. Henry's letters to Anne, the deceits which he practised for her sake, the wreck that he made of his life and of his conscience, remain as evidence that, at the time of More's challenge, Henry was not fully in control of himself. Many small incidents survive as proof of the enduring vindictiveness of the Boleyn faction; it was known in Stapleton's day that whereas Henry merely intended to keep More a prisoner in the Tower, Anne, it was, who insisted on his death. We need not accept all the posthumous stories, but two of these, however much exaggerated, emphasize the point. It was said that Henry was deeply moved when they brought him the news of More's death. He was dicing with Anne at the time. "You are the cause of this man's death," he remarked, rising, and immediately left the room to shed bitter tears. The sequel to this, from a far distant source, reports how Anne, seeing the Holbein portrait of More, opened the window and threw the painting into the street with her own hands.[48]

How far More accepted in the first place the story of Henry's scruple we cannot now tell. Knowing his charity and deep un-

[48] Stapleton, p. 212; Morison, *op. cit.*, p. 8.

derstanding, we may suppose that he took it as genuine. Though long uncertain of the King, he yet loved him and would have been the first to make allowance for religious doubts. Further, a great many sincere and learned men supported the King's view. More probably judged these doubts about the marriage to be genuine. He was also plainly touched by the King's willingness to respect his disagreement, a tolerance which went as far as entrusting him with the Chancellorship.

The constant pressure put on More by the King and his followers must surely have roused his suspicions, for any genuine acceptance of another's freedom of conscience would exclude such badgering.

In the last stages of More's life, Roper becomes our chief witness, for he alone lived in More's house, saw the Chancellor daily, and shared his anxieties. Roper reports the pressure thus:

> 1. The King, not sorry to hear it, opened it first to Sir Thomas More whose counsel he required therein; showing him certain places in Scripture that somewhat seemed to serve his appetite; which when he had perused, and thereupon as one that had never professed the study of divinity, himself excused to be unmeet many ways to meddle with such matters. The King not satisfied with this answer, so sore still pressed upon him therefore, that in conclusion he condescended to His Grace's motion. And further, forasmuch as the case was of such importance as needed great advisement and deliberation, he besought His Grace of sufficient respite advisedly to consider of it. Wherewith the King, well contented, said unto him that Tunstall and Clerk, Bishops of Durham and Bath, with other learned of his Privy Council, should also be dealers therein [49]

More returned to the King, after having studied the matter carefully in the Scriptures and the Fathers, and gave him his opinion.

> 2. To be plain with Your Grace, neither my Lord of Durham nor my Lord of Bath, though I know them both to be wise, virtuous, learned and honourable prelates, nor myself with the

[49] Roper, p. 17.

rest of your Council, being all Your Grace's own servants, for your manifold benefits daily bestowed on us so most bounden to you, be, in my judgement, meet counsellors for Your Grace herein. But if Your Grace mind to understand the truth, such counsellers may you have devised as neither for respect of their worldly commodity, nor for fear of your princely authority, will be inclined to deceive you. To whom he named then St Jerome, St Augustine and divers other old Holy Doctors, both Greeks and Latins, and moreover showed him what authorities he had gathered out of them, which although the King (as disagreeable with his desire) did not very well like of, yet were they by Sir Thomas More, who, in all his communications with the King in that matter had always most discreetly behaved himself, so wisely tempered, that he both presently took them in good part and ofttimes had thereof conference with him again.[50]

3. Now upon the coming home of the Bishop of Durham and Sir Thomas More from Cambrai, the King was earnest in persuading Sir Thomas More to agree unto the matter of his marriage as before, by many divers ways provoking him thereunto. For the which cause, as it was thought, he the rather soon after made him lord chancellor. . . . yet there was another thing found out of late, he said, whereby his marriage appeared to be so directly against the law of nature that it could in no wise by the Church be dispensable, as Dr. Stokesley (whom he then preferred to be Bishop of London, and in that case chiefly credited) was able to instruct him with whom he prayed him in that point to confer.[51]

4. But for all his conference with him, he saw nothing of such force as could induce him to change his opinion therein. . . .

5. Of the cardinal, whom His Highness therefore soon after of his office displaced and to Sir Thomas More, the rather to remove him to incline to his side, the same in his stead committed.[52]

6. Now shortly upon his entry into the office of the chancellorship, the King yet oftsoons again moved him to weigh and consider his great matter, who falling down upon his knees

[50] *Ibid.*, pp. 17–18.   [51] *Ibid.*, p. 19.   [52] *Ibid.*, p. 20.

humbly besought His Highness to stand his gracious Sovereign, as ever since his entry into His Grace's service had found him, saying there was nothing in the world had been so grievous unto his heart as to remember that he was not able as he willingly would with the loss of one of his limbs, or for that matter anything to find whereby he could with his conscience, safely serve His Grace's contention, as he that always bare in his mind the most Godly words that his Highness spake unto him at his first coming into his noble service, the most virtuous lesson that ever Prince taught his servant, willing him first to look unto God and after God to him, as, in good faith, he said he did, or else might His Grace well account him his most unworthy servant. To this the King answered, that if he could not therein with his conscience serve him, he was content to accept his service otherwise, and using the advice of other of his learned Council whose consciences could well enough agree therewith, would nevertheless continue his gracious favour towards him.[53]

It would seem from this final passage that the King now finally knew that he would never change the Chancellor while More knew that he could not continue in office any more. To his conscience, the duties of the office proved embarrassing. Thus he had to announce to the Lords and Commons the findings of the Universities on the subject of the King's marriage and to proclaim that the King was pursuing the subject from a scruple of conscience and not because he was in love with any other lady. Again, a petition was to be sent to the Pope, signed by all the leading people, and More could not bring himself to sign.

He resigned the Chancellorship on the plea of ill health, "for he was troubled with a disease in his breast, which continued with him many months, after he consulted with the physicians, who made him further answer that long diseases were dangerous, adding further that his disease could not shortly be helped, but by a little and little, with continuance of long time, by rest, good diet and physic and yet could they not appoint any certain time when he should recover or be quite rid and cured". More persuaded

[53] *Ibid.*, p. 25.

the Duke of Norfolk to place his resignation before the King. It was granted with a special show of friendliness. Yet few were fooled by this. More's friends all knew the reason for his resignation, though they admit that his illness was not merely a pretence. The Imperial Envoy reported exactly on the matter: "The chancellor has resigned, seeing that affairs were going so badly and likely to be worse and that if he retained office, he would be obliged to act against his conscience or incur the King's displeasure, as he had already begun to do, for refusing to take his part against the clergy. His excuse was that his salary was too small and that he was not equal to the work. Everyone is concerned for there never was a better man in the office."[54]

More delivered the seals into the hands of the King at Whitehall on 16th May, 1532.

We may conclude this account of More's service at Court—his career was finished with his resignation—with the mention of two gestures which show the courage of the man. First, immediately after his resignation he drew up the famous epitaph to be erected in Chelsea parish church. He did this, we know, to silence gossip and malicious rumours that he had been dismissed. Stories were going around that he was a disloyal servant who had abused the King's friendship and More was determined, even at the risk of appearing conceited, that the full story of his service to his King and country should be proclaimed. For once he blew his own trumpet, "not so much in regard to himself or his own estimation as to God's cause and religion", which might be impaired if it was noised about that he had been dismissed through his own fault.[55]

Secondly—one of the bravest acts of his life—he refused, a month after his resignation, to attend the coronation of Anne Boleyn. We may still read the golden accounts of this spectacular occasion, the bands, the barges, the great city men all dressed in scarlet, Anne carried through the city, seated in a litter "covered with cloth of gold shot with white". At Cheapside Cross stood all

[54] Harpsfield, p. 87; Stapleton, pp. 78–80; Bridgett, p. 240.
[55] Harpsfield, pp. 87–88.

the aldermen, at the conduit "was a rich pageant and Pallas, Venus and Juno handed Anne an apple made of gold". The conduit in Cheapside ran at one end white wine, at the other claret, all that afternoon.

More was invited to attend. The bishops of Winchester, Bath and Durham not only begged him to ride with them in the procession but, knowing his poverty after leaving office, offered him £20 to fit himself out. For a man in his position to miss such a function, especially on such an occasion, might well prove a fatal step. Yet More stayed away. He could not do what to him would be treachery. In place, he told the bishops a long and slightly inelegant story and ended with a remark which still carries a note of challenge:

"It lies not in my power but that they may devour me, but God being my good Lord, I will provide that they shall never deflower me."[56]

[56] Roper, p. 29.

CHAPTER SEVEN

Tragedy and Triumph

I. TRAGEDY

THE STORY OF More's death need not be recounted here. Few incidents in Tudor history have been more fully reported or better described. Eyewitnesses, hostile and friendly, saw More in the Tower, stood in Westminster Hall to hear his condemnation, followed his slow progress towards the scaffold on Tower Hill. Each new biographer quotes from the letters which he wrote in prison, letters as beautiful as any known to literature. More's masterly defence at his trial has been the subject of a recent study in which every detail of his death and burial is also supplied. Professor Chambers, too, in his great biography, has weighed up More's success and failure in paragraphs which, surely, will never be excelled. The facts are all known and may never now be altered; any change must be a change in ourselves.[1]

Should anyone ask why such a change is needed, his question would be answered by two others, for how are we to explain the fact that only two public men in England were prepared to make a stand against such unparalleled corruption and that the noblest figure in our history remained forgotten for three hundred and fifty years after his death? Only at the turn of the nineteenth century did More begin to come into his own. Millions of Englishmen had hardly heard his name when Robert Bolt with his powerful play *Man for All Seasons* drew and held such impressive audiences. Now, at last, and all of a sudden, the English-speaking nations are beginning to grasp the greatness of this forgotten English-speaking saint.

[1] Reynolds, *The Trial of St Thomas More*; Chambers, pp. 360–371.

As the prejudice of the Reformation fades and men cease to think in terms of Protestant v. Catholic, More's courage and integrity may be more easily recognized and shared. Partisan spirit should have no place. He was not killed by Protestants. Nor did he lay down his life in support of a Roman Catholic party, for he died before the iron curtain divided Christendom into warring camps. Before Luther's name was ever heard in England, More had stated the dilemma which the men of his decade would have to face. Discussing the arguments for avoiding public life, he wrote (and I have here modernized his English): "Either I must hold differently from the crowd and then it would be safer for me to say nothing or I must hold with them and thus help to further their madness."[2]

It was sheer madness in this particular case. The marriage between Henry and Anne was already falling to pieces when More stood his trial in Westminster Hall. The Act of Succession, to be supported by oath, establishing the rights of Anne's children was a dead letter within a few months of More's death. Not only was the Act dead but Anne herself had been two months in her dishonoured grave in the Tower of London chapel when More's friends kept the first anniversary of his martyrdom. The girl who caused the death of the two noblest men of their generation survived them a little over ten months.

The collapse of the much vaunted marriage which had rocked Europe took few wise men by surprise. English comment is slight because Englishmen at this time were far too frightened to commit themselves to paper, but the crowds had their jokes at the expense of the royal mistress while naughty pictures of Henry and Anne were popular on the Continent. On the other hand, so observant if prejudiced a witness as Chapuys, the Imperial envoy, could report home, six months after More's execution, that the King had spoken to Anne not more than ten times in four months. Stories leaked out that he had shouted at her after her miscarriage and Chapuys could remark that he would have divorced her long before only he did not want to play into the hands of the Pope.

[2] *Utopia*, p. 49. More is quoting Terence.

Anne's days were already numbered when More and Fisher died.[3]

When, finally, she was arrested and lodged in the Tower, she was accused of misconduct over many years. The King himself declared in private that as many as a hundred gentlemen were involved. Both King and Queen were so utterly untruthful that we will never now know where the truth lies. Henry, with tears in his eyes, told his bastard son, the Duke of Richmond, how Anne had planned to poison him. She was charged with incest and adultery.

Another more trivial but significant charge against her was that she had mocked the King with her friends, had joked about his clothing and had declared that he was impotent. Indeed it was asserted that various clerics of the progressive type had justified her seeking pleasure elsewhere because of her husband's deficiency. How far such gossip was true cannot now be ascertained. The scandals were certainly reported and show the kind of world which contrived More's death. Part hysterical, part contrite, mainly innocent, in her last days devout in her religious practice, Anne went to her death. Two of her set, Norris and her brother, were also killed. When More spoke to Meg about Anne Boleyn as they sat in his cell in the Tower, his kindly words, "It pitieth me to remember into what misery poor soul she shall shortly come" were, maybe, based on first rather than on second sight.[4]

The years of profligacy at Court which brought Anne to the scaffold played havoc with Henry too. A habit already mentioned is often repeated, and we find the King cutting all business and retiring to hunt for a whole month. Chapuys reports when More was still alive that though the King put a bold face on things in public, "inwardly, as I have already hinted, he is very far from being pleased and seems agitated and thoughtful". On several occasions we hear of the King being in tears. His is a tragic case for secretly he loved his daughter Mary whom now by his own folly he could not see. He appears in the documents as touchy,

---

[3] *Calendar of State Papers (Spanish)*, Vol. 5, Part 2, N. 29.
[4] *Ibid.*, N. 54; Roper, p. 38.

self-pitying, righteous, utterly lacking in self-control. While Anne lay in the Tower awaiting execution, he was out each day dining with women and was seen cruising down the river, reading his own verses to the accompaniment of the Tudor equivalent of our modern guitar. His child by Anne was now said to have been sired by Norris, and on the day before her execution Anne was taken to Lambeth to face her old friend Cranmer and to hear her marriage with Henry declared null. Just three years before, at Dunstable, this same Cranmer had nullified Henry's first marriage on the same grounds. The King's scruple about marrying his brother's widow had now been extended to entangle his second Queen. As Anne's sister Mary had once been his mistress, his scruple, deftly adjusted by a subservient Primate, proved useful once again. Henry's scruple did not prevent him from sending Sir Francis Bryan posthaste to alert Jane Seymour. On the day following Anne's execution, Henry, with a group of flattering courtiers around him, married for the third time.[5]

Anne, her brother George, Norris her friend, Catherine of Aragon, Thomas More and John Fisher all died within twelve months.

One would have preferred not to discredit Henry whom More loved and served so faithfully. Yet, without some appreciation of the King's moral squalor, it is hard to assess our national cowardice. This evil man, by any standards an adulterer and not squeamish about murder, decided to declare himself the supreme head of the English Church. The famous oath which Fisher and More refused but to which bishops, priests, courtiers subscribed with astonishing expedition, must be regarded as one of the most diabolical jokes in our long history.

The image of Hitler flits across the mind as one reads of Henry, for though the two tyrants were so different, they neither could have achieved their evil mastery without compromise, subservience and corruption on a national scale. Henry's world was trivial when set beside Hitler's, but evil is evil in any century and any country and its methods are invariably the same. England was

[5] *Spanish Papers*, N. 54; Strickland, *op. cit.* passim.

ruled by fear. Reported Chapuys: "At present, it is true, the people are kept with so tight a hand and in such fear that no one, great or small, dare say a word of complaint but when the opportunity comes their real feeling will show itself." Vives, who escaped to Bruges, wrote to Erasmus while More was lying in the Tower: "One can neither speak nor be silent without danger." Secret police, spies, informers made their appearance and the State Papers abound in cases of men being made to answer to every kind of trumped-up charge. More had, thus, the added sorrow of knowing that his family would be molested in his place. After he was dead, Meg was summoned before the Council on the charge of hiding his papers, his son John went to prison, his son-in-law Giles Heron was hanged at Tyburn for "sundry detestable and abominable treasons" five years after More's death.[6]

The simple, ordinary folk whom More so loved, whom he knew so well, whose hard lot in life he so well described in *Utopia*, cannot be held responsible. They lived in ignorance, were neither heeded nor consulted, lacked sufficient power to assert themselves. They were the victims of a conspiracy which turned into a system and held them bound for centuries. Alone among the intellectuals, More voiced their cause. Nor did they lack all courage, for their jokes, their lampoons, their affectionate applause for Queen Catherine embarrassed the Government. The Pilgrimage of Grace, the one forlorn revolt against a tyrant, was inspired by the anger of poor men. They shouted against Cromwell and Rich, and as they straggled south, demanded for these two wicked men a suitable punishment.

Reginald Pole, a clever man, then living in exile, knew well the sentiments of London when he penned this tribute to the memory of More:

> O City of London, you saw led out from prison on a charge of treason the man at whose tribunal you had so lately beheld others standing for a similar crime; the man whom you had known as a boy, a youth, and whom you had marked in later life as, amid the applause and congratulations of all, he mounted

[6] *Spanish Papers*, Vol. 5, Part 1, p. 130; *Letters and Papers*, Vol. 7, N. 635.

through every grade of honour until he reached the very highest office. And because he was your citizen and child, not without a secret sense of joy, you beheld his prosperous career tending always to your own praise and honour. You saw him at last led out a criminal from prison in sordid dress and grown old, not by lapse of years but by the squalor and suffering of his dungeon, and, for the first time you beheld his head made white by long confinement; you saw his weak and broken body leaning on a staff and even so scarcely able to stand and dragged along the way that led to the place of trial or, rather, of certain condemnation. Could you see this spectacle with dry eyes?

Pole had been the friend of More and the friend of Henry; his was a frightening decision for his mother had to pay for his defiance with her life.[7]

No, cowardice was not the sin of the poor but of the monied classes, of the sycophants "who do shamefully and flatteringly give assent to the fond and foolish sayings of great men". Of those who tendered the oath to More, Cranmer was to assert that one should follow the King's command in any doubt of conscience; Audley was to say of More to Alice Middleton, "I would not have your father so scrupulous of his conscience"; Norfolk warned More that the wrath of kings meant death and received the perfect answer, "then in faith there is no more difference between your Grace and me but that I shall die today and you tomorrow".

What arrant cowards they all proved to be. Norfolk presided at the court which condemned Anne, his niece, to death; the Earl of Wiltshire, her father, anticipated no embarrassment in seeing his son and daughter sentenced, Bryan picked a timely quarrel with George Boleyn and was, thus, able to help in his cousin's degradation and to enjoy the royal favour for many more years. Bryan's reputation for dissolute living was so notorious that even Cromwell could refer to him as "the Vicar of Hell". What did it matter? Cromwell himself was to be the next to go to the scaffold,

---

[7] Pole's appeal to London, cf. Reynolds, *St Thomas More*, p. 362.

making at the end a speech worthy of a Russian in the age of
Stalin, "I am by law condemned to die; I have offended my
Prince, for which I ask him heartily forgiveness". His friend
Richard Rich was the chief prosecution witness at Cromwell's
trial.

When we meet Richard Rich, we are forced to wonder whether
More made a mistake when he chose to serve the King of England
instead of following Hythloday to Utopia. The wickedness of
Henry and the corruption of the Court is seen most fully in this
despicable man. Here is the only man whom More publicly
attacked. So great was his charity that we search in vain through
his words and writings for any bitter, personal invective against
his enemies. More always spoke kindly of Anne, he loved Henry,
never criticized the actions of men like Tunstall, implied no condemnation of Norfolk, Audley, FitzJames, Cranmer, who played
their mean little parts in his death. Only once did he call up his
unparalleled gifts as an advocate to crush an individual and this
in his trial when he came face to face with Rich. For Rich came
from the same London parish as More himself, had used his
friends for his own promotion, betrayed each one in turn to
curry favour and build a prosperous career on perjury. Rich had
been knighted and appointed Solicitor General in the previous
year. He served Henry by entering into private confidential
conversation with the King's victims and then betraying them
publicly. His first recorded perjury was in the trial of John Fisher
and, after speaking secretly with More in the Tower, he appeared
again as the only witness against the ex-Chancellor.

Few men in history have been publicly discredited in so sharp a
way. Hearing the perjury of this unworthy man and goaded by
the shame thus brought on his own honourable profession, More
challenged Rich to his face:

> If I were a man, my Lords, that did not regard an oath, I
> needed not, as is well known in this place, at this time or in
> any case to stand here as an accused person. And if this oath of
> yours, Master Rich, be true, then, pray I that I never see God
> in the face, which I would not say, were it otherwise, to win

the world. . . . In good faith, Master Rich, I am sorrier for your perjury than for mine own peril. And you shall understand that neither I nor any man else to my knowledge, ever took you to be a man of credit as in any matter of importance, I, or any other, would at any time vouchsafe to communicate with you. And I, as you know, of no small while have been acquainted with you and your conversation, who have known you from your youth hitherto; for we long dwelled both in one parish together, where, as yourself can well tell (I am sorry you compel me so to say) you were esteemed very light of your tongue, a common liar, a great dicer and of no commendable fame. And so in your house at the Temple, where hath been your chief bringing up, were you likewise accounted. . . .[8]

Here was More's agony. He, the most distinguished lawyer in the land, a man who loved the poor, who had served the King and London so faithfully, had to sit in Westminster Hall and watch while Audley and FitzJames for their own safety accepted against him the perjury of a man like Rich. Not one of them was fooled, not one of them believed Rich against Fisher or More or any other of his victims, but they were all compelled to ascribe to Norfolk's cliché "the wrath of the King means death".

More died and Richard Rich marched on to fame. As Speaker of the House of Commons in 1536, he, in a speech, compared Henry to Solomon for justice, Samson for strength, Absalom for beauty; he saw him as the bright sun withering the weeds. This London boy from the same parish as More, of the same Mercers' Company, exactly followed More's successful public career. In due course he was appointed Chancellor. As his biographers record, he played an active part in destroying Wolsey, Fisher, More, Cromwell, the Dukes of Somerset and Northumberland. He persecuted Catholics and Protestants as occasion offered and grew wealthy from his share of the monastic lands. When Mary Tudor rode into London as Queen, Richard Rich and his wife were there to welcome her. We find him busy in old age restoring the

[8] Roper, p. 43.

old faith in Essex, beautifying the church at Felsted and setting aside money for Masses to be said for his soul. He had the blood of two saints for which to atone.

Unscrupulous as was Rich, his perfidy did not take Thomas More by surprise. Men of the class of Rich and Cromwell paid only lip service to religion while manipulating the King's passion so as to get a grip on the monastic lands. The behaviour of the churchmen comes as a shock to us. The bishops and abbots were devout men—many of them of exceptional talent—all of them friends who had loved More and shared his views. Except for Cranmer, few of the Church party were fooled. The King's men expected resistance from the bishops and plans were made to commit some of them to jail. Such preparations proved unnecessary. Perhaps the saddest case for More was that of Cuthbert Tunstall, More's most intimate friend. These two had worked together for nearly twenty years. They shared two diplomatic missions and Tunstall was with him when More wrote his *Utopia*. Tunstall dedicated his book to More, and More, possibly to protect Tunstall, proudly proclaimed their friendship in his epitaph.

With Erasmus and Bonvisi, Tunstall was a lifelong friend. Perhaps More loved him best for the two had most in common, especially in the last ten years. They shared a common anxiety for the future of the English Church, discussed together the King's marriage scruples at the King's request. Tunstall was known as a Queen's man, had been assigned to her defence at the Legatine court at Blackfriars; one may feel a slight surprise that Henry should have picked on him to give More advice. It was Tunstall who commissioned More to write his great controversial books in defence of the Church. Yet, he also invited More to the coronation of Anne Boleyn.

It seems clear from the State Papers that many people expected Tunstall to refuse the oath. Henry was afraid of his opposition and for a time confined him to his diocese. When he was finally called to Court, the royal bailiffs entered his house in his absence and made an inventory of his effects. Chapuys, who reports the fact, clearly took it as a threat. The Imperial envoy describes Tunstall as "one of the most learned, prudent and honest prelates in the kingdom and has, hitherto, upheld the Queen's cause by his words as well as by his writings".

Tunstall took the oath. While John Hussy could write to Lord Lisle, "Most part of the City was sworn to the King and legitimate offspring by the Queen; it is thought that Tunstall will be arrested", Chapuys, the Queen's most devoted adherent, tells the final story bitterly:

"Not choosing to become a martyr and lose such ecclesiastical benefice as his, bringing him 15,000 ducats annually, he has been obliged to swear like the rest though under certain reserves and restrictions to satisfy, as he thinks, his conscience."[9]

Poor Tunstall was like his fly in amber and took the oath. Once he had taken it " he began to say in public that the statute was a most considerate and well established act for the quietness of this Kingdom". We last see Tunstall down at Buckden with Archbishop Leigh, another of More's great friends. The two were trying to persuade poor Catherine of Aragon to take the oath in her supplanter's favour but here they met more than their match. When they threatened her, Catherine answered at once that she was ready to die at any moment. Her magnificent statement, "I ask only that I may be allowed to die in the sight of the people", defeated them.

Chapuys gives his impression in a vivid sentence; after remarking that Leigh and Tunstall looked quite pleased to hear their arguments refuted the ambassador adds, "they were obliged to stifle the truth and yet look approvingly on the occasion".[10]

So Tunstall took the oath and passed out of More's life. More seems to have made but one comment on his friend and that in a message which he sent from the Tower when Burton, one of the bishop's servants, called on him. More asked Burton how his master was and whether he was likely to join them in the Tower and when Burton replied that he did not know his master's

---

[9] *State Papers (Spanish)*, Vol. 5, p. 159.
[10] *Ibid.*, p. 159; Mattingly, pp. 279–280.

mind on the matter, More said, "If he do not, no matter, for if he live he may do more good than to die with us".

How did More feel about this desertion by his friends? He differed from Catherine, from Chapuys, from Harpsfield, Stapleton, Roper and the later biographers in refusing to attribute personal blame. Indeed, apart from his attack on Richard Rich, he was totally unwilling to imply bad motives to any of his former friends. From his letters in the Tower we may see that he still regarded Audley and Cromwell as his benefactors and nursed no grievance even against the King. Such an astonishing attitude was in no sense artificial, an attempt to forgive his enemies for Christ's sake. He never thought or spoke in terms of enemies and, as he said at the end of his trial in a famous passage, he sincerely hoped to meet them all in heaven again:

> More I have not to say, My Lords, but that like the Blessed Apostle Paul, as we read in the Acts of the Apostles, was present and consented to the death of St Stephen and kept their clothes that stoned him to death, and yet be they now both twain holy saints in heaven and shall continue there friends forever, so I verily trust and shall therefore right heartily pray that though your Lordships have now here in earth been judges to my condemnation, we may yet hereafter in heaven merrily all meet together to our everlasting salvation.[11]

More died as he had lived, without resentment or enmity. Yet there is no room to doubt that he was both saddened and indignant that Christian men could behave so shortsightedly. The indignation and sarcasm which marks the opening pages of *Utopia* is still heard in the Tower in his words to his daughter: "And surely, daughter, it is a great pity that any Christian prince should, by a flexible council ready to follow his affections and by a weak clergy lacking grace constantly to stand to their learning, with flattery be so shamefully abused."[12]

By the time that More went to the Tower, he stood entirely alone. Gone were the days when he could consult Colet, Lillie

[11] Roper, p. 47.   [12] Roper, p. 38.

or Erasmus; his intimate circle of friends had dissolved for good. His beloved Meg took the oath to the King and tried hard to persuade him to follow her example, while Dame Alice could write in a letter of him that he suffered from "a long continued and deep-rooted scruple as passeth his power to avoid or to put away". Just before the news of his execution was known abroad, Erasmus also made an unsympathetic judgement in a letter: "Would that he had never embroiled himself in this perilous business and had left theological questions to the theologians." More certainly discussed the papal supremacy and other points with Antonio Bonvisi but not with any hope of explaining his own attitude.

Six brave men opposed the King with him and died for their principles. More must have known the three Carthusian priors, though none of them were monks at the Charterhouse during his stay. He was intimate with Richard Reynolds and with John Fisher over many years. All three were great scholars and Henry was, in fact, challenged by the three most learned men in the England of that day. But More seems to have made no great effort to consult with these two fellow martyrs, indeed he appears anxious not to involve himself in any way. One of the very few times when he sounded mildly indignant even with Margaret was when it was suggested that he was following Fisher's example in resisting the King. More's reply is interesting as a comment on the situation in which he found himself. He said to Meg:

For whereas you told me right now that such as love me would not advise me that against all other men, I should lean unto his mind alone, verily daughter, no more I do. For albeit, that of very truth I have him [Fisher] in the reverent estimation that I reckon in this realm no one man, in wisdom, learning and long approved virtue together meet to be matched and compared with him, yet that in this matter I was not led by him, very well and plainly appeareth, both in that I refused the oath before it was offered to him and in that also his lordship was content to have sworn to that oath (as I perceived since by you when you moved me to the same) either somewhat more or in some other manner than ever I minded to do. Verily, daughter, I never intend (God being my Lord) to pin my soul at another man's back not even the best man that I know this day living; for I know not whither he may chance to carry it. There is no man living of whom, while he liveth, I may make myself sure. Some may do for favour, and some may do for fear and so might carry my soul the wrong way. And some might hap to frame himself a conscience and think that while he did it for fear, God would forgive it. And some may, peradventure, think that they will repent and be shriven thereof and that so God shall remit it them. And some may be, peradventure, of that mind that if they say one thing and think the while the contrary, God more regardeth their heart than their tongue and that therefore their oath goeth upon what they think and not upon what they say. ... But in good faith, Margaret, I can use no such ways in so great a matter, but like as if my conscience served me, I would not let to do it, though other men refused, so though other refuse it or not, I dare not do it, mine own conscience standing against it.[13]

2. TRIUMPH

The last phase of our story may be quickly told. More triumphed but only after two years of anguish which exacted from him physically a terrifying toll.

Always an apprehensive man, gazing far ahead and examining both sides of every question, he must have known well enough when he retired to Chelsea just how his life might end. His objections to the second marriage had not been kept secret, indeed he had told the King to his face. At the time, the deep affection between them had seemed sufficient and Henry had graciously agreed to tolerate his scruple and to let him depart in peace. The King was genuinely sorry to lose him and not only praised the outgoing Chancellor but declared that he would welcome him back to his service again. For his part More fully intended to quit public life, to keep his own counsel, to avoid all controversy. The epitaph which he planned would serve as a cover for this escape.

[13] Margaret Roper to Alice Alington, Rogers, p. 514.

His immediate preoccupation after his retirement was to clear his name. The Continent abounded with rumours that he had been disgraced. Erasmus wrote, both puzzled and worried, and More sent him a copy of the epitaph. He charged his old friend to make the news public that he had retired freely owing to ill-health. At home, More avoided all contact with any faction, rejecting alike the money offered by the bishops and the protection of the Emperor Charles V. He begged Chapuys "for the honour of God" not to visit him or to allow the Emperor to write. Any such letter from the Emperor he would take straight to the King.

He had also to clear his name of other malicious charges brought by his enemies. Few seriously believed that More had accepted bribes in return for favours, but the Earl of Wiltshire and the Boleyn faction wanted to. More's scrupulous honesty over so many years not only saved him but made his antagonists look ridiculous. The accusation of cruelty to heretics could also be brushed aside. More quitted public life with a reputation rarely if ever equalled in English history.

He retired to Chelsea and there lived in poverty for two years. His household economies have been described. He found homes for all his servants, divided up his property among his children, consoled Dame Alice on her painful loss of money and dignity. He seems to have fulfilled few public engagements, visited few friends, written few letters save two or three to Erasmus and a long and beautiful defence of the Blessed Eucharist for John Frith. We know that Father Risby, a Franciscan, stayed a night with More at Chelsea, that More went over to Syon Abbey and spoke to the fathers at the grille. He spent most of his time at home and in the New Building, leading his Carthusian life again.[14]

The famous epitaph, still to be seen at Chelsea, exactly describes his state of mind. After honouring his father, listing the offices which both had held, praising Tunstall, More sums up his ambitions thus:

[14] More to Frith, Rogers, pp. 439 seq.

He therefore irked and weary of worldly business, giving up his promotions, obtained at last by the incomparable benefits of his most gentle prince, if it please God to favour his enterprise, the thing from which as a child in a manner always he had wished and desired, that he might have some years of his life free, in which, little and little, withdrawing himself from the business of this life, might continually remember the immortality of the life to come. And he hath caused this tomb to be made for himself, his first wife's bones hither too, that might every day put him in memory of death that never ceases to creep on him. And that this tomb made for him in his lifetime be not in vain, nor that he fear death coming upon him, but that he may willingly for the desire of Christ, die and find death not utterly death to him but the gate of a wealthier life, help him, I beseech you, good reader, now with your prayers while he liveth and when he is dead also.[15]

This is an astonishing testimonial. We have his whole life in stone, the Barge, the Four Last Things, the Court, the King, his deep longing for the contemplative vocation and, both in the spirit and the style of writing, More's desperate desire to escape.

More wanted to hide. It was not that he doubted his position but that he could not feel sure of himself. He was clear in his attitude to the Royal Supremacy and to the marriage with Anne, for this had been reached over years of study; he could quote the Fathers, his greatest prop, to justify his stand. It did not much trouble him that all the most learned in the land would not agree with his opinion; when Meg in the Tower urged just this in an effort to persuade him, he disposed of her arguments easily.[16] Nor, after so many years of meditation, was he afraid of death. His great doubt lay much deeper than physical panic; he was desperately doubtful about his own strength. Spiritually More had the lowest opinion of himself. He felt that it would be presumption on his part to step forward as a candidate for martyrdom. So severe was his judgement of his past, so unsure his trust in his present determination, so insecure his hope that God

---

[15] The epitaph is given in Rastell's Works. Here quoted from Bridgett, p. 251.
[16] Margaret Roper to Alice Alington, Rogers, pp. 514 seq.

would sustain a sinner of his type if he put himself forward, that he decided to dodge the issue and to hide himself. Hence the restless weary nights, hence the epitaph, the hope expressed in stone that he might be overlooked, forgotten, finally buried quietly in his newly purchased vault.

We may gather the strain which he endured spiritually by the sudden collapse of his physical health. He had retained his good looks and good health until he was over fifty; only one bout of illness, a tertian ague, is recorded throughout this span of years. After his retirement, his health rapidly declined. The complaint in his chest proved painful, and, as he tells Erasmus, he only went to the doctor "when it had plagued me without abatement for some months". One may sense his anxiety in this further note: "I suffer less in present pain than in fear of the consequence."

By the time that he reached the Tower of London, he was physically a wreck. He wrote: "I have, since I came in the Tower, looked once or twice to have given up my Ghost ere this; and in good faith mine heart waxed the lighter with the hope thereof." He described himself in the *Dialogue of Comfort* as a candle, spluttering before being finally snuffed. Meg, when she visited him, found that as well as the pain in his chest he was also troubled "by reason of gravel and stone and of cramp also that divers nights grippeth him in the legs". That More was not imagining these illnesses may be seen by Pole's account. In his appeal to London, already quoted, Pole paints a true but pathetic picture of More's decline. As he went to his trial and to execution, he could only move slowly with a stick. His hair was white and he found it difficult to stand. More was but fifty-seven when he died. His favourite meditations in the Tower turned on the sufferings of Christ in the agony of the garden; if we read them we see, too, what More endured.[17]

More would have chosen the contemplative life as an escape from martyrdom with the qualifying condition set out in his epitaph, "if it please God to favour his enterprise". God saw things otherwise. So, therefore, did the King, the Boleyns, the Council

[17] *Ibid.*

who could not suffer the passive resistance of so famous and holy a man. More was the only layman in the country whose support Henry had to have. If the world of scholars and statesmen, if the monks and bishops knew that More was not in favour of the King's new powers, the Tudor despot would lose face. All despots eventually are driven to persecuting the just. So began a series of rumours, suspicions, investigations, unnamed charges which must have made clear to More that he could not escape. His nephew Rastell was questioned about a book which attacked the King. It was suspected that More was the anonymous author but he was able to answer convincingly. Next came the Holy Maid of Kent, a brave but unbalanced nun, who condemned the King's licentiousness publicly. The Government suspected that both More and Fisher were behind her in a resistance which was judged treasonable. Again More was able, with greater effort, to prove his innocence. We now know that he escaped arrest because the Council feared his reputation and thought it better to wait for a less doubtful issue on which to challenge him. Audley, Cromwell and the others persuaded Henry to yield in this. Such was the ex-Chancellor's reputation that a Tudor was forced to take account of it.[18]

Henry may have been forced to yield to More but More in his turn made great concessions to Henry; in the last few months of his anguish he was painfully anxious to please. He would go to the limit permitted by his conscience to pacify the King. He wrote to the Maid of Kent begging her to be prudent and not to involve him, he wrote two long letters to Cromwell justifying his behaviour, in one of which there was a note of pleading, not characteristic of More. Most astonishing of all is More's last letter to the King. If he does not retract in any way, he yet seeks to win Henry in language which sounds astonishing now. He writes to Cromwell: "So am I he that among other of his Grace's faithful subjects, his Highness being in possession of his marriage and this noble woman really anointed Queen, neither murmur at it, nor dispute upon it nor never did nor will but, without any other manner

[18] Roper, p. 35.

meddling of the matter among his faithful subjects, faithfully pray to God for his Grace and hers both, long to live and well, and their noble issue too, in such wise as may be to the pleasure of God, honour and surety to themselves, rest, peace, wealth and profit unto this noble realm." Clearly there is no word in this or indeed in any of More's letters to suggest that he is wavering, but the language is very different from the earlier statement on Anne's coronation, "they may devour me but I will provide that they shall never deflower me".[19]

Let me quote here the passage from More's meditations on the Passion which Fr Bridgett also inserts in his narrative at this point. Written soon after the struggle with himself was over, it most perfectly describes More's attitude. He has been talking of the brave martyrs of old who gladly and freely went forward to their death. Now suddenly he turns to his own case:

> But yet God of his infinite mercy doth not require us to take upon us this most high degree of stout courage which is so full of hardness and difficulty. And therefore I would not advise every man at adventure rashly to run forth so far forward that he shall not be able fair and softly to come back again, but unless he can attain to climb up to the hill-top, be haply in hazard to tumble down even to the bottom headlong. Let them yet whom God especially calleth thereunto, set forth in God's name and proceed and they shall reign. But yet, before a man falleth in trouble, fear is not greatly to be discommended, and so that reason be always ready to resist and master fear, the conflict is then no sin nor offence at all but rather a great matter of merit. ... Unto one that were likely to be in such a case, Christ saith "Pluck up thy courage, faint heart; what though thou be fearful, sorry and weary and standest in great dread of most painful torments, be of good comfort; for I myself have vanquished the whole world and yet felt I far more fear, sorrow, weariness and much more inward anguish too, when I considered my most bitter, painful Passion to press so fast upon me. He that is strong-hearted may find a thousand glorious, valiant martyrs whose example he may right joyously follow. But

[19] Rogers, pp. 480–490.

thou now, O timorous and weak silly sheep, think it sufficient for thee only to walk after me which am thy Shepherd and Governor, and to mistrust thyself and put thy trust in Me. Take hold of the hem of my garment therefore; from hence shalt thou perceive strength and relief to proceed."[20]

It should be encouraging to us to grasp that More, after so many years of prayer and penance, so great fidelity, so much love, so earnest a desire to Godward, came to the full understanding of trust in God only at this point. One cannot pinpoint the precise moment when he "took hold of the hem of Christ's garment" but it must surely have occurred somewhere on the Thames, as he went in his barge to Lambeth for the first time to face the Commissioners. For when the Commissioners Norfolk, Cranmer and Cromwell spoke to him of the favours which the King had granted him, More was in complete agreement; when they turned to the anger of the King and to the punishments which he would impose on those who resisted, More suddenly found himself. "My Lords," said he, "these terrors be arguments for children and not for me."

It was after these bold words had been said that More returned home so merry, having given the devil so foul a fall that without great shame he could never go back.

His progress was relatively simple after that. It certainly broke his heart to part from his wife and children, and for that one, agonizing moment, he could not bear to have them with him on the landing-stage. Yet, on what should have been the saddest and most agonizing day of his life, he speedily recovered his humour, a humour sadly strained in the last few worrying years. He sent to Meg a long and detailed account of the second session at Lambeth in which he was sent into the garden to think things over, after he had refused to take the oath. More is back to his Utopian form:

I was in conclusion commanded to go down into the garden. And thereupon I tarried in the old burned chamber that looketh into the garden and would not go down because of the heat.

[20] Cf. Bridgett, p. 352.

In that time I saw Master Doctor Latimer come into the garden
and there walked he with divers other doctors and chaplains
of my Lord of Canterbury. And very merry I saw him, for he
laughed and took one or twain about the neck so handsomely,
that if they had been women I would have weened he had been
waxing wanton. After that came Master Doctor Wilson forth
from the Lords and was with two gentlemen brought by me
and gentlemanly sent straight unto the Tower. What time my
Lord of Rochester was called before them that can I not tell.
But at night I heard that he had been before them but where he
remained that night, and so forth till he was sent thither, I
never heard. I heard also that the Master Vicar of Croydon and
all the remnant of the priests of London that were sent for, were
sworn; and that they had such favour at the Council's hand
that they were not lingered or made to dance any long atten-
dance to their travail and cost as suitors were sometimes wont
to be, but were sped apace to their great comfort; so far forth
that the Master Vicar of Croydon either for gladness or for
dryness or else that it might be seen *quod ille notus erat pontifici*,
went to my Lord's buttery bar and called for a drink and drank,
valde familiariter. When they had played their pageant and were
gone out of the place, then was I called in again.[21]

More was lodged in the Tower of London for nearly fifteen
months. Tradition used to favour the Beauchamp Tower, today
they show you his cell in the Bell Tower, but neither choice is
supported by hard fact. We know for certain that he and Meg
watched the Carthusians going to martyrdom from the window
of his cell. It would seem, too, that he was imprisoned near to
John Fisher, and that both, as prisoners of importance, would
have been placed somewhere in the vicinity of the King's House.
Cardinal Pole is exaggerating when he describes More as looking
old and ill "not by the lapse of years but by the squalor and
sufferings of his dungeon", for both Meg and her stepmother on
their visits to him found him tolerably comfortable. He himself
described his cell as "a chamber meetly fair and, at leastwise, it was
strong enough". By the use of straw mats on the floor and round

[21] Rogers, More to Margaret Roper, p. 501.

the walls, he was able to keep the cold from his feet. Fisher complained bitterly of the cold in winter, so More, too, may have suffered from this.

We know that More had sufficient clothing with him and that he wore his best tippet on St James's feast. For the first year he was not harassed and had with him a goodly number of his books. John a Wood, his servant, lodged in the Tower and cared for him. The door of his cell was locked only at night time and he seems to have been able to walk at times in the garden and to assist at Mass. For this he would have gone either to the Tower chapel in which, later, he was to be buried or to the lovely Norman chapel of St John. Antonio Bonvisi presented him with wine daily, and also sent in a fine silk garment for his execution which More, after much discussion, did not wear. He rewarded Bonvisi with a last most tender letter, one of the few he wrote from the Tower to a friend.

After the weariness and panic of the past few years, More found his days in the Tower very peaceful though he suffered much from physical debility. Meg visited him, perhaps, once a month, maybe more often, and Dame Alice came once or twice. Apart from the visits from these two and from occasional conversations with the resident Governor, More spoke to no one and spent his days and nights in study and in prayer. He found his cell commodious and on many occasions remarked that he was as happy in the Tower as at home. That grim fortress rarely housed a more contented prisoner. More wrote his impressions to Meg:

> I believe, Meg, they that have put me here ween they have done me a high displeasure; but I assure thee on my faith, mine own good daughter, if it had not been for my wife and ye my children, I would not have failed, long ere this, to have closed myself in as strait a room and straiter too. But, since I am come hither without my own desert, I trust that God of his goodness will discharge me of my care and with his gracious help supply my lack among you. I find no cause, I thank God, Meg, to reckon myself in worse case here than at home; for methinketh

God makes me a wanton and setteth me on his lap and dandleth me.[22]

This book should end on a peaceful, spiritual note for it has always seemed to me certain that More's fidelity to prayer and his strong contemplative attraction found their full reward in this world during the last harrowing months of his life. All other considerations lapse into unimportance when placed next to this. His conversations with his beloved Meg, comparable to the similar bond between Monica and Augustine, have been fully recorded in so many of More's biographies. His letters to her, his messages to his school, his long interviews with the Privy Council, seem to take the mind from the true fulfilment of his holiness. Soon after Christmas the regulations were severely tightened and, for his last months, More was in solitary confinement, deprived of Mass and with his books trussed up and taken away. One need hardly stress the normal strain of solitary confinement to grasp that, in this, More was no longer a normal man.

Meg knew her father as no one else would ever know him; he paid her the superb compliment of stressing this when they said good-bye. I think Meg knew that her father had lost his hold on this world and was longing to die. It was her own ardent love that forced her to wait for him, somewhere by the Tower Wharf, as he was led back to prison after his trial. His son John also said farewell to him on the same sad journey but, possibly, in the neighbourhood of Westminster Hall. Meg broke through the crowd, kissed him farewell, knelt for his blessing, stood back ten paces and then ran forward to embrace him again. More's words to her were measured and she alone would have allowed for this. "Have patience, Margaret, and trouble not thyself. It is the will of God. Long hast thou known the secrets of my heart."

Of this most moving scene, surely one of the most tender in all our history, Harpsfield alone notes the most significant point. After describing Meg's last embrace, "like one that had forgotten herself, being all ravished with entire love of her dear Father", he turns his eyes to More. Now Harpsfield was not present him-

[22] Roper, pp. 37-38.

self but he had almost all his information from Roper and, thus, from Meg. One feels that this next passage of his, at least in substance, came from Meg herself. She was weeping, we know, and so were many of the bystanders:

> yet for all this, Sir Thomas More, as one quite mortified to the world and all worldly and natural affections also, and wholly affixed to heavenward, albeit he were a most loving, tender and natural father to his children, and most dearly and tenderly affectionated above all others to this his daughter, having now most mightily subdued and conquered even nature itself for God's sake, with whom he looked and longed every hour to be and eternally to dwell with, neither fell to weeping nor showed any token of grief or sorrow nor once changed his countenance.[23]

There was no trace of hardness in More. In his last moving letter to Meg came the charming expression, "I never loved you better than when you kissed me last". Yet in all his letters from the Tower one senses the increasing reticence to which contemplatives attain. Meg, who had always known his secret, was not surprised by this. During his last sojourn in the Tower, the first faint vision seen in the Charterhouse turned into reality. In those long hours, ten thousand of them, spent by himself in the royal fortress, More's ties with this world seemed to fall away. It is this fact which makes his *Dialogue of Comfort* one of the most extraordinary books known to literature. Here, at last, we have the whole More. He was now old, sick and garrulous, writing in jail, writing only for his school, writing with no great care of style or arrangement, pouring out the secret experiences and aspirations of his most unusual life. We go back to Old Maud, to the kids playing funerals, to the boy with his cherry stones, leaving home late to be punished at school. All the scruples, the fears, the imaginings of a lifetime are skilfully expressed. Cardinal Wolsey appears again, the King, the ridiculous courtiers, the folly of counterfeit and fashion, the grave temptation to make passive contemplation an escape from the imitation of Christ.

[23] Harpsfield, pp. 164–165.

How little More changed in fifty years. Yet in the *Dialogue of Comfort*, amid all the suicides, reminiscences, fables and merry stories, one notes with awe that the author could now clearly discern a more splendid vision and was aching to be off. He still uses the language of Picus, Earl of Mirandola, but the reality was his own. His yearning to Godward was so intense that, in his own words, he could regard the King's threats as no more than a flea bite, when set beside the happiness ahead. More knew "that secret, inward pleasure of the spirit" of which, as he says, our hearts may have little sips in this world and the very full draught in the next. "Then shall I be satiated, satisfied and fulfilled when Thy glory, Good Lord, shall appear with the fruition of the sight of God's glorious majesty, face to face." More wanted to die. The longing to see God became all absorbing, "for the essential substance of all celestial joy standeth in the blessed beholding of the Glorious Godhead face to face, and this, no man may presume to look or to obtain in this life."[24]

We may end our story of Thomas More in either of two ways. Both show forth part of his indomitable spirit, for his words and behaviour on the scaffold are the complete expression of his contribution to Christian history. Only More could have summed up his whole public life in one short sentence, "The King's good servant but God's first". And only More could have been so much at home in those few, last, fatal moments, as to stay the executioner and to die with a joke on his lips. When he checked the axe to remove his beard from the block, "for this has committed no treason," he had reached the triumphant moment in which he could not take even death too seriously.[25]

But the courage of the scaffold was but the outward sign of that inward victory over diffidence. It had taken a whole lifetime

---

[24] *Dialogue of Comfort*, pp. 410–412.

[25] Roper, Stapleton and Harpsfield make no reference to More's last jest about his beard. Under-Sheriff Hall wrote the first account of More's execution, one not very favourable to the martyr, for Hall was very much a King's man. He tells us however how More, "even when he should lay down his head on the block, he having a great grey beard, sticked out his beard and said to the hangman, 'I pray you let me lay my beard over the block lest you should cut it'." Cresacre More gives the further words, "for this has done no treason".

of faith to conquer this. He had won his battle by painful stages, when he went to the Charterhouse and left the Charterhouse, when he married and married twice, when he went to Court and when he resigned the Chancellorship, faced the Commissioners at Lambeth, left his children and grandchildren on the Chelsea landing-stage. I would like to part from him, not on the scaffold, for only his body perished there. See him sitting in his cell with his feet on a straw mat, writing to his daughter or see him saying these words to her as they sat together in his cell:

Mistrust him, Meg, I will not, though I feel me faint; yea, and though I should feel my fear even at the point to overthrow me; yet shall I remember how St Peter, with a blast of wind, began to sink for his faint faith and shall do as he did, call upon Christ and pray him to help. And then I trust he shall set his holy hand unto me and, in the stormy sea, hold me up from drowning. Yea, and if he suffer me to play St Peter further and to fall full to the ground and swear and foreswear, which Our Lord for his tender passion keep me from doing . . . yet, after shall I trust that his goodness will cast upon me his tender, piteous eye, as he did upon St Peter, and make me stand up again and confess the truth of my conscience afresh and abide the shame and the harm here of my own fault.[26]

Small wonder that More was laughing when he died.

[26] Margaret Roper to Alice Alington, Rogers, p. 351.

Notes

1. Though historical research continues and from time to time provides new information, most of the facts about Thomas More are now well known. The bulk of available material has been printed many times. All modern biographers copy from each other and must turn to the chief contemporary sources, Erasmus, Roper, Harpsfield and Stapleton. Here these have been followed closely and less attention has been paid to later writers, e.g., Cresacre More.

2. Of modern biographers, three have proved outstanding; Fr Bridgett, the first in the field, remains in many ways the most sympathetic, especially in his treatment of More's spiritual life. Professor Chambers has produced the classic biography while, in recent years, E. E. Reynolds has not only added to our knowledge of More but has presented the saint to us in a vivid and most attractive way. These three biographies have been consulted on every subject with mounting gratitude.

3. In the main, the author has tried to rely on More's own writings, a source of information not yet fully known. He may claim to have read at one time or another most of St Thomas's writings but, for this book, attention has been deliberately confined to those most easily available. *Utopia* and the *Dialogue of Comfort* have now been published in Everyman's Library. Miss Rogers has collected all More's letters into one volume, while his early poems, his Life of Picus, of Richard III, his *Four Last Things* and the *Dialogue Concerning Tyndale* are available in the modern edition of his English Works. Add to these the letters of Erasmus and "Letters and Papers, Foreign and Domestic" and the student has available a mass of first-hand material about More.

4. Those familiar with the period will appreciate the problems of translation, not only from Latin into English but from Old English into a contemporary form. With clarity only in mind, the author has picked that translation which seems to him to suit More best. In certain cases, duly noted, he has himself risked a rendering, keeping as close as possible to More's words. More's English is magnificent but the long sentences, so fashionable in his day, might only confuse us now.

On the other hand a version which is entirely modern misses much of More's charm.

5. The author could have given a reference for every statement put forward, but to avoid pedantry and pretension he has restricted his notes to the larger quotations and more significant facts. To avoid breaking the text, references are normally given at the end of the complete paragraph.

Bibliography

No attempt has been made to include in this bibliography all the books consulted in the preparation of this book. References are given thus:

1. BIOGRAPHIES

Stapleton: *The Life of Sir Thomas More*, Thomas Stapleton. English translation by Philip Hallett. Burns and Oates, 1928.

Roper: *Lives of Saint Thomas More*, William Roper and Nicholas Harpsfield. Dent, Everyman's Edition, No. 19, 1963.

Harpsfield: Ditto.

Ro. Ba: *The Lyfe of Syr Thomas More*, Early English Text Society, 1950.

Bridgett: *Life and Writings of Sir Thomas More*, T. E. Bridgett, Burns and Oates, 1891.

Chambers: *Thomas More*, R. W. Chambers, Penguin Edition, 1963.

Reynolds: *St Thomas More*, E. E. Reynolds, Burns and Oates, 1953.

Margaret Roper, Burns and Oates, 1960.

The Trial of St Thomas More, Burns and Oates, 1964.

2. MORE'S WORKS

The Workes of Sir Thomas More, Rastell, London, 1557.

English Works of Sir Thomas More, 2 vols, Edited by W. E. Campbell, Eyre and Spottiswoode, 1931.

Utopia and Dialogue of Comfort, Dent, Everyman's Library, No. 461, Revised Edition, 1962.

The Correspondence of Sir Thomas More, Elizabeth Rogers, Princetown University Press, 1947.

Latin Epigrams of Sir Thomas More, Bradner and Lynch, University of Chicago, 1953.

Thomae Mori . . . Omnia, Louvain, 1565.

Philomorus. Notes on the Latin poems of Sir Thomas More, Second Edition, Longmans, 1878.

The Yale Edition of More's works, *Richard III* and *Selected Letters*, Yale, 1963.

3. OTHER WORKS

Opus Epistolarum Des. Erasmi. Roterodami, P. S. Allen, 11 vols, 1906.

The Epistles of Erasmus, F. Morgan Nichols, 3 vols, Longmans, 1901.

Praise of Folly, Erasmus, English translation, Reeves and Turner, 1876.

Letters and Papers, Foreign and Domestic of the Reign of Henry VIII. Edited by J. S. Brewer and J. Gairdner, 21 vols, 1862–1910.

Lollardy and the Reformation, J. Gairdner, 5 vols, 1908.

The Reign of Henry VIII, 1509–1530, J. S. Brewer, 2 vols, 1884.

The Likeness of Thomas More, Stanley Morison, Burns and Oates, 1964.

Life of Dean Colet, J. H. Lupton, London, 1887.

Jean Pic de la Mirandole, Pierre Marie Cordier, Debresse, Paris, 1957.

The Oxford Reformers, Frederick Seebohm, 3rd Edition, Longmans, 1887.

Catherine of Aragon, Garrett Mattingly, Paperback Edition, Jonathan Cape, 1963.

The Reformation in England, G. Constant, Sheed and Ward, 1934.

Lives of the Queens of England, Vol. IV, Agnes Strickland, 1844.

Early Tudor Drama, A. W. Reed, Methuen, 1926.

Mary Tudor, H. F. M. Prescott, Eyre and Spottiswoode, 1958.

Blessed John Fisher, T. E. Bridgett, Burns and Oates, 1888.

Index